Southern Living.
1993
Garden Annual

Southern Living
1993
Garden Annual

Oxmoor
House

ISBN: 0-8487-1101-7
Manufactured in the
United States of America
First Printing

Southern Living® *Magazine*
Garden Editor: Mark G. Stith
Associate Garden Editors:
    Stephen P. Bender,
    Linda Askey Weathers
Senior Garden Photographer:
    Van Chaplin
Associate Projects Editor:
    Julia Hamilton Thomason
Contributing Editors:
    Lois Chaplin, Rita W. Strickland
Production Manager: Kay Fuston
Assistant Production Manager:
    Amy Roth
Production Traffic Manager:
    Vicki Weathers
Editorial Assistant: Tena Z. Payne

Oxmoor House, Inc.
Editor-in-Chief: Nancy J. Fitzpatrick
Senior Homes Editor:
    Mary Kay Culpepper
Senior Editor, Editorial Services:
    Olivia Kindig Wells
Director of Manufacturing: Jerry Higdon
Production Manager: Rick Litton
Art Director: James Boone

Southern Living 1993 Garden Annual

Editor: Rebecca Brennan
Southern Living Editor:
    Linda Askey Weathers
Designer: Barbara Ball
Editorial Assistant: Roslyn Oneille Hardy
Associate Production Manager:
    Theresa L. Beste
Production Assistant: Pam B. Bullock

To subscribe to *Southern Living*
magazine, write to:
Southern Living, P.O. Box C-119
Birmingham, AL 35283

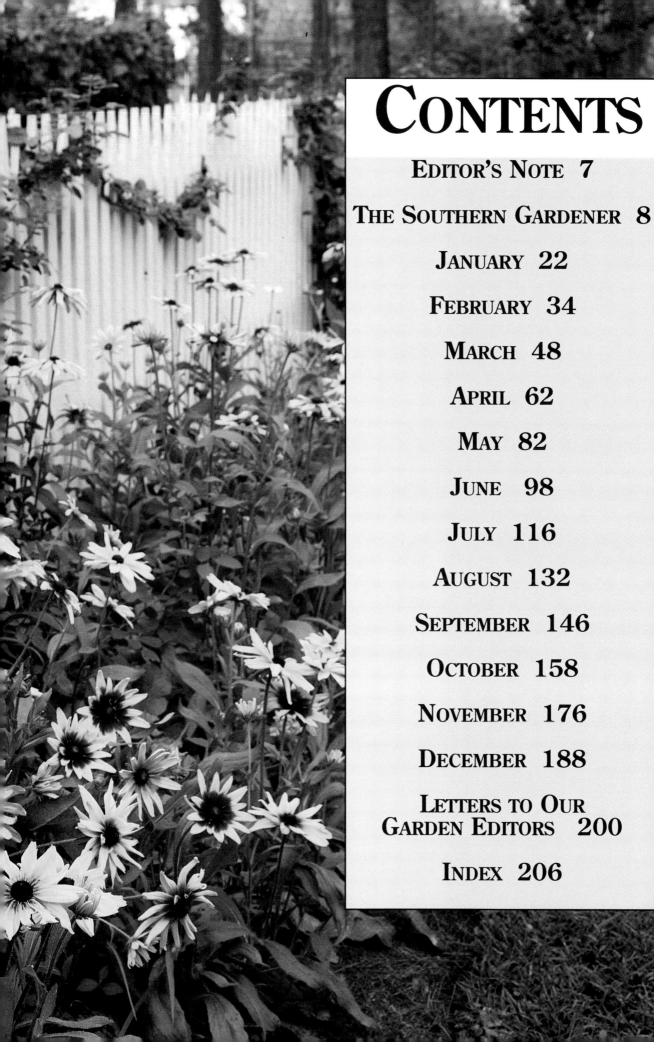

CONTENTS

EDITOR'S NOTE 7

THE SOUTHERN GARDENER 8

JANUARY 22

FEBRUARY 34

MARCH 48

APRIL 62

MAY 82

JUNE 98

JULY 116

AUGUST 132

SEPTEMBER 146

OCTOBER 158

NOVEMBER 176

DECEMBER 188

LETTERS TO OUR
GARDEN EDITORS 200

INDEX 206

I f the home is a castle, the garden is the kingdom. Because we rule our little plots, they give us freedom to express ourselves artistically and intellectually. We nurture the feeble shoots and hack back aggressive sprouts. We turn the soil, joining our ancestors in an almost primal ritual of life. And we garner and possess the newest and best plants that modern genetics has to offer.

One characteristic all gardeners share is that we are always looking forward to next year. But before we do, it is good to look back over our collective shoulder. In the pages that follow, we retrace the year past. We hope you will find helpful hints and exciting ideas, lots of garden know-how and compelling examples of how Southerners have planned their personal kingdom.

Each year we delve into one subject in a special section we call The Southern Gardener. This time we explore the front yard—from the automotive realities to the aesthetic possibilities. This begins our book, and leading each monthly chapter thereafter is a garden checklist, reminders of little tasks that will keep your garden looking great all year long. Because every year and every garden is different, we have added space for you to customize the checklist to suit your needs. It is our fondest hope that our year in the garden, our *1993 Garden Annual*, will be your companion in the seasons to come.

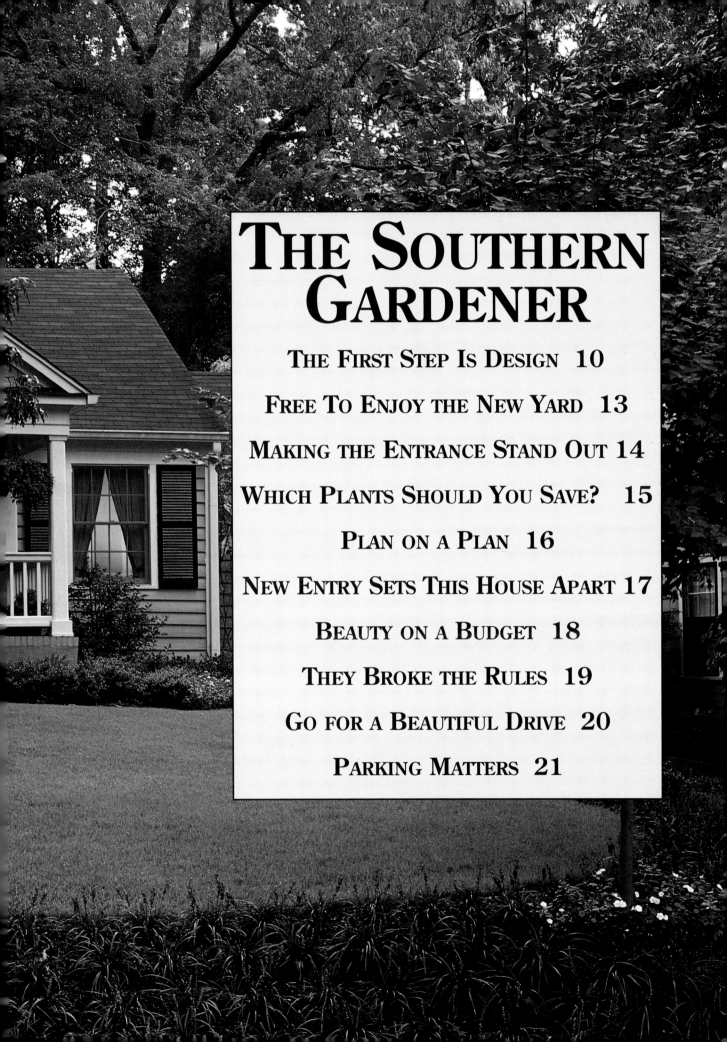

The Southern Gardener

The First Step Is Design 10

Free To Enjoy the New Yard 13

Making the Entrance Stand Out 14

Which Plants Should You Save? 15

Plan on a Plan 16

New Entry Sets This House Apart 17

Beauty on a Budget 18

They Broke the Rules 19

Go for a Beautiful Drive 20

Parking Matters 21

Deciding where you need plants is critical to a successful design. Ground covers, shrubs, and trees surrounding the lawn offer year-round interest.

The First Step is
Design

If your front yard needs sprucing up, this Special Section is for you. On the following pages, you'll find practical advice on such subjects as designing plantings and walkways, determining the right size and shape for the lawn, and reducing maintenance. Also you'll meet Southerners who have solved common problems to fashion front yards that truly are assets to their homes.

The foremost function of a front yard is circulation, both for cars and people. Too often, homeowners turn most of their attention to how it looks rather than how it works. Although eye appeal is important and a pleasing look is an ultimate goal, think about function first.

Parking should be easy to identify, enter, and exit. If possible, provide off-street parking (see page 21). From the parking area, the path to the front door should be clearly marked, invitingly wide, comfortable, and an all-weather surface. Steps should be low, deep, and well lit at night. If possible, avoid having a single step; a lone step can be hard to see and invites injury.

When it comes to planting for front yards, the question asked first is usually, "What kind of shrubs should I plant up against my house?" To begin with, that's the wrong question. This custom of lining the foundation of a house with shrubs is a throwback to the days when houses were built on pilings and plants were used to screen the view underneath. While a conventional foundation planting can be attractive and suits some architectural styles, it is overused and certainly not for every home.

The right question to ask, then, is, "Where in my front yard do I need plants?" If your home is built on a slope, for instance, a mass of shrubs on the low side can keep it from looking as if it's sliding down the hill. You can use plants to screen unwanted views or mask unfortunate architecture.

Conversely, plants can call attention to your home's good features. A specimen shrub or small tree might accent your front door or landing, and well-placed shade trees can frame your house like a picture.

Many homeowners are also perplexed about whether to plant along the front walk. Often nothing is needed, but you can make getting to your door an enjoyable experience by using color, texture, and fragrance. Avoid spiny plants, such as Chinese holly or barberry, anywhere people walk or stand.

Long walkways especially need variety to keep them interesting. You can accomplish that by presenting several different moods along the walkway. For instance, low plants on either side might give one section of the walk an open feeling, while a canopy of small trees can make the next area seem somewhat enclosed. Remember, if you simply outline the walk with a single type of plant, it will seem even longer.

Once your foundation and walkway plantings are designed, turn your attention to the rest of the front yard.

LANDSCAPE DESIGN: TERRY LEWIS, ASLA, SAN ANTONIO

Bordered by shrubs, ground cover, and flowers, this small lawn can be maintained with just a few minutes effort each week.

"But isn't the rest of the front yard just grass?" you may ask. We certainly hope not, for too much grass serves little purpose, and maintaining it can eat up much of your precious time and money.

Rather than just green grass and a row of shrubs, front yards can be three-dimensional spaces formed by the house on one side, and a foreground of trees and other plants toward the street. (Built elements, such as fences or walls, also may be part of this foreground.)

When well designed, this buffer of green gives the front yard privacy and lessens traffic noise, but still allows views of the house from points along the street. Glimpsed between trees or over low shrubs, the house can retain its dominance without its hoop skirt of lawn. And it may become even more inviting when partially concealed.

That is not to say, of course, that the lawn has no place in today's front yard. Naturally, it does. Its color and texture offer a great contrast to the rest of the garden. It also provides a soft, durable play surface for children and overflow space for entertaining. But today's lawn, like today's foundation planting, has a purpose. Use turf like you would any other plant: Decide where and how much of it you need; don't just fill up empty space with grass.

Having decided exactly where plants are needed—near the house, by the street, or along the walk—you can select the best plants for a particular job. Following these guidelines should help simplify the process:

Limit your thinking to plants that will ultimately reach the size you want. For example, if you need a plant 2 feet tall to underscore low windows, don't even look at plants that will grow to 6 feet. Save the 6-footers for screening.

Four stately boxwoods are the only plants required along the foundation of this Williamsburg-style home. Additional planting would simply detract from the architecture.

LANDSCAPE DESIGN: J.D. MARTIN, ASLA, GREENVILLE, SOUTH CAROLINA

A buffer of trees and low shrubs separates this front lawn from the street, providing a safe space for family activities.

From the correct size group, consider only those with cultural requirements that correspond to your site and your desired maintenance level. If you have full sun, forget about the shade-lovers. If you don't want to spray frequently, eliminate plants prone to insects and diseases.

Of the remaining plants, choose the ones that give you the most in terms of texture, color, and seasonal interest. Willow oak is a good shade tree, for instance, but a maple has better fall color. Crepe myrtles have colorful flowers in the summertime, but some selections also have showy bark, which is a fascinating addition to the winter landscape.

Repeat plants throughout the design; too much variety looks chaotic. Use bright colors and coarse textures sparingly; they tend to dominate. Make sure the colors you've chosen work well together; bloom times aren't exact, so try to avoid clashing colors that may overlap. And don't forget fragrant plants; fragrance is a wonderful bonus in any planting.

Rita Strickland
and Linda A. Weathers

LAWN TIPS

—Plant a lawn for a specific purpose, even if the purpose is strictly aesthetic. Turf is the finest texture in the garden. Use it to carpet the "outdoor room" in front of your home. You may also need turf in play areas and other spaces with light foot traffic. Heavy traffic requires pavement or mulch.

—It is much better to have a small, good-looking lawn than a large, poorly kept one. If your time is limited, a small lawn may be all you can manage.

—Shape the lawn to suit your garden. Geometric shapes look formal; free-form lines are casual.

—If there are existing trees, draw the lines of your beds to encompass the trunks of the trees, leaving the lawn as unobstructed as is practical. Most grass has difficulty growing beneath trees, and mowers can seriously damage tree trunks.

—Choose mulch, shrubs, or ground covers for slopes because mowing these areas is dangerous.

—Reduce lawn maintenance by using a mowing strip (a paved strip at soil level) around the edge of your lawn. Do not overfertilize; this increases the frequency of mowing and incidence of disease. Raise the cutting height to the maximum level for your grass to reduce weeds.

Choose grass to suit your climate and preferences. If you live in the Middle and Upper South and prefer a green lawn in winter, select a tall fescue type, bluegrass, or a cool-season blend. Gardeners in the Lower and Coastal South should stay with warm-season grasses, such as Bermuda, centipede, St. Augustine, or zoysia. Gardeners in the Middle South and portions of the Upper South that are in the transition zone can choose almost any grass. The lowest maintenance grass is centipede, and the highest is hybrid Bermuda. St. Augustine is a good choice for warmer coastal areas. The best grasses for shade are St. Augustine and tall fescue.

The
Southern
GARDENER

Bordered by low-maintenance liriope and evergreen shrubs, the small Zoysia lawn is in perfect scale with the house.

For James and Jean Boohaker of Homewood, Alabama, adding new columns and railings to their front porch was only the first step in improving their property. They realized that no amount of time and effort spent on the house would ever pay off until they did something about the front yard. At the same time, they didn't want to become slaves to a garden. So they asked Birmingham landscape architect Charles Sowell, ASLA, to draw an appropriate plan.

"Our yard was an eyesore that we needed to spruce up without surrendering our freedom," says James. The biggest problem initially confronting the Boohakers was too many trees. Deep shade prevented them from growing a nice lawn. But even after they removed several pines, the edges of the lawn were still too shady. Moreover, the bare front bank facing the street began to erode. So their first two decisions were where to place the lawn and what to do about the bank.

Sowell advised regrading the yard to level it, then locating a small lawn in the center, where the yard was sunniest. Around the shadier edges of the lawn, he designed flowing shrub beds that contain mostly easy-to-grow evergreens, such as dwarf yaupons, Satsuki hybrid azaleas, and dwarf Burford hollies. Next, he carpeted the bank with liriope, which helped frame

Free To Enjoy the
New Yard

the lawn and control erosion. Just as important, it eliminated the need to mow, which would have been difficult and dangerous had the bank been planted with grass.

Today, the softly curving lawn acts as a living stage, accentuating the house and garden. Its small size and lack of sharp corners allow James to cut it in 10 minutes. "And that's with picking up clippings and everything,"

he boasts. Furthermore, pruning the shrubbery is a once-a-year chore. "An hour or two once a year is certainly something I can handle," he says.

Planted in the spring of 1990, the yard is the toast of the neighborhood. "The neighbors across the street are thrilled," states James, "because they've been living there for 45 years and this is the first time this yard has looked right." *Steve Bender*

(Before) *Prior to planting, the front yard was sparse and shapeless.*

Hollies, azaleas, and native shrubs in mulched beds need little attention.

FRONT YARD FACTS

■ No gardening task takes more time and toil than maintaining a lawn. The smaller you make your lawn, the less work you'll have maintaining it.

■ Don't waste time and money trying to grow grass in shade. Plant shade-tolerant ground covers and shrubs instead.

■ Oval or rounded lawns take less time to cut than square or rectangular lawns of the same size because you don't have to stop or turn around in corners.

The front entry of a house should act as more than just a portal. It should also guide visitors to the door and give them a warm feeling of welcome. But when Donovan and Linda Hamm moved into their Baltimore home, the entry was anything but inviting. With assistance from Landscape Architect Catherine Mahan, ASLA, they turned things around.

Several problems beset the original entrance as well as the front of the house. Dark-green shutters and brown awnings gave the house a somber appearance. The front door and steps were so small that you could easily mistake them for a secondary or side entrance. The narrow walk leading to the steps forced visitors to approach single file. Finally, a

Before

This side walk comes from the parking area and front steps and leads to the deck in back of the house.

Making the Entrance
Stand Out

formal row of boxwoods planted at the foundation was out of place in the woodsy surroundings.

As part of a complete remodeling of the home, the Hamms removed the shutters and awnings and installed new windows to let in more light. To emphasize the new front door, they painted its frame red and flanked it with a pair of handsome brass lamps.

Mahan designed a wider, more attractive flagstone walk to guide visitors from the driveway to the door. Then she replaced the original boxwoods with a graceful and naturalistic planting of dogwoods, paperbark maple, serviceberry, azaleas, juniper, yew, and ferns to settle the house into its surroundings. To take people from the front door to a deck along the back of the house, she added a flagstone side walk and steps. A low retaining wall of stacked native stone borders this walk.

The new entrance makes ap-

A wider walk and more naturalistic planting welcome guests to the front door.

Which Plants Should You Save?

If you think redoing an older front yard means ripping out all the existing plants, think again. In many cases, you can bring new life to trees and shrubs by moving them to different locations or surrounding them with new plantings.

How do you decide which plants are worth saving and which aren't? Here are some guidelines.

• First, assess the health of the plant. If the plant is diseased, insect-ridden, in decline, or contains a lot of dead wood, remove and discard it.

• Second, evaluate how a plant looks in its present spot. If it looks fine, leave it alone. If it's obviously badly placed, and its size allows, move it. If the plant isn't in an ideal location but is a magnificent specimen, think of alternatives to moving it.

• Third, consider the size and age of the plant. In general, the larger and older a plant is, the more difficult it is to transplant. This is because old, established plants usually have extensive root systems. If you cut off too many roots while transplanting, the plant won't survive the move. You probably shouldn't try to transplant a tree that's taller than 6 feet or a shrub that's wider than 3 feet.

• Fourth, calculate the value of the plant and whether it's worth the trouble to transplant. For example, you may not want to dig up a Japanese holly when you can buy a new one for as little as $9.99.

• Finally, if you decide to transplant, do so when the plant is dormant to minimize transplanting shock. Get as big a root ball as possible. Make the new hole at least twice as wide as the root ball. Plant the tree or shrub at the same depth that it had been previously growing. Firm the soil around the roots, and water thoroughly. Water the plant regularly during the next year, until it becomes established.

If you have a large Burford holly, sasanqua camellia, or similar plant that has outgrown its place, consider removing the lower limbs. By simply pruning, you can convert an overgrown shrub into a handsome small tree. Then add additional small shrubs or ground cover as needed.

proaching the house an event, instead of an afterthought. "We're very pleased with the way it turned out," remarks Linda." And everyone who comes to the house is pleased with it, too."

Steve Bender

FRONT YARD FACTS

The front entry of a house should be easy to identify from the parking area and comfortable to approach. Make the front walk and steps at least 5 feet wide so that two people can advance toward the door side by side.

Native plants, gentle curves, and muted colors usually suit wooded lots better than formal plantings do.

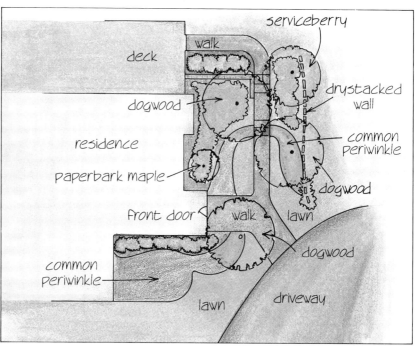

Plan on a Plan

There is something exciting and promising about a new home. It's the best time to think ahead instead of going for the "quick fix." By using part of your landscape budget for a master plan today, you can avoid a lot of landscape problems tomorrow.

The price of most new homes includes a landscape budget between 1% and 2% of the cost of the house. Typically, drives and walks don't come from this budget. If you deduct $500 or so for a long-term plan, you aren't left with much to work with. But a good plan will help you prioritize where to put the remaining dollars; trees first, a basic shrub backbone second, and the balance of the budget can be used to sod or seed a lawn and mulch for bare ground.

If possible, try to get a landscape architect involved—the earlier the better. Sometimes he can make helpful suggestions to the builder on how to position the house on the site, where to put the driveway, and other considerations.

For example, the cost of an extra course of cinder blocks on the foundation wall may raise the house a little higher and avoid additional grading or potential drainage problems. This saves money and may even look better. You simply need to talk to the builders and find out what your options are. In most cases, they aren't

going to care where the money is spent. You can decide.

Developing a landscape plan is not something the builder always does. "We frequently work with a crew of landscapers that come out, grade the soil, and plant. In a case like that, we never really see a formal plan," explains Jim Scott, builder with Executive Homes.

Often the result is functional, but not necessarily attractive. "On the other hand, we've also worked with landscape architects," Scott continues, "which has been a good experience for us. I can see the value in spending part of the landscape budget for a plan."

Having the house and its landscape look good immediately is not as hard as you might think. The house shown here was well under construction when Scott met Landscape Architect J. Kelvin Terry with Barnett and Terry, Inc. Together they determined the final grade and the location of the walk. Terry then had nothing but a patch of red clay with a lone pine tree to work with as he developed a planting plan.

"I wanted instant impact but had a limited budget. Still, I wanted something that looked as if it had been there for a while," Terry says. "I tried to create a pleasant approach to the house, adding a small landing off the drive and curving the front walk instead of having a straight shot."

Perhaps one of the more significant design decisions was to reduce the lawn area by having large mulched areas. This is a great way to cut back on costs if your budget is tight.

"My only regret," Scott recalls, "is that we didn't go ahead and put in a sprinkler system. If you're going to pay for a plan and plants and labor, you may as well spend a little more and get automatic irrigation. It really increases the likelihood of the plants and turf staying healthy."

Todd A. Steadman

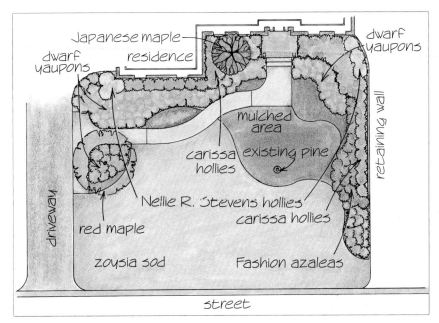

The world may not be flat, but you would never know it by driving through River Oaks in Houston. The biggest hill in the neighborhood doubles as a curb. This lack of topography can make for a pretty boring front yard, as Fred and Hulda Schubert discovered when they moved into their house.

Compounding matters was the fact that their property resembled many others on the block—a rectangular lot bisected by a straight concrete walk between the street and door. "Neither Fred nor I like squares and straight lines," comments Hulda. "We prefer the softness of curves." With this thought in mind, the Schuberts asked Houston landscape architects Lawrence Estes, ASLA, and Richard Dawson to devise a new approach.

Estes and Dawson responded by designing a handsome entry that features a curving brick walk and low wall. Now, instead of walking straight to the door, you ascend a single step, stroll leisurely around a water oak, amble past lush beds of Japanese star jasmine, azaleas, and tree-form privets, then step up to the front door.

The new entrance accomplishes several goals. First, the steps and wall provide a welcome hint of elevation. And the wall furnishes a nice place for kids to sit while waiting for a carpool or a ride. The wall also visu-

Lush beds of Japanese star jasmine, azaleas, and tree-form privets leading to this entry give year-round color and need little care.

New Entry
Sets This House Apart

ally separates the house from the street. With the house number prominently displayed, it seems to transform the yard behind it into a sort of garden anteroom. Finally, the distinctive entrance tells neighbors that *this* is where the Schuberts live.

Both the Schuberts and their neighbors appreciate the change. "We could not be more happy," says Hulda. "We've had people ring the doorbell and ask who did our landscaping. The yard is a constant source of enjoyment." *Steve Bender*

A curving brick wall separates the house and street, while adding a welcome grade change.

A semicircular terrace set into the bank serves as an outdoor living room.

A big change doesn't always require big bucks. As proof, just look at Eleanor Griffin's new entry garden. By combining her own good ideas with sage advice from experts, she replaced a front walk, installed a terrace, fixed a drainage problem, and added attractive plantings. And she did the entire renovation for only a few thousand dollars.

When Eleanor bought the house, she saw two basic problems with the front yard. "One was a nasty, ancient, poured-cement walkway that ran straight from the driveway to the door," she recalls. "The other was that water would run down the front bank and just pool at the bottom. In wet weather the yard looked like a ricefield."

Eleanor asked Eastside Nursery & Landscaping of Birmingham to regrade the front yard and add a French drain (a large hole filled with gravel that collects excess water). Then, with the help of Horticulturist Charlie Thigpen, she set to work on the walk, terrace, and plantings. "One morning," she remembers, "we got a can of spray paint and drew on the ground where we wanted the walk and terrace to go." They decided the walk should gently curve to soften the straight lines of the house. A semicir-

Beauty on a **Budget**

cular terrace, set into the bank, incorporated an existing cinder block retaining wall. They faced the cinder blocks with native stone and used the same stone for the walk.

To save money, Thigpen transplanted all the existing shrubbery still in good condition from the front of the house to new locations. Then he developed a front planting of broadleaf evergreens—azaleas, Japanese holly, Foster holly, sweet olive—plus seasonal annuals.

Eleanor regards her new terrace and entry garden as an outdoor living room. "It's where I entertain friends, read the Sunday paper, and just hang out. If the temperature is between 50 and 90 degrees, I'm out there," she explains.

Steve Bender

FRONT YARD FACTS

■ Solve the big problems before doing any planting. This homeowner improved the drainage and walkway, then added new shrubs and grass.

■ By retaining existing plants still in good condition, you'll save lots of money when it comes to landscaping an older home. See information at right for guidelines on evaluating and transplanting existing trees and shrubs.

The gently curving front walk softens the lines of the house and lends a looser, more natural shape to the shrub bed.

L ong hair, rock music, and deficit spending weren't the only trends that arrived in the sixties. Many homeowners also fell into lockstep with what they perceived to be the Two Immutable Laws of Residential Landscape Design: 1) *You must cover up the front of your house with bushes;* 2) *The bushes on each corner of the house must be tall and pointy.* Trouble was, following these landscaping laws would of-

Before

ten mean hiding attractive homes behind unattractive shrubbery.

This was the situation facing Ed and Pat Hearle when they bought their home in Bethesda, Maryland. Huge hemlocks overpowered the house. Together with pyramidal Japanese yews flanking the front door, these conifers also exaggerated the home's vertical lines. The house looked as welcoming as a fortress.

Garden designer Jim Sines of Garden Gate Landscaping provided the answer. Following his advice, the Hearles replaced the hemlocks and yews with a low tier of China Girl blue hollies. These compact hollies screen basement windows without blocking

A stone retaining wall divides the yard into two distinct levels.

They Broke the Rules

light to the living room. Out in the yard, new Redspire callery pears frame the front of the house, but they don't dominate the setting.

To further soften the yard's straight lines, the Hearles removed the original front walk that ran from the house to the street. They supplanted it with a flagstone landing and curving walk that takes you from the driveway to the front door. A serpentine retaining wall divides the front slope into two

separate levels. Undulating sweeps of spreading English yew (*Taxus baccata* Repandens) and Japanese pachysandra edge a very small lawn above the retaining wall.

Today, with its "twin towers" gone, the house appears larger and its good looks show through. As this example so admirably demonstrates, the Two Immutable Laws are often false. For few people *really* want their home to look like their castle.   *Steve Bender*

FRONT YARD FACT

One way to make your house appear larger is to buffer its vertical lines by planting spreading or rounded plants near the corners. Good selections for this include crepe myrtle, wax myrtle, waxleaf privet, dogwood, rhododendron, Japanese pittosporum, Burford holly, sourwood, sweet bay, and boxwood.

Framed by planting beds, the new walk guides visitors to the front door, while new shrubs, trees, and ground covers complement the house.

The Southern GARDENER

PHOTOGRAPH: VAN CHAPLIN

Interior Designer Reid Pasternak and Building Contractor Tim Melvin have rescued several Orlando homes from the ravages of time. Yet when they came upon this long-neglected residence, they feared at first that they'd bitten off more than even they could chew. "We had a feeling that the house had good bone structure, but we weren't sure," Pasternak says. "It was so overgrown out front that we couldn't really see it until we could get in there and rip everything out."

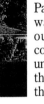

Before

Pasternak and Melvin handled the redesign of the structure from start to finish. But, for the exterior parts of the project, they relied on Landscape Architect Joe Brooks. "They called me even before they bought the house," says Brooks. "We looked at what was existing and decided none of it worked, so we started from there."

Perhaps the most important improvements the front yard needed were circulation and parking. Two concrete pads—one on either side of the lot—gave access from the street. One led to an old lean-to carport, and the other went nowhere. "We decided to connect the two aprons with a cir-

Sheltered by trees and bounded by masses of shrubs, this parking court becomes a separate space between house and lawn.

Go for a Beautiful
Drive

cular drive and car court that would create a foreground for the home, in addition to providing off-street parking," Brooks says.

Brooks's design was influenced by the low horizontal profile of the house. "To simply underline it with a row of shrubs would only emphasize that," he explains. So he used the car court, enclosed by trees overhead and partially bounded by masses of plants, to extend the house toward the street.

Like many residential streets in Orlando, the one in front of this house is brick, so they used brick to pave the drive as well. "We chose brick that matched the street and also picked up the roof color," Pasternak says.

The 12-foot-wide drive allows people to walk around cars parked there. "You don't want them to teeter off into the planting or brush against the cars," Brooks explains. The court itself is twice as wide as the rest of the driveway so that two cars can park there, or pass each other.

According to Pasternak, the arrangement works. "If you have small gatherings, everybody can park in the driveway," he says. "And I can pull around without having to back out into the street."

steps · residence · additional parking · car court · brick drive · concrete edging · brick drive · lawn

Please move your car—I'm blocked in! If this sounds familiar, then you have a parking problem. But you are not alone. Inadequate parking space is especially common with homes more than 25 years old, built when the average family owned only one automobile. Here are a few suggestions on adding parking space.

Pull-Off Parking

Your new parking area may be parallel to, perpendicular to, or angled off the driveway. Each option has advantages and drawbacks.

Parallel parking intrudes the least on the remaining yard (see sketch A). But it's usually designed to handle only one car because if one car parks behind another, the car closest to the house can become blocked in. Perpendicular parking requires the most space, but can accommodate several cars (see sketch B). A big advantage is that cars can back up, turn around, and head straight down the driveway when exiting. Angled parking, on the other hand, takes slightly less space than perpendicular (see sketch C). But cars must back out of the driveway when exiting.

If you are planning perpendicular or angled parking for several cars, consider using individual bumper strips to indicate where the parking spaces are. This will help alleviate the problem of someone taking up more than one space when they park.

For a finished look, the surface of the pull-off parking should match the existing driveway. To match an asphalt driveway, just topcoat the driveway when you surface the new parking area.

Blending a new concrete parking area with an existing concrete driveway can be done in several different ways. St. Petersburg landscape architect Phil Graham, ASLA, suggests coating both areas with a cement-sand mixture that has an acrylic binder. The coating, which is available in a wide range of colors through franchised installers, provides a flexible, waterproof, ⅛-inch-thick protective covering for both old and new concrete.

Another method is to wash the old concrete with muriatic acid, and then stain both the old and new with a commercial concrete stain. This method, however, does not give an exact match.

Brick pavers offer yet another way to blend old and new concrete. Graham recommends using ½-, 1-, or 2¼-

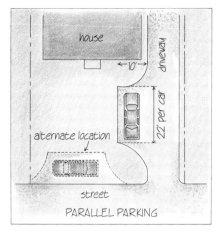

PARALLEL PARKING

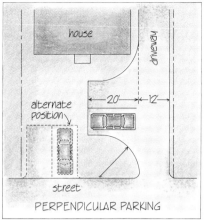

PERPENDICULAR PARKING

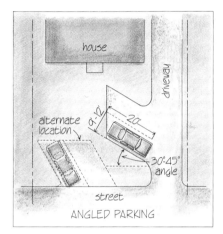

ANGLED PARKING

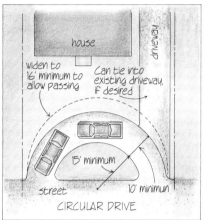

CIRCULAR DRIVE

Parking
Matters

inch-thick brick pavers, gluing them over both old and new concrete with a bituminous mastic, and then washing sand into the joints. "Plan ahead, and place the pavers carefully," Graham advises. "Once glued down, they are there to stay."

Yet another method is to pave the new parking area with brick, cut grooves in the existing concrete drive, and then inset strips of matching brick to visually unify the parking and driveway areas.

Separate Parking

If you have enough space, you might want to add a separate parking area for guests or family so the main driveway is not blocked. This could be either a parallel pull-off at the street or a perpendicular or angled parking area with access to the street. If the new parking area

doesn't touch the existing driveway, matching surface materials and colors will not be as great a concern.

If you are adding a family parking area, it should be close to the family entrance and convenient to the kitchen for carrying in groceries. Also consider secondary uses for the driveway and parking areas, such as play spaces or basketball courts.

Circular Driveways

A final option is to add parking along a circular driveway. Be sure that the distance from the center point of the half-circle (most circular drives are really half-circles) to the inner curve of the drive is at least 15 feet. This allows cars to turn easily. The drive should be at least 10 feet wide—16 feet wide to allow cars to pass each other.

Louis Joyner

JANUARY

CHECKLIST
24

PLANTED SCREENS, THICK AND GREEN
26

WINTER IS THE TIME FOR PRUNING
28

MEET THE SPRING MAGNOLIAS
29

GROW GRAPES FOR THE SHADE
30

GLORIOUS GLOXINIA
31

FLOWERS GREET THE NEW YEAR
32

CHECKLIST
for January

BROMELIADS

These tropical plants, available in sizes from tiny to tremendous, thrive indoors with little care. Just place room-temperature tap water in the bromeliad's cup about every two weeks; refill when the cup is nearly empty. Keep the soil moist, but not soggy.

CHRISTMAS TREES

Recycle your tree. If you have a chipper, you can turn it into valuable garden mulch. (Many communities have programs for collecting and shredding trees for this purpose.) Weighted down and dropped into a pond or lake, the trees provide a good spawning ground for fish. Some areas along the Florida coast collect old Christmas trees to use in sand dune stabilization.

CLEANUP

This isn't the most colorful time of year, but if your garden is tidy, the subtle features of the season will show through. Cut back browned perennials. Blow or rake up remaining leaves. Mulch to make vacant beds appear tended.

COVER CROPS

If you are growing crimson clover or other cover crops in the Middle or Lower South, consider turning it into the soil with a fork or tiller during the next few weeks. That will give the green materials time to break down and enrich the soil before planting time. Two to three weeks before planting is a good time to turn the crop.

GARDEN JOURNAL

A good New Year's resolution for gardeners is to keep a journal of daily or weekly activities and observations. Besides being fun for you, it will provide a valuable reference for planning next year's garden.

HELICONIAS

In the event of a freeze in South Florida or South Texas, cut the tops of these tender perennials back to about a foot from the ground. Unless the cold was severe and lasted more than a day, the buds beneath the ground should give rise to new shoots in spring. When new growth begins, fertilize with ¼ cup of a 6-6-6 slow-release fertilizer per plant.

HERBS

Plan your herb garden now; then order seeds as soon as possible. Include plants used in vinegars, potpourri, or dried wreaths, as well as those you'll need for cooking. In the Lower South you can begin sowing dill, chives, and coriander.

HOUSEPLANTS

Plants on the windowsill need attention on cold nights. Tender leaves will be killed if they touch the windowpane. However, if you pull plants away from the glass or close the curtains or blinds, they will be protected.

LAWNS

Take advantage of cooler weather to edge the lawn. Even where lawns are dormant, you can trim away runners that stretch onto the sidewalk and driveway. If using a motor-powered edger, wear protective goggles. Don't delay if you plan to apply a pre-emergence herbicide, such as Dac-thal, to kill seeds of crabgrass and broadleaf weeds in Bermuda, centipede, St. Augustine, Zoysia, fescue, and bluegrass lawns. Pre-emergence herbicides are ineffective after active weed growth has begun.

PALMS

In areas where palms grow outdoors, fronds may turn yellow due to a lack of potassium, iron, or magnesium. Supply iron and magnesium with a solution of minor elements sprayed on the foliage or poured into the soil. Potassium leaches from the ground very easily, but some fertilizer manufacturers make a slow-release form, such as 0-0-46, made especially for palms. It is applied to the base of the palm like a granular fertilizer.

PLANNING

If you can't garden now, plan to garden. Winter is a good time to prepare the soil for new beds. Whether your soil is clay or sand, it will benefit from the addition of compost, manure, or other organic matter. Plan changes and additions to your garden, and then order seeds and plants. If you have not received mail-order catalogs already, look for advertisements in your mail and magazines. Garden catalogs are a wonderful resource for hard-to-find plants and seeds.

PLANTING

When selecting a spot for new shrubs, remember that areas that are sunny now may be in shade when deciduous trees are in leaf. Good shrub choices for shade include aucuba, azalea, camellia, gardenia, hydrangea, leucothoe, and mahonia. All of these shade-lovers will grow better under pines and oaks than they will under maples, crepe myrtles, elms, Japanese cherries, and other trees with shallow roots that make it hard to establish a new planting. Unless the ground is frozen, continue planting trees and shrubs this month. Keeping them well watered throughout the coming year will be crucial to their survival.

ROSES

For Florida gardeners, now is the time to plant bare-root roses. Local garden centers carrying roses grafted onto *Rosa fortuniana* rootstock are your best source for plants. This rootstock is highly resistant to disease and nematodes prevalent in Florida. If you purchase roses grafted onto other rootstock, don't expect them to live more than three years. In the rest of the South, prepare beds now for rose planting later. Select a location that is well drained and receives at least six hours of full sun per day. In areas with poor soil, consider growing roses in raised beds.

TRANSPLANTING

A cool damp winter day is ideal for moving shrubs. Dig up a root ball at least the width of the plant. (Large plants will be heavy, so plan to ask someone to help you.) Replant immediately in a previously prepared planting hole.

TREE PLANTING

This is a perfect time to set out trees because their roots have time to establish before hot weather arrives. Prepare an area of ground at least five times the diameter of the root ball by loosening with a tiller or turning fork to a depth of 8 to 12 inches. Then dig a hole for the tree in the center of the circle, digging only to the depth of the root ball. Smaller holes can constrict the roots, and deeper ones sometimes allow the root ball to sink, which can cause rot.

WATERING

Plants get dry even in the winter; evergreens particularly are susceptible to drought. If you live in the Upper South where the soil freezes for any length of time, listen carefully to forecasts. Water plants well when cold fronts are predicted, because after the

soil has frozen, roots cannot supply moisture to the leaves.

WINTER-BLOOMING SHRUBS

This is a good time to plant winter-blooming shrubs in the Middle and Lower South. Try winter honeysuckle (*Lonicera fragrantissima*), winter jasmine (*Jasminum nudiflorum*), and leatherleaf mahonia (*Mahonia bealei*). Gardeners in the Lower South can also plant winter daphne (*Daphne odora*) or common camellia. (Other types of camellias are fine to plant, too.) In areas where the soil is alkaline or winters are severe, grow camellias in containers.

WINTER FRAGRANCE

Begin a winter potpourri by saving needles from your Christmas tree. Allow them to dry completely by spreading them on newspaper in a well-ventilated location. Collect hemlock cones, juniper berries, sumac berries, seed pods, and other fragrant or visually appealing items from the garden. You can even stuff a small pillow with the short needles of Fraser fir.

TIP OF THE MONTH

I make my own medium for growing orchids by recycling corks from wine bottles. I save my own corks, scrounge them from my friends, and even endure the stares of restaurant waiters when I ask them for used corks. I thoroughly soak the corks in water to remove wine traces and tannic acid and wash them in a light detergent solution. Then I cut them into half-inch slices and mix them with peat moss and perlite to make a quick-draining mix for cattleya and Phalaenopsis orchids.

Adele Kleine
Winnetka, Illinois

JANUARY NOTES

To Do:
- Force spring bulbs for early blooms indoors
- Brush heavy snow from shrubs to prevent breakage
- Recycle cut Christmas trees
- Cut boughs from discarded Christmas trees to mulch perennial beds
- Scan garden catalogs to plan orders for spring
- Mist houseplants to maintain humidity

To Plant:
- In Middle, Lower, and Coastal South, trees and shrubs
- In Coastal South, cool-weather annuals and vegetables

To Purchase:
- Flowering houseplants for winter color

_____

_____

_____

_____

_____

_____

_____

_____

_____

_____

_____

_____

GARDENING
PLANTS AND DESIGN

Soft, billowy wax myrtles disguise a parking area at the rear of this home and direct your eye to the front.

Planted Screens, THICK AND GREEN

BY STEVE BENDER / PHOTOGRAPHY VAN CHAPLIN

Carefully chosen screening plants can provide privacy, frame a view, block the wind, and much more. And unlike fences and walls, they offer handsome foliage.

Most of us don't mind keeping up with the neighbors. We just don't want them keeping up with *us*. This need for privacy often leads us to erect barriers in the landscape. If your initial impulse is to make such a barrier a wooden fence or stone wall, pause for a moment and consider a planted screen.

To be sure, fences and walls do have advantages over plants. For one thing, they perform their duties immediately; you don't have to wait for them to grow. They may also cost less to install. Moreover, they take up relatively little space and don't need pruning, watering, or fertilizing. On the other hand, according to Dallas landscape architect Steve Dodd, ASLA, people generally prefer the look of plants. "A wooden screen, even one that is very attractive, is a hard, flat object," he explains. "Most homeowners want to

use plants to soften up things."

Though desire for privacy is a common motivation, it's not the only reason for planting a screen. For example, screens can enclose and define space, separating one area of the garden from another. They can block unpleasant views or frame desirable ones. They can control movement and limit access. They can serve as a backdrop for colorful flowers, trees, and shrubs. And they can trap blowing dust coming from nearby busy streets or empty lots.

That's not all. If street noise bothers you, a tall screen of dense, small-leaved evergreens planted close to the street will reduce the problem significantly. And if sweeping winter winds play havoc with your tender, ornamental plants, you might consider planting a screen on the northwest corner of your property to act as a windbreak.

Advantages Over Fences

Living screens can sometimes provide the needed height that a fence can't. In many places, local ordinances forbid fences and garden walls taller than 5 to 7 feet. Obviously, if you're trying to block the view from a neighbor's second-floor window, this size fence won't do. But a row of mature Leyland cypresses or Savannah hollies will.

Because trees and shrubs will grow, consider a plant's mature size when planting a living screen. Many people start out with small plants and mistakenly place them too close together. The plants fill in too quickly, but soon crowd each other out. In general, you should space plants slightly closer together than their expected mature width (see spacing chart on page 27). You can plant closer than this for immediate screening, but eventually you'll have to remove

DESIGN: ROBERT P. KIRK, ASLA, BIRMINGHAM

A row of upright junipers screens this small yard from the condominiums in back.

some plants as they become over-crowded. And remember, no plant is one-sided, so don't locate the screen directly on the property line. If you do, your screen will eventually en-croach on your neighbor's yard.

According to Dodd, a sense of scale is essential when deciding the size of your planted screen. "If you have a small backyard, about 20 x 30 feet," he observes, "and you plant a screen that grows 15 feet tall and 6 feet wide, you'll either be pruning it all the time, or you'll feel intimidated by its size." A properly sized screen not only performs its function but also adds to a garden's visual appeal. If it makes the garden feel crowded, overly small, or foreboding, it's prob-ably out of scale.

Formal and Informal Screens

You can plant screens as single rows or as mass plantings consisting

COMMON EVERGREEN SCREENING PLANTS		
NAME	RECOMMENDED SPACING	HEIGHT AFTER FIVE YEARS*
Dwarf Burford Holly	3 feet	5 to 6 feet
Foster Holly	4 to 8 feet	8 to 10 feet
Japanese Black Pine	8 to 15 feet	8 to 10 feet
+Japanese Cleyera	3 feet	5 to 6 feet
Leyland Cypress	4 to 8 feet	12 to 18 feet
Nellie R. Stevens Holly	6 to 10 feet	10 to 12 feet
Pfitzer Juniper	6 to 10 feet	6 to 8 feet
Savannah Holly	6 to 10 feet	10 to 12 feet
Thorny Elaeagnus	4 to 8 feet	8 to 10 feet
Upright Juniper	3 to 6 feet	6 to 8 feet
Wax Myrtle	4 to 8 feet	10 to 15 feet

* Assumes plant is 3 feet tall at planting.   + Hardy only in Lower and Coastal South.

Tall hollies separate this front yard from parking and the street beyond, providing needed privacy.

WINTER
Is the Time For Pruning

of several layers of plants. Single rows tend to be formal in nature and appropriate for settings where the screen is a major design element. Mass plantings tend to be informal because they often contain a mixture of different plants. When deciding which style is right for you, keep in mind that formal screens demand more maintenance because each plant must be pruned to the same height, width, and shape as the others. Moreover, if one plant in the screen should die, you'll have a difficult time finding a new plant to match those remaining.

Most screens depend on dense, year-round foliage to fulfill their purpose in the landscape. For this reason, people generally opt for evergreen screens. Broadleaf evergreens offer more variety in terms of color and texture of foliage. In addition, many broadleaves adorn themselves with colorful flowers and fruits. However, as Atlanta landscape architect Rick Anderson, ASLA, points out, needleleaf evergreens do have one advantage. You can shear them without leaving a lot of conspicuous brown or jagged edges on the leaves.

Once you've determined which plants to use in your screen, do one more thing. If the screen is going to be close to a property line, consult the affected neighbor. Remember that a screen planted to limit access or block a view will do so on both of its sides, not just the one facing you. In such a case, Dodd suggests involving the neighbor in the design process so that the proposed screen benefits both parties. This way, you'll get the privacy you need without the hard feelings you don't. ◇

As a confirmed gardener, what I appreciate most about living in the South is that our winters are relatively short and mild. Thus, there are only a few days when I can't be outside working in the garden. Believe it or not, one winter task I really look forward to is pruning trees.

Pruning appeals to the puritan side of my personality that likes restoring order and discipline to free-form nature. And now is a good time to prune because trees are dormant. Moreover, deciduous trees have lost most or all of their leaves, making it easier to see what work needs to be done.

There are plenty of reasons for pruning a tree. Perhaps a branch is too low and gets in your way. Maybe a branch hangs over the house. Or a dead branch could be posing a safety problem.

No matter the circumstance, properly removing the offending branch or branches is the answer. For small branches, 1½ inches or less in diameter, pruning shears or loppers will do the job. But for larger branches, you'll probably need a pruning saw.

Avoid Flush Cuts

In the past, conventional wisdom advised cutting branches off flush with the trunk. However, more recent research demonstrates that flush cuts actually harm trees by opening them up to fungal and insect attack. Arborists now recommend cutting branches back only as far as the branch collar—the raised or swollen area at the base of the branch where it joins the trunk.

On most trees, this collar appears as a knob of concentric rings of bark. Each year the tree adds a new ring. The collar forms a protective barrier against disease and insects. It also promotes healing of the wound made when you prune. Even after you remove the branch, the collar continues to grow.

Pruning a branch correctly leaves

a wound that's roughly circular in shape. To produce this, you'll have to make three cuts for each branch you remove (see sketches). Make the first cut on the underside of the branch approximately 6 to 8 inches out from the collar. Cut about a fourth of the way through. Make the second cut on the top side, slightly farther out than the undercut, cutting the branch through. Because of your first protective cut, the branch will fall without tearing away any bark. Finally, cut the remaining branch back to the collar. Don't leave a stub beyond the collar—it will only rot. And unless the tree is an oak, don't bother painting the cut. Research shows that tree paint does little good, except in preventing oak wilt.

Although winter is the best time to prune, it may be another season when you spy a branch that needs removing. Unless it poses an immediate problem, just mark it with some bright paint so you won't forget it. Then when winter rolls around and you're searching for an outside activity, your task will be clearly before you.

second cut
First cut
third cut
branch collar
Correct Three-Cut Pruning

Incorrect One-Cut Pruning

only one cut
bark torn from tree

Saucer magnolia offers huge blossoms that are typically white inside and pink or rose outside.

Meet the Spring Magnolias

The magnolias of spring have a host of virtues, but patience isn't one of them. In fact, many of these trees refuse to wait until spring to bloom. Just three to four days of unseasonably mild weather in January or February often coaxes them to unfurl large, fragrant blossoms.

About a third of the time, a sudden cold snap rebukes the trees for such impetuousness, freezing their new flowers into brown mush overnight. But more often, merciful weather lets magnolias off the hook, and the resulting show is magnificent. Here's a look at some of the South's most popular magnolias, along with hints for curbing their restlessness so you'll have flowers to enjoy when spring *really* rolls around.

Star magnolia (*Magnolia stellata*) is the earliest magnolia to bloom. A dense, shrubby plant, it slowly grows 10 to 15 feet tall and wide. Its name comes from the shape of its starlike, 3- to 5-inch blooms. They're usually pristine white, but some selections feature pink blossoms.

Saucer magnolia (*M.* x *soulangiana*) claims the title of the South's favorite and showiest spring magnolia. Growing 20 to 30 feet tall and wide, it bears colossal, cuplike blossoms from 5 to 10 inches across. The flowers are usually bicolored—white on the inside and pink, rose, or purplish-red on the outside. Its blooms usually appear a week or two after those of star magnolia.

Lily magnolia (*M. quinquepeta* formerly, *M. liliiflora*) is the most disciplined member of this trio. In an average year, it opens its 5-inch blooms a month or so later than the other two. Like star magnolia, this one is slow-growing and shrubby, topping out at 8 to 12 feet tall and wide.

Spring magnolias grow well throughout the South, except South Florida. They do best in deep, rich, acid (pH 5 to 6.5) soil that contains plenty of organic matter. Excellent drainage is essential. Plant them in late winter, spring, or fall in a spot where they'll get full sun during most of the day, but light shade in the afternoon. Make the hole at least twice as wide as the root ball. Set the root ball so that the top half-inch is exposed after you have filled in around it with soil. After watering well, cover the top of the root ball with a 3-inch layer of mulch.

There are several ways to delay the characteristic early blooming. First, plant in the coolest area of your yard that still receives summer sun. Avoid planting near walls, paving, or the house, which radiate warmth. Second, mulch thoroughly around the tree following a hard freeze in late autumn. This will help to keep the roots cool and "asleep." Finally, you may want to plant a late-flowering form of either saucer or star magnolia (lily magnolia usually blooms late enough to escape frost).

Late-blooming selections of saucer magnolia include Alexandrina (pink and white flowers), Brozzonii (white and purple), and Verbanica (deep rose and white). For a later flowering star magnolia, try any one of the Little Girl hybrids produced at the U.S. National Arboretum by crossing Nigra lily magnolia with Rosea star magnolia. Named Ann, Betty, Jane, Randy, and Susan, these hybrids possess the shape and size of their parents and display rose-purple and white flowers.

Steve Bender

If you would like a list of mail-order sources for spring magnolias, send a stamped, self-addressed, business-size envelope to Magnolia Editor, *Southern Living,* P.O. Box 830119, Birmingham, Alabama 35283. ◇

Star magnolia's blooms usually open in late winter or early spring.

The tulip-shaped flowers of lily magnolia escape most spring frosts.

Growing on a wire trellis, bunch grapes shade a porch from the afternoon sun.

PHOTOGRAPHS: VAN CHAPLIN

Muscadines, native Southern grapes, provide poolside shade as well as delicious fruit.

Grow Grapes for the Shade

More and more, when Southern landscapes call for a vine, Southern gardeners are turning to grapes. Whether they grow natives, such as muscadines or American bunch grapes, or fancier hybrid table grapes, the wealth of delicious fruit is a bonus too good to pass up. And because grapes and muscadines ripen over a short period of time, keeping the fruit picked shouldn't become a hassle.

Although you'll enjoy both the fruit and foliage of your grapevines most during the summer months, winter is the time to plant. Bare-root plants should be available in garden centers soon. Grapes prefer deep, sandy soils that are rich in organic matter. They need full sun and excellent drainage, and they must be supported on an arbor or trellis.

At the Oklahoma City home pictured (above, left), Landscape Architect Robert Lewis, ASLA, used the luxuriant foliage of grapes to shade a porch plagued by hot afternoon sun. "Even though the porch faces southwest, the large leaves cut the sun's heat dramatically," he explains. And

their clusters of fruit are as pretty as they are delicious.

In Jackson, Mississippi, Landscape Architect Rick Griffin, ASLA, found a similar solution for creating shade at poolside (above, right). "We didn't want a tree that would shed a lot of leaves into the water," he says. "In addition, the homeowners wanted plants that would do something besides just look good," so he used blueberries as ornamentals, strawberries as ground cover, and planted muscadines on a rustic arbor. After

providing shade all summer, the deciduous vines allow warming sunshine through on winter days.

Choosing a bunch grape that's adapted to your part of the South is the key to success. Certain selections simply will not grow in some areas. In Florida and the Lower South, for instance, you must pick a type that is resistant to Pierce's disease, a bacterium that loves hot, humid weather. Resistant selections include Blanc du Bois, Blue Lake, Conquistador, and Orlando Seedless.

In the Middle and Upper South, hybrids such as Saturn, Mars, and Reliance are often recommended. In general, muscadines are somewhat less persnickety than bunch grapes. Cowart, Scuppernong, and Magnolia can be grown over a wide range. Check with your county Extension agent for specific suggestions for your area. Grapes are subject to fungal diseases, such as black rot, downy mildew, and powdery mildew. Different fungicides are recommended for different areas; your Extension service can tell you what to spray when.

Rita Strickland

RECOMMENDED GRAPES FOR LANDSCAPE USE

	Selection	*Type*
Upper and Middle South	Concord	Native bunch
	Mars Seedless	Hybrid
	Scuppernong	Muscadine
Lower South	Orlando seedless	Hybrid
	Cowart	Muscadine

Gloxinias add spectacular color to any room. Their velvety, trumpet-shaped blooms appear for weeks.

Glorious Gloxinia

The first time I ever saw a gloxinia in bloom, I thought the plant was fake. Almost everything about this spectacular relative of the African violet supported such a conclusion. The bell-shaped blossoms seemed too big, too numerous, and too bright to be real. And the thick petals felt like velvet, not living tissue.

But make no mistake, the gloxinia (*Sinningia speciosa*) *is* real. Though it originated in Brazil, the form we see today resulted from over a century of work by European hybridizers. Its single or double blossoms, from 4 to 6 inches long and up to 3 inches wide, may be crimson, carmine, pink, white, violet, or bicolored. Flowering extends over a two-month period each year; individual blossoms last a week or more. Because of their dazzling color, gloxinias often bedeck greenhouse benches during the holidays. But they can bloom in any season—it all depends on when the plants were started.

If you receive a gloxinia as a gift this year, handle it carefully—the brittle leaves snap easily. Place it near a window where it receives bright, filtered light, but not hot sun. While it's actively growing, feed every two weeks with general-purpose house-plant fertilizer. Allow the soil to go barely dry between thorough waterings. Always use tepid water, and never wet the foliage because this could cause leaf spots.

After the final blossoms fade, the plant enters a dormant stage. At this point, you can either discard the plant or save it for another season. If you choose the latter, stop watering and feeding when the leaves begin to yellow and droop. Let the foliage wither completely, leaving you with what looks like a barren pot of soil. Place the pot in a cool, dry place for two to three months. When the tuber is ready to sprout again, it will do so on its own. As soon as it does, resume your previous schedule of watering and feeding. The plant should bloom again in several weeks.

You can buy additional plants in full bloom from a garden center or start your own from tubers planted in spring. To start your own, fill a 6-inch azalea pot with a soil mixture consisting of 2 parts potting soil to 1 part sand. Plant the tuber 1 inch deep with its rounded side down. Thoroughly moisten the soil. Be sure not to wet the sprouts that emerge from the soil, as this could lead to rot.

To propagate a gloxinia, detach a leaf and a bit of leaf stem from the "mother" plant. Dust the cut end with rooting powder; then stick it into moist potting soil. The cutting should root and reward you with blossoms in less than a year.   *Steve Bender*

White gloxinias lend a cheery touch to this breakfast table. The plants are large enough to make an impact, but not so large that they block vision.

PHOTOGRAPHS: MARY-GRAY HUNTER

Karren King shows how plants kept in their original pots can be easily arranged in a planter. If you do it yourself, even a large arrangement like this costs less and lasts longer than a florist's arrangement of the same size.

Flowers
Greet the New Year

BY STEVE BENDER
PHOTOGRAPHY VAN CHAPLIN

If you're like me, you find it hard to say nice things about January. The weather is cold, daylight is short, the football season ends, and tax forms arrive. To compound matters, the tinsel, greens, and flowers of the holidays have all been packed up or thrown away, restoring Spartan order to rooms that still cry out for warmth and life.

We can't change the weather. We can't lengthen the day. We can't reschedule college football. And we can't avoid taxes. But one thing we *can* do to raise our spirits is take advantage of the beautiful flowers now available at local greenhouses and florists. Christmas may be officially over, but exuberant flowers displayed throughout the house will help us hang onto the festive feeling of the season well into the new year.

Believe it or not, greenhouses carry as big a selection of indoor flowers in January as in almost any other month. They usually have plenty of poinsettias, kalanchoes, Christmas cacti, cyclamen, and amaryllis remaining from Christmas. Most of these have weeks of bloom left in them. You'll probably find them on sale to boot.

January also marks the start of the season for forced bulbs. Look for greenhouse benches lined with pots of tulips, daffodils, hyacinths, paperwhites, and crocuses. Later in the month, primroses, Rieger begonias, and forced hydrangeas make their appearance in anticipation of Valentine's Day. And, of course, African violets and greenhouse mums are always for sale.

As the photographs on these pages attest, such variety encourages some wonderful floral combinations. If you wish, you can blend a half-dozen different kinds of flowers together inside a large, ornate planter so splendid it seems fit for a palace. Or take the opposite tack and house a single flowering plant in a modest terra-cotta pot. Either way, match the size and style of the container to the setting where it will be displayed.

One option when creating larger arrangements is re-

Baskets and pots of primroses take the chill off winter days.

PHOTO STYLING: JULIA THOMASON

Paperwhites, tulips, cyclamen, hyacinths, kalanchoes, and African violets fill this ornate planter.

Dwarf narcissus, grape hyacinths, and a small mum harbored in a basket foretell the approach of spring.

moving plants from their original pots and growing them together in a handsome planter filled with potting soil. However, it's much easier to leave plants inside their pots, then conceal the pots in the planter. This way each plant can be individually watered. And when one plant begins to fade, you can quickly replace it without disturbing the entire arrangement. Thus, the display can last for weeks.

While vivid flowers will undoubtedly dominate your planter, don't overlook the important contribution that foliage plants can make. Ferns, small palms, and other leafy plants can provide a deep-green backdrop for flowers and also fill in gaps between flowering plants. Vines, such as creeping fig and heart-leaf English ivy, draping over the edge of the planter will give it extra depth and lushness,

while at the same time obscuring the line between plants and container.

Keep in mind that because your flowers aren't cut but are still growing, you'll need to expose them daily to bright light to keep them alive. However, shield them from hot sun or the blossoms will quickly fade. Cool indoor temperatures of 60 to 65 degrees will also extend the life of the blooms. When selecting forced bulbs for your planter, choose those whose flowers haven't fully opened yet. Fully opened blooms last only a few days.

January may mark the end of the holidays, but it also signals the start of a new year. So bring in 1992 with flowers. Beautiful blooms indoors won't eliminate all of life's worries ahead. But they'll help you face them in a better frame of mind. ◇

FEBRUARY

CHECKLIST
36

**DAFFODILS WAKE UP
THE GARDEN**
38

GOING WITH THE FLOW
41

**THE WAY TO
A BEAUTIFUL GARDEN**
42

**A GARDEN
DESIGNED FOR FAMILY**
44

LET'S LOOK AT GARDENING
45

**DRESS UP
YOUR HOUSEPLANTS**
46

CHECKLIST
for February

ANNUALS

Set out transplants of cool-weather annuals as soon as they become available at your garden center. You'll be surprised how many don't mind the cold. Pansies can freeze solid and then perk back up as the sun melts the crust of frost. Other choices include snapdragons, English daisies, sweet William, and calendulas.

BIRDS

If you haven't been feeding birds, it's never too late to start. Set out your feeder this month. You'll have a parade of migratory birds passing through your garden all spring.

CHIVES

To start transplants, place potting soil in a plastic flowerpot, moisten thoroughly, sprinkle chive seeds over the surface, and cover them lightly with soil. Stretch clear plastic over the pot, and place it in bright, indirect light. After seeds sprout, uncover the pot and feed with soluble fertilizer every two weeks. Transplant outdoors after danger of frost has passed.

CITRUS

Florida and Texas gardeners, apply a citrus fertilizer at the rate recommended on the label now. It's also time to apply a solution of extra zinc, iron, and other minor elements that citrus trees may need. Mix the solution, and pour it evenly under the canopy of the tree.

COMPOSTING

A compost pile can be more than convenient. In Florida, state law now calls for garden refuse to be separated from household garbage. In addition to dealing with spent plants and other garden refuse, composting provides organic matter for planting beds. Start your pile in a hidden but accessible corner. You can purchase a ready-made composter, or make your own from hogwire bent into a circular bin 3 to 4 feet in diameter. Sprinkle fertilizer on the pile each time a 2-foot layer of refuse is added. Keep the pile moist, and the material will compost within a season.

LILIES

To prevent the tall stems of lilies from flopping over when big, heavy blooms appear, drive a thin stake into the ground about 3 inches away from the base of the plant. Tie the stems with pliable plant tape or other soft material, but don't use string, as this will cut into the stems.

FERTILIZE

This is a good time to fertilize shrubs and perennials. Apply 12-6-6 or similar analysis fertilizer as directed on the label. However, if you have a good supply of nutrient-rich compost, use it instead. Spread generously around your plants.

FLOWERING BRANCHES

Pussy willow, forsythia, flowering quince, and azalea can easily be forced to bloom indoors. Cut stems, bring them inside, and place in water. Keep them in a cool place. Change the water, and recut the ends of the stems every three to four days. Bulbs will swell and bloom in 1 to 2 weeks.

HOUSEPLANTS

Scale insects can multiply rapidly. The first signs will probably be a coating of sticky sap on the leaves and floor around the plant and brown specks on the underside of leaves, especially along the midribs. You can scrape them off, but the eggs and crawling stages will remain. Spray leaves with insecticidal soap until runoff occurs to kill the more vulnerable stages, or use horticultural oil to suffocate both juvenile and adult insects. Water houseplants only when they need it. Stick your finger into the soil 1 or 2 inches. If the soil feels damp, don't water; wait until it feels dry. Watering frequency will depend on the type of plant you have, size and type of pot, and growing conditions.

MAIL-ORDER PLANTS

As soon as plants arrive, open the package to check the contents against the invoice. Notify the nursery immediately if items are missing or damaged. Keep all invoices, shipping labels, and guarantee policies. Plant as soon as possible. If planting must be delayed, heal in (cover lightly with moist soil or mulch) bare-root items, and keep all plants well watered.

NASTURTIUMS

It soon will be time to plant seeds of nasturtiums. They will germinate even when the soil is cool, and by giving them a headstart, you will have larger plants. For best results when planting, soak the pea-size seeds in a saucer of water overnight; then push them about an inch deep into containers or garden beds. Start them now in the Lower South, the last week of  the month in the Middle South, and the middle of next month in the Upper South.

POINSETTIAS

Gardeners in South Florida and South Texas may prune garden poinsettias that have lost their color. Cut the plants back to about 6 inches from the ground, and fertilize with a slow-release plant food, such as organic 6-6-6. As the plants grow, pinch the ends of each stem every time they grow 6 inches. This encourages branching so there will be more flowers next season. You should continue monthly watering, fertilizing, and pinching until Labor Day. Then, the plants will begin to set flowerbuds for the holidays; further pinching will delay blooming.

PRUNING

By forcing new sprouts, pruning actually invigorates your plants. Remove dead or diseased branches first. Cut others just above a bud that points in the direction you want the branch to grow. To rejuvenate a tired hedge, cut it down below the desired height, and then shape the new growth as it emerges.

ROSES

This is the last month to prune hybrid tea roses for spring. Even if the plants aren't dormant, they can still be cut back to reduce their size and ensure good form. Pruning helps reduce black spot, too, by removing infected stems and leaves. Removing old mulch and replacing with fresh also helps control the disease. After pruning, strip any leaves that remain and fertilize with a high-quality, slow-release rose food.

STORAGE

Store opened bags of fertilizer, potting soil, and sphagnum peat moss in plastic trash cans. This will shield them from moisture and help keep the toolroom neat.

VALENTINE BASKET

For a different Valentine's Day gift this year, make a garden basket that will last for weeks. Just combine small containers of flowering and foliage plants in a basket, and cover the tops of the pots with Spanish moss. For inspiration, see "Flowers Greet the New Year," page 32.

For inspiration, see "Flowers Greet the New Year," page 32.

TIP OF THE MONTH

Those clear plastic food containers you get from supermarket delicatessens or bakeries make ideal seedling trays and miniature greenhouses. Just fill the container bottom with potting soil, sow your seeds, moisten the soil, and close the lid to retain moisture. Check the moisture level periodically. Once seedlings sprout, open the lid. Transplant the seedlings when their first set of true leaves appear

John Zaparyniuk
Montgomery, Alabama

VEGETABLES

It's hard to believe, but it's already time to plant vegetables in the Middle and Lower South. Make the most of the growing season by starting early. Sow seeds of carrots, English peas (including edible podded peas), beets, kale, turnips, Chinese cabbage, and radishes now. In the Upper South, get ready to plant by turning the soil and buying seeds. Set out transplants of cabbage, broccoli, cauliflower, and collards. In the Coastal South, watch cool-weather crops, such as broccoli, greens, and Chinese cabbage, for signs of cabbageworms and cabbage loopers. Both are green caterpillars 1 to 1½ inches long that chew holes in leaves. To control them, sprinkle plants with Dipel at the first sign of infestation. Farther north, get set for planting as the weather warms.

FEBRUARY NOTES

To Do:
• Prune summer-flowering trees and shrubs
• Cut back wisteria
• In Lower and Middle South, apply pre-emergence weed killer to lawn
• Trim old foliage of liriope
• Spray fruit trees with dormant oil
• Clean foliage of houseplants
• Force cut branches of forsythia, quince, spirea, redbud, and azalea into early bloom indoors
• Send in spring seed orders
• Lime lawn and garden beds, if necessary

To Plant:
• In Lower and Coastal South, cool-weather vegetables, summer bulbs, and annual flowers
• In Middle, Lower, and Coastal South, trees, shrubs, and roses

To Purchase:
• Mail-order seeds and plants
• Pre-emergence weed killer
• Dormant oil spray
• Lime

_____

_____

_____

_____

_____

_____

_____

_____

_____

_____

_____

_____

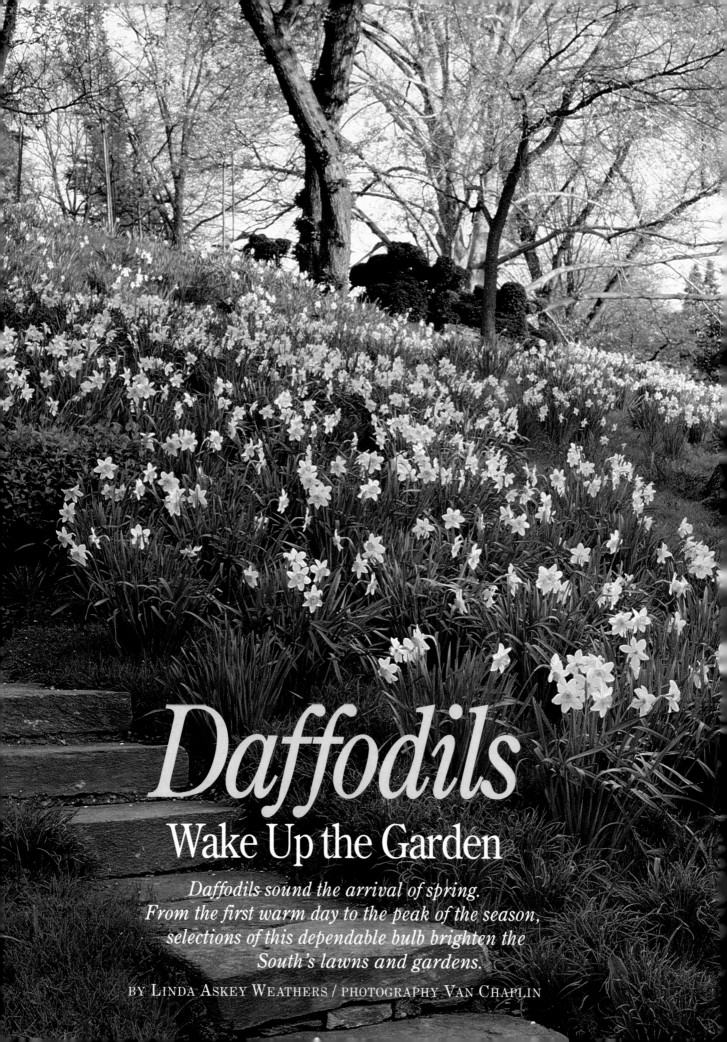

Daffodils

Wake Up the Garden

*Daffodils sound the arrival of spring.
From the first warm day to the peak of the season,
selections of this dependable bulb brighten the
South's lawns and gardens.*

BY LINDA ASKEY WEATHERS / PHOTOGRAPHY VAN CHAPLIN

GARDENING
PLANTS AND DESIGN

*A hillside of daffodils welcomes spring at Dumbarton Oaks in Washington, D.C., (**left**), while Peeping Tom daffodils (**above**) tilt toward the sun.*

These are daffodil days. The green buds push through the warming soil, bend their necks, and open wide. First one, then another and another until they become a chorus facing the spring sun.

Do you recall fragrant jonquils (that's probably what your mother called them) blooming as soon as it was warm enough to play outdoors? Jonquils are daffodils, too—one of several different types. Actually, all of them could be called narcissus, their botanical name. But most of us just say daffodils.

Although transplanted from Europe and Asia, daffodils behave as if they were Southern bred. You can find them growing profusely beside an old chimney or on the wayside, far outliving the hands that planted them. In those older plantings are lessons on spacing bulbs in your garden today.

"You want them to look wild, as if the Lord had planted them," explains Brent Heath, owner of The Daffodil Mart in Gloucester, Virginia. "You want the center to look tight, and then sweep loosely outward." Darrel Morrison, dean of the School of Environmental Design at the University of Georgia, agrees. He found that in

Ice Follies

nature there is often a dense clump of plants with drifts trailing off in one or more directions. These drifts thin out as they move away from the clump and merge softly with surrounding plants. If you were applying this to daffodils, you would begin planting one selection at its tightest recommended spacing, and then let bulbs drift ever thinner in one or two directions. You might even try to overlap this drift with the drift of a second selection. Those recommended for naturalizing include Ice Follies, Carlton, Bravoure, Salome, Cassata, and Colblanc.

Whether you naturalize daffodils or plant them in a more formal setting, be sure to plant enough to have impact. If you only want to start with a dozen, then plant them in a clump, and add more the following years.

By choosing a variety of daffodils, you can possibly have a 6- to 8-week flowering season. Dr. August De Hertogh, professor of Horticulture at North Carolina State University, likes to plant an assortment, from the very early to the late selections, starting with February Gold and ending with Geranium.

When making your choice, keep in mind that

bigger isn't always better. While much can be said for the fist-size blossoms of Unsurpassable and the magnificent show they put on, smaller-flowered selections are more in scale with a smaller garden. Miniatures are kindling much excitement at The Daffodil Mart, where Brent and Becky Heath are breeding smaller selections. "Primarily our effort has been toward small and fragrant daffodils," Brent explains, "because we think gardens in the future will be in small areas and in containers." Some of his favorites for the South include Baby Moon, Hawera, Jumblie, Little Beauty, Little Gem, Minnow, Sundial, Sun Disc, and Tête-à-tête.

Pink cups are another recent fashion in daffodils. "We really like Ac-

cent, and it's become readily available," says Becky. Other choices include Passionale, Roseworthy, and Bell Song. Of course, some may appear to be apricot- or peach-colored. "Color is in the eye of the beholder," Becky continues. "I have had people tell me that they have never seen a pink daffodil because they all are salmon to them. But they look pink to me."

Just as Ice Follies opens with a yellow cup and turns white, many of the pink selections turn as well. Becky gives an example. "Most pink daffodils bloom some shade of yellow the very first day."

In any color, daffodils endure, and that's good news for gardeners. Because whether daffodils are planted

as part of a formal design or naturalized in an open woodland, they can be counted on for years to come.

GROWING DAFFODILS

Choose early-, mid-, and late-season selections to extend the flowering season.

Choose a spot that receives at least a half day of sunlight.

Plant bulbs 8 inches deep for consistent performance.

Fertilize when you plant with a slow-release fertilizer formulated for bulbs.

In spring, let the foliage remain for at least 12 weeks after flowering to replenish the bulb.

Give Daffodils a Good Start

Daffodils are among the most dependable of bulbs, and even beginning gardeners can dig a hole, drop one in, and have a flower next spring. But success with daffodils is probably best judged by their performance in future years. If they are treated right, they will not only return each year, but they will also multiply.

Begin by choosing the right daffodil for your climate. In the frost-free regions of the Coastal South, select paperwhites for winter blooms. In the Lower South most daffodils perform well, but you should avoid double-flowered forms that may abort their blossoms in a warm spring. In the Middle and Upper South, choose whatever selections you like. By planting early-, mid-, and late-season selections, you can have daffodils blooming for six to eight weeks.

"Always plant in a well-drained spot; that is paramount," assures Dr. August De Hertogh, who specializes in bulb research at North Carolina State University. "Secondly, plant them deep enough." His research has shown that shallow planting exposes bulbs to variable winter temperatures, yielding variable results. By planting the base of the bulbs 8 inches deep, they are insulated. In situations where the soil is hard or too shallow, shallower planting is adequate if supplemented with 6 inches of pine bark mulch.

"All daffodils grow better in full sunlight; however, color tends to be better in partial shade," notes Becky Heath, who with her husband, Brent, owns The Daffodil Mart in Gloucester, Virginia. De Hertogh agrees, "As you go into more Southern zones, you must block out the midday sun by whatever means you have. You can do it by using the north side of your house or the shade of your trees." He cautions not to plant daffodils directly under shallow-rooted trees that would compete with the bulbs for water and nutrients.

Lay your bulbs out as you intend to plant them on the surface of a prepared bed, and work your way across. Use care to plant at a consistent depth so your flowers will bloom in unison.

Brent Heath's recipe for success with daffodils includes the key ingredients of water, light, and food. Give them a location where they receive at least one-half day of sun, and then water in spring when there is less than ½ inch of rain weekly. On food, Heath and De Hertogh agree: Fertilize when you plant, and don't use bonemeal.

Bonemeal is the traditional fertilizer, but it is primarily phosphorus. Daffodils need nitrogen and potassium as well, and they need it during the winter when their roots are active in the soil. If the fertilizer is a slow-release type, it provides a continuous supply of nutrients. A good

example is Bulb Booster (9-9-6), which was formulated at North Carolina State for tulips but also gives good results with daffodils. Apply it as directed on the label, working it into the soil for new bulbs, and top-dressing established beds. (Don't put fertilizer in the planting hole and then plop the bulb on top. This can burn the roots.) The Heaths' experience has shown that daffodils require higher levels of potassium than tulips. The Daffodil Mart's 5-10-20, slow-release fertilizer was developed with that in mind.

Do not fertilize after flowering as was once the custom. "You can ruin the bulb, rather than help it," says De Hertogh. "The uptake has already taken place. All you are doing is encouraging fusarium rot."

If given proper care, your daffodils will increase the number of flowers each year. But they can only do it if the leaves catch sufficient sunlight and manufacture food for the bulb. The latest research indicates that the foliage should be left standing (and eventually flopping) for a minimum of 12 weeks after flowering for adequate bulb growth. This means that another old practice, that of bending or tying the foliage, is also detrimental.

Because developing seed heads drain energy, cut them off after the flowers fade. If you cut your flowers and bring them indoors, they will last about a week in water.

As if entranced by the beauty of the spot, a concrete raccoon perches atop the sandstone bridge.

Embellished with plants and native stone, this natural drainage ditch has become a garden feature.

Going With the Flow

According to *Webster's*, a gully is a trench worn in the earth by running water after rains. Not a pretty image, huh? Yet water will inexorably run downhill and, in its running, cut the earth to suit, sometimes leaving scar-like gullies in its wake. A common solution is to install drains to gather the water and bury pipelines to spit it into some anonymous storm sewer.

Although such subterranean structures get the job done, Sandie and Donne Pitman of Tulsa decided instead to just "go with the flow." The Pitmans' backyard collected most of the rainwater runoff from neighboring properties as well as their own, and the result was an unattractive drainage swale that carried water across their backyard to a nearby creek.

According to Sandie, the previous owners of the property began the process of turning this eyesore into an attractive feature. "Instead of putting in a huge drain and sending the water underground, they just decided to take what was existing and enhance it to bring out the natural beauty," she explains.

Landscape Architect Donald S. Kauffmann, ASLA, worked with both sets of homeowners to accomplish the effect pictured here. To prevent damage to existing trees along the swale, Kauffmann left the original grade in the area unchanged. He simply used native brown sandstone, evergreens, and herbaceous perennials to transform the gully into a garden.

To break the force of the moving water, Kauffmann constructed the floor of the dry streambed with boulders and smaller stones, carefully placed to mimic a natural creek. "Although the streambed is manmade, it doesn't look that way," Kauffmann says. Designed to channel water in wet weather, the swale is used as a casual walkway during dry periods. "It's multipurpose, but it has become as much a visual feature as a functional one," he adds.

In addition to stones, planting helps prevent further erosion. "The area lends itself to a lot of variety," says Kauffmann. "We've just kept adding to it over the years." According to Sandie, one of the most important plants in the scheme, if not the largest or most showy, is ajuga. "It's great for keeping erosion down because it gets into the cracks and crevices between the rocks and just grabs hold," she says. In addition, azaleas, mondo grass, liriope, irises, hostas, and daylilies keep the banks of the dry stream green in winter and colorful come springtime.

Toward the lower end of the swale, near where it empties into the creek, a large slab of sandstone forms a bridge from one side to the other. There Sandie added her personal, crowning touch—a concrete raccoon purchased at a local garden show. "He really does look natural sitting there on the rock," Sandie says. "A lot of people do a double take when they see him." Perched atop the rough stone bridge, he seems to be admiring the shrubs and flowers, as if the whole garden had been built for him alone. *Rita Strickland*

Cut stone

Flagstone

The Way to a Beautiful Garden

Man probably invented the garden path about the same time he invented the garden. After all, it couldn't have taken him long to discover the practical value of a few strategically placed stepping stones. Since that time, however, paving has assumed much more than a purely functional role. Indeed, it is often one of the most important elements in the garden.

A paved walkway beckons the visitor to enter, leads him on a self-guided tour, tempts him to follow it around a corner, to discover what lies beyond. The paving material itself reveals much about the character of a garden. Whether it's formal or casual in style, a path or a promenade, the paving helps set a mood and influences the visitor's perception of the place.

When you choose a paving surface for your garden, consider the options carefully. Paving can be expensive both to install and to remove. And make sure the material you choose is compatible with your architectural, gardening, and life styles. For example, if your home is brick, you might use similar brick for the walkways. And if you don't enjoy performing

Exposed aggregate

Scored concrete

PHOTOGRAPHS: VAN CHAPLIN, TINA EVANS, MARY-GRAY HUNTER

mundane garden chores, you probably shouldn't use gravel, which will need to be raked and replenished regularly.

Costs for paving materials and labor to install them will vary greatly depending on where you live. Generally, materials that are native to your area or are manufactured nearby will be less expensive due to the lower cost of shipping. Likewise, craftsmen may be more adept at working with materials that are common locally. But don't eliminate a choice just because you think it will cost too much. Do some checking first. Sometimes the cost of higher priced materials may be offset by lower fees for labor. For instance, limestone may be more expensive than brick, but a mason should be able to install a few large pieces of cut limestone much more quickly than he could hundreds of small bricks. This may make the total cost for a brick surface and a limestone one more comparable than you'd think.

To help you in your decision, here are a few examples of the endless variety of paving materials available to the Southern gardener.

Flagstones are derived from a number of types of hard rock that split easily into flat, irregularly shaped pieces. Color will depend upon the particular kind of stone and its area

Interlocking pavers

of origin. Flagstones are usually set in mortar, but can be laid out on a bed of sand.

Cut stone often has a more elegant appearance than flagstone, especially if laid in a regular, repeating pattern. Among the many types of stone suitable for cutting are slate, limestone, coquina, Pennsylvania bluestone, and crab orchard stone.

Pea gravel, waterworn stones of about ½ inch diameter, is suitable for use on level walks that are subject to occasional foot traffic. Apply it about 2 inches deep inside a permanent edging over well-compacted subgrade. And keep in mind that the gravel can be difficult to walk on and maintain.

Concrete is a mixture of a cement, an aggregate or gravel, water, and sand, poured in place into forms.

The surface of the concrete then can be finished or scored in a variety of patterns. It's one of the least expensive paving materials.

Exposed aggregate is concrete with the upper mortar surface washed away to expose the gravel with which it was made. Decorative pebbles, such as pea gravel, are usually used when making exposed aggregate.

Stamped concrete is colored and has various patterns imprinted on it with metal presses. This is not a simple process, so ask to see completed examples of a contractor's work before you decide to hire him. If not properly installed, stamped concrete may crack and crumble.

Interlocking pavers are made of concrete and can be placed on a bed of sand to form walkways or terraces. They come in a variety of shapes and sizes, and are easy for the experienced do-it-yourselfer to install. Like brick laid on sand, they require some sort of hard edging to hold them in place.

Tiles of many different types are suitable for landscape construction. Make sure to select a style with a finish that does not become dangerously slippery when wet. And make sure it will stand up to the temperature extremes in your area.

Rita W. Strickland

Stamped concrete

Tile

Pea gravel

PHOTOGRAPH: VAN CHAPLIN

The lattice fence does not stop at the corner of the garage, but continues in front of the dark wall as a screen.

A Garden Designed for Family

"I'm not worried about keeping the yard beautiful," says Beth Henry. "Our children like to be right underfoot, and we like to be with them. Frankly, it's for us to enjoy, and if it takes a little wear and tear, it doesn't really bother us." This is real life for Beth Henry and husband, Rich Stephens, who are balancing two careers and their family responsibilities.

A ground-level deck covers most of the yard immediately outside the back door. Opting for a low deck provides a safe, close-by play area for the children and eliminates mowing from a list of Saturday chores. The deck, designed by Dave Wagner, AIA, encompasses two beautiful willow oaks that shade the area.

Beth and Rich also enlisted the help of Landscape Architect Brian Zimmerman, ASLA, to make a garden of the space that remained. One of his greatest contributions is a division of the backyard into functional spaces, screened from each other

The ground-level deck provides a comfortable place just outside a new family room addition.

and from the adjacent backyards common to their older neighborhood in Charlotte.

Their own garage was also a problem. Zimmerman recommended painting the garage wall dark green, almost black. Then he designed lattice panels for the wall that were consistent with the design of the fence. He remarks, "We were trying to

make the structure disappear and make the space seem even larger."

Beth enjoys the plants in the garden. "I love the sweet bay magnolias," she adds, "especially when they're blooming." Other plants in the garden include mondo grass, white gumpo azaleas, Otto Luyken cherry laurels, and annual white-flowered waxleaf begonias. All in all, it's a low-maintenance garden, and Beth appreciates that most of all. "With both of us working full time and having two children, we couldn't manage it if it required much attention."

However, the garden is not just for adults. The area under the hammock will be planted someday, but for now it has another purpose. Beth explains, "In summer we keep a little plastic pool there. It's right by the house, so when I come home from work I can fill it up with water, keep the children happy, and run back and forth to the kitchen to fix supper."

Beth and Rich enjoy the garden too. "I like the mondo grass because it handles traffic well." Beth explains, "Really, our children just get out there and walk all in it. We plant begonias every year, but they have not been as healthy this year. Our 2-year-old has just loved them."

Linda Askey Weathers

Let's Look At Gardening

Last spring I asked my friend Rob Curl, age 8, to help me grow transplants from seeds. An articulate young man, Rob climbed down from his tree fort and pitched right in.

We used a kit with bright-yellow trays, a bag of soil, and interesting seeds like pumpkins, cosmos (a bright flower), and sunflowers. Rob filled the trays with soil and decided where to plant everything—carrots went here, popcorn there.

He watered them all carefully, and put on the lid to make a little greenhouse. Green sprouts appeared in a few days. Some were more successful than others, but Rob was undaunted and transplanted the healthy ones to the garden when they were big enough.

Spring passed into summer, and we met again. The Braves monopolized much of our conversation, but then our talk turned to Rob's rookie year as a gardener. "So how was your garden this year?" I asked. "We got all of the carrots and started eating some of them," he remembered, "One of them was *this* fat."

"Have you ever done anything like this in school?" I asked. "Yes, once we did a science experiment," Rob said. "We tried planting seeds in all this different stuff—lint from the dryer, plastic, dirt in a pot with a hole, dirt with no hole, toothpaste." Which gave the best results? "The dirt with the hole."

So I asked, "Do you have any advice for other kids planting seeds?" Rob nodded, "Oh yeah, give 'em lots of sun, take care of 'em, and water 'em every day. I did that. But when they get too big, you had better start putting them out in the garden."

Linda Askey Weathers

If you've enjoyed this feature and have any suggestions on future topics for kids, please send them to *Southern Living*, Kids Corner, P.O. Box 523, Birmingham, Alabama 35201.

Rob Curl carefully prepares his seed flat.

PHOTOGRAPH: TINA EVANS

TIPS FOR GARDEN ROOKIES

■ Begin with fresh seeds, and read the packages carefully. Some can be sown directly in the garden, which is the easiest way. But it helps to give others, such as cabbage and broccoli, a headstart by growing transplants indoors.

■ It helps to have a tray called a "flat." You can buy one with a cover like Rob's and reuse it next year. Or even use paper cups. Using individual containers makes the young plants easier to transplant. And remember: You need a hole in the bottom of any container so water can drain away.

■ Label each cup with the name of the seed and the date it was planted. Some seeds take longer to come up than others. The seed packets will say how long you'll have to wait.

■ When the seedlings start to grow, the first leaves (called seed leaves) are oval or round. The next set of leaves (called true leaves) look more like the big leaves will. When these appear, remove the cover, and place the flat in bright light. Water with a solution of half-strength 20-20-20 fertilizer every other week.

■ If you planned ahead, the roots will have filled their container about the time that the weather is right for planting outdoors.

This variegated dwarf schefflera serves as a centerpiece to a buffet luncheon. Boston ferns, pothos, fragrant rubrum lilies, and floribunda roses fill the blue-and-white jardiniere.

The simplicity of a Benjamin fig in a basket is the perfect counterpoint for the combination of spathiphyllum, dieffenbachia, and variegated Canary Island ivy.

Dress Up Your Houseplants

BY LINDA ASKEY WEATHERS

Any collection, especially plants, can quickly take over a home, but more and more gardeners have put plants in their place—as part of the decor. In fact, it's become rather fashionable to create the illusion of a miniature garden growing beneath an indoor tree.

Although it looks extravagant, this design idea is not nearly as difficult to implement as it might seem—the plants don't even need to grow in the same pot. Usually the bigger plant has a utilitarian plastic container. Slip this into a basket or other decorative container. Then set the smaller plants, still in their pots, on top of the soil of the large plant. Nestle enough small plants to conceal their pots, and water them right where they are, which reduces maintenance as well. Nothing could be easier, but you have to make

sure you choose the correct companion plants.

Karin Purvis of The Houseplant in Greenville, South Carolina, cautions, "If the plants' water needs vary greatly, as it would with maidenhair fern under a ficus tree, you could end up drowning the ficus tree. My favorite plant to put under ficus trees is grape ivy. It's soft, the leaves hang down, and they have very similar watering habits.

"Then for special occasions you can add small pots of flowers—begonias for summer, poinsettias at Christmas, or mums for fall. The grape ivy under

Alii ficus is a sturdy choice for an indoor tree. Handsome all by itself, it's dressed up here with grape ivy and a Fascini bromeliad at its base.

PHOTOGRAPHS: VAN CHAPLIN, MARY-GRAY HUNTER / STYLING: KARIN PURVIS, JULIA THOMASON

Coral impatiens highlight this elegant jardiniere of dwarf spathiphyllum and variegated English ivy. This blend of textures and colors works well as a dining room centerpiece.

Beneath the fronds of a pygmy date palm are dwarf spathiphyllum, variegated ivy, gerbera daisies, and a Rieger begonia. Overturned pots hold these plants at the right height.

the ficus tree is the base, and then you add color."

But don't be limited to flowering potted plants; for a party you can include more perishable color. During spring and summer when bedding plants are readily available, buy inexpensive packs of four or six flowering transplants, and tuck them into the trailing foliage. For a shot of color, buy flowers from the florist or gather them from your garden. Cut the stems the appropriate length, place them in water picks, and stick the water picks into the soil surface.

You can also apply this concept of displaying plants under trees to smaller plants. The dominant plant can be a 3-foot kentia palm on a buffet or sideboard. Even a dwarf spathiphyllum becomes lush and full when supplemented in this fashion (see photo above). Just select smaller plants to go beneath it, such as variegated English ivy, and be sure they trail over the edge to complement the more upright forms.

MAKE IT EASY ON YOURSELF

Choosing the right container and preparing it properly makes watering a lot easier. The idea is to be able to water the entire group of plants as they are, without having to take the group apart and then put it back.

A ceramic container with no drainage hole is moisture proof, so you don't have to worry about leakage on floors or furniture. On the other hand, be cautious not to water so much that the container fills up and drowns your plants.

Baskets are inexpensive, but you have to take extra care to contain the water that will drain from the pots. Line the basket with a heavy-duty garbage bag, put one or two plastic saucers in the bottom, and then set the main plant within the basket, still in its own container. Trim the excess plastic around the upper edge of the basket, and set additional potted plants in place.

You can also use a large container that requires several plants to fill it up, as with the copper kettle shown above. In this example, blocks of plastic foam and overturned pots are used to position plants at the appropriate height.

From time to time you will need to exchange your plant combinations. Sometimes one will fade and need to be replaced, which can change the entire composition. Once in a while you will want to repot your plants and treat them for insects. And all plants will need to be refreshed by an occasional spray from the hose or shower to wash away the inevitable dust that builds up. ◇

MARCH

CHECKLIST
50

IN STEP WITH THE SEASON
52

BET ON BLUE STAR
55

**SHRUBS FROM
GRANDMA'S GARDEN**
56

FOR THE LOOK OF LEAD
60

CHECKLIST
for March

AMARYLLIS

As soon as amaryllis finish flowering outdoors in Lower and Coastal South gardens, fertilize with bulb food. This supplies the foliage with nutrients needed to manufacture plenty of food and ensure a large cluster of blossoms next spring. To control red blotch disease, which disfigures leaves and blossoms with red blotches up to 2 inches long, spray with copper. Also remove badly infected leaves.

ANNUALS

Several annuals can be planted now including snapdragons, dianthus, sweet William, sweet alyssum, calendulas, and English daisies. All can be set out as transplants, but wait until mid-March in the Upper South. You can also directly sow seeds of larkspur, baby-blue-eyes, forget-me-nots, Johnny-jump-ups, and sweet peas in the Middle and Lower South.

BOOKS

Two new books with good information for gardeners in the Lower South are *Garden Guide to the Lower South,* 2nd Edition ($12.95 plus $1.75 postage and handling from Trustees' Garden Club, P.O. Box 24215, Savannah, Georgia 31403-4215) and *Design & Care of The Southern Landscape* by David W. Marshall. (Check your local bookstore or send $23.85 postpaid to Know 'N' Grow Publications, 2437 Wintergreen Road, Tallahassee, Florida 32308.)

HERBS

As soon as the last frost is over, plant seeds or transplants of basil, oregano, dill, borage, ginger, lemon balm, and other herbs that do well in warm weather. Herbs are most convenient near the kitchen door where they're close at hand. Ornamental herbs, such as chives, can also be worked into flowerbeds or little corners of the garden. The colors and textures of herbs make them as tempting to the eyes as to the taste buds.

LAWNS AND SHADE

For shady lots in the Lower and Coastal South, try shade-tolerant types of St. Augustine grass—Seville, Bitter blue, Jade, or Delmar. While Floratam is the most popular St. Augustine because it resists chinch bugs, it doesn't like shade. If chinch bugs are such a problem that you can't grow the nonresistant varieties, consider using mulch or a ground cover instead. Feed cool-season grasses (fescue, bluegrass) early this month in the Middle South and anytime this month in the Upper South. Fertilize warm-season grasses (Bermuda, St. Augustine, centipede, Zoysia, Bahia) about two weeks after they have begun to turn green. Apply the amount recommended on the label, and use a fertilizer spreader as hand application results in spotty coverage.

PEAS

Plant English peas in the Lower South before the middle of the month, throughout the month in the Middle South, and from now until early May in the Upper South. Good selections include Wando, Little Marvel, Thomas Laxton, and Maestro, as well as edible-podded peas such as Sugar Snap, Sugar Ann, and Sugar Daddy.

ROSES

Just before leaf buds break open, thin out the oldest canes of shrub roses, leaving only young, vigorous wood. Also, remove any canes that are crossed. Prune back all remaining canes to 15 inches. When leaves appear, begin spraying with a fungicide, such as Funginex, according to the label directions.

SHRUBS

For spring-flowering shrubs, such as forsythia, spirea, azalea, virburnum, deutzia, and weigela, pruning before they bloom will remove this year's flowerbuds. Get out your clippers immediately after they've bloomed.

TOMATOES

Sweet 100 cherry tomatoes will set fruit throughout the summer. You may have trouble finding transplants, but you can mail-order seeds. It will take about four weeks after seeds are sown before transplants can be set.

TWIG GIRDLER

If you find an abundance of tiny twigs on the ground under trees or shrubs, twig girdlers are probably at work. Small white beetle grubs chew through tiny twigs so they fall to the ground. They are common pests of

pecan, hickory, persimmon, oak, and poplar trees, and may also attack pyracantha. Their damage is usually tolerable, but the best control is to pick up the fallen twigs and destroy them. The twigs harbor eggs and grubs that will attack next year.

WILD ONIONS

One way to remove wild onions from your lawn is with a standard bulb planter. Slip the planter over the clump, and twist to penetrate the soil deeply. The clump and onion bulbs will come up with the soil plug. Dispose of the plugs (do not compost), and refill the holes with fresh soil.

TIP OF THE MONTH

Here is a wonderful, inexpensive way to make solar greenhouses for young vegetable plants. Save all of your plastic, gallon milk jugs during the winter. When you plant your squash, cucumbers, and tomatoes in spring, fill the jugs with water. Place four jugs around each plant or hill. The sun will warm the water and protect your plants from cool spring winds. During hot, dry days, you can use the water from the jugs to water the plants. I had the best garden ever by doing this!
Mrs. Lois Spencer
High Point, North Carolina

MARCH NOTES

To Do:
- Dig and divide crowded perennials
- Fertilize trees, shrubs, ground covers
- Feed the lawn
- Lime lawn, perennial beds, rose beds, and vegetable garden, if necessary
- Sow seed for cool-season grasses
- In Upper South, apply pre-emergence weed killer to prevent crabgrass

To Plant:
- Bare-root roses
- In the Lower and Middle South, broccoli, cabbage, lettuce, peas, carrots, potatoes, spinach, asparagus, collards, kale
- Trees, shrubs, perennials
- In the Upper South, pansies, Johnny jump-ups, ornamental cabbage and kale

To Purchase:
- Seeds
- Vegetable transplants
- Fertilizer
- Pots, stakes, tomato cages
- Pre-emergence weed killer

_____

_____

_____

_____

_____

_____

_____

_____

_____

_____

_____

_____

_____

_____

Above: Planting pansies is equally challenging and rewarding for Sylvia and Noah Larsen. Right: The Larsen family enjoys a spring day and prepares the garden for the season at hand.

In Step With
THE SEASON

With spring just around the corner your garden's success depends on what you do now.

by LINDA ASKEY WEATHERS
photography VAN CHAPLIN

The Larsen family members, like gardeners all across the South, are getting ready for spring. Sylvia, David, Hope, and Noah all help with the preening and planting. It's a family activity, an outing in their own yard.

We visited the Larsens on a spring day and talked about their garden experiences in Mountain Brook, Alabama. Sylvia echoes the feelings of many: "I have a love/hate relationship with the garden. Sometimes I get really mad and think I had better prune all this back, but I don't want to get rid of it. Then there are these wonderful days when I'm glad I have all this space, and I enjoy it."

Most gardeners have generous spirits. If they are not sharing seeds of this or cuttings of that, it's information that they offer. Such was the case on our visit with the Larsen family.

• Sylvia remembers early experiences that got her started gardening, and she tries to provide similar ones for her **children.** "I've let each of them have an area to

plant. I've made it a point to let them destroy things if necessary to keep their interest up. They are not going to sow in straight rows, and they might pick something before it's ready. They will not be perfect, but if you are going to be a perfectionist, you can't be a gardener."

• Although Sylvia knows fall **pansies** are stronger plants than those planted in spring, she's a busy mother and doesn't always manage to get them out in the fall. Even spring transplants, though, bring several months of color to the garden and give the children flowers to pick. Because they will not grow as large as those planted in fall, she reduces the usual 5- to 6-inch spacing to about 4 inches. She's learned not to skimp, setting out several flats of pansies for an effect appropriate to the bounty of spring.

• Sharpening the edges of **tools,** such as a shovel or hoe, makes work in the garden a lot easier. Also, after each use, the Larsens clean their tools by plunging them two or three times into a bucket of sand moistened throughout with oil. This wears away any remaining soil while the oil coats metal surfaces to prevent rust.

One of Sylvia's prized tools is her grandmother's hoe. "My father was cleaning out the garage and found the head of it," she remembers. "I took it to the hardware store, and they put a nice handle on it. We keep it sharp. When I use it, I think of her."

Sharp shovels make garden work easier.

Above: By transplanting daffodils in bloom, Sylvia can arrange the flowers by color and height in their new bed. Right: David sows additional seeds into the existing fescue each spring to keep the lawn thick and healthy.

• **Organic matter** is essential for good, fertile soil. The Larsens use leaves from their oak trees. "We leave them in the garden in autumn, and then in spring we fork them under with the soil amendments," Sylvia explains. "We put down pine straw mulch, mainly for appearance, but also to control weeds." A thick layer of pine straw helps keep the garden neat and weed free.

• **Herbs** play an important role in Sylvia's garden. "I grow the perennial herbs [sage, thyme, chives, garlic chives, and mint] because they are lower maintenance," she explains. "Later in the year, we'll make mint water. We take a fistful of mint, wash it off, put it in a gallon container in the refrigerator overnight, and then strain it. This water tastes like cool mint; we just use it for drinking water."

Sylvia's thyme doesn't have a chance to get woody in the center. "I think I prune it enough by making thyme tea and thyme-rosemary bread."

One annual herb that she grows is dill, which she plants from seeds saved each season. "I sow it along the border of the garden in February. I'll sow again in June, but the early dill is stronger."

• Sylvia is growing fewer **vegetables** and more perennial flowers, but Swiss chard is a must. "It's not a popular vegetable, but I love it. If you pick the outer leaves regularly, the plants will last from spring to early October. And they are beautiful. I braise the leaves in butter and lemon."

Since Sylvia discovered Sweet 100 cherry tomatoes, she seldom grows any other kind. "Sweet 100s are not bothered by the birds like the big ones," she says. She also plants cucumbers to climb on the picket fence, and sweet bell peppers that ripen yellow and red.

• "Most of the things that I love, friends have given to me," she remembers. That includes her old **roses**—a 150-year-old purple/lavender rose and a 100-year-old chestnut rose called Ma's Favorite. She favors these because they are hardy. "I'm not interested in anything that is subject to insects. With a family, I don't have time to spray—and I wouldn't want to even if I could."

• Although it is usually recommended to move **daffodils** when they are dormant, this is not always practical. And it's difficult to remember which clump bloomed what color. The Larsens have learned that daffodils in bloom can be lifted, divided, and transplanted without disrupting the bulbs' growing cycle. If the flower stems get bent or broken in the process, Hope and Noah are always willing to pick them to bring indoors.

• Because of shade, tree roots, a sloping lot, and the wear and tear of little feet, the Larsens periodically sow **grass** seed to thicken the existing lawn and help prevent erosion. They sow ryegrass each fall and fescue each spring, loosening the soil in bare areas to be sure the seed does not wash away.

Perhaps it's her sunny disposition or the joy her garden brings, but Sylvia is an optimist. She says, "Gardening gives me hope for the future. I can think of things I haven't done yet, so it's always a hopeful experience to be a gardener. Even if things get torn down by a storm or they freeze and die, there's always a new package of seeds to try, or somebody willing to share a plant, or a nice place where you can go buy plants and try again. I'll never stop gardening, wherever I am."

Blue star blooms well in sun or shade. It sparkles with ferns and Alleghany pachysandra in a woodland garden.

Bet On Blue Star

It's a mystery why some of the prettiest and easiest to grow plants are seldom found in home gardens. Such is the case with blue star (*Amsonia tabernaemontana*), also known as willow amsonia. Native to the South and Midwest, this hardy perennial is one of the few wildflowers that provide bright color in both spring and fall. On top of that, it blooms equally well in sun or light shade.

The show begins in early spring, when stems carrying narrow, willow-like leaves sprout from a crown near the soil surface. When fully grown the foliage stands 2 to 3 feet tall. Clusters of star-shaped, five-petaled flowers appear atop the foliage in April and May. The floral display lasts for around 2 to 3 weeks. In autumn the foliage changes to clear yellow or orange yellow. Curiously, the leaf color is usually more intense in the South than in the North.

Several of blue star's first cousins also deserve attention. Dwarf blue star (*A. tabernaemontana montana*) grows 15 to 18 inches tall and boasts fuller clusters of darker blue flowers than the species. Arkansas blue star (*A. hubrectii*) resembles dwarf blue star, but grows slightly taller. Sandhills blue star or feather amsonia (*A. ciliata*) sports narrower leaves than blue star and tolerates drier soil.

Few wildflowers can match blue star's versatility in the garden. As

Blue Star at a Glance

Height: 2 to 3 feet
Light: Full sun or light shade
Soil: Moist, fertile, well drained, pH adaptable
Pests: None serious
Propagation: Seed or division
Range: Throughout the South, except South Florida

Nancy Goodwin of Montrose Nursery in Hillsborough, North Carolina, remarks, "I can't think of any plant it would clash with." She adds that it's a "see-through plant"—open enough to let you see other plants behind it. You can combine blue star in a sunny border with peonies, irises, columbines, lamb's-ears, and tulips. Or plant it in a woodland garden next to ferns, hostas, primroses, daffodils, mayapples, and spring wildflowers. If you can bear to sacrifice a few of blue star's blossoms, you'll find they make fine cut flowers, too.

Considering how finicky some wildflowers can be, care-free blue star is one native plant you really shouldn't do without.

For mail-order sources send a stamped, self-addressed, business-size envelope to Blue Star Editor, P.O. Box 830119, Birmingham, Alabama 35283.   *Steve Bender*

Southern Living®
MARCH 1992

Shrubs From Grandma's Garden

These tough, hardy plants from the South's romantic past have been largely forgotten. But decades of neglect haven't dulled efforts to bring them back.

BY STEVE BENDER

PHOTOGRAPHY VAN CHAPLIN AND TINA EVANS

Many objects in life seem to possess little outward value. They don't help us eat, drink, clothe, or defend ourselves. We could easily live without them, but don't want to. Their value lies not in material concerns, but rather in the way they make us feel. So it is with the hardy, old-fashioned shrubs we remember from childhood. Tending them conjures up fond images of places and people that belong to the past—the sweet roses in the churchyard down the street; the gnarled pearlbush by grandma's fence; the quince that your great-aunt used to make jelly.

Though some antique shrubs originated in the South, many arrived aboard ships in the 18th and 19th centuries from Japan, China, Korea, and

This American Pillar rambling rose hugs a rail fence in Alexandria, Virginia.

Beautybush (Kolkwitzia amabilis) *is another forgotten Southern treasure. At Annetta Kushner's garden in Annapolis, it's been trained into a romantic arbor.*

Decades of Southern gardeners have regarded the blossoms of flowering quince as a welcome herald of spring.

India. Their extraordinary blooms led to quick distribution throughout the region—well, as quick as could be accomplished at a time when traveling overland from Richmond to Memphis often took weeks or months.

Most of these plants were tough old birds, perfectly capable of surviving years of utter neglect. You see them today eking out livings in old, overgrown gardens, abandoned lots, fencerows, and cemeteries. A few, such as spirea and French hydrangea, were tamed for mass production and are sold by the thousands each year. But others, like Confederate rose, slender deutzia, beautybush, and flowering almond, have all but vanished from the marketplace. About the only way to obtain such a plant is to beg a piece from a fortunate friend.

The disappearance of heirloom shrubs can be traced to several factors. First, many of them are deciduous, and Southerners traditionally favor evergreens. Second, some are hard to propagate. Finally, such shrubs as weigela, mock orange, and winter honeysuckle aren't naturally *kempt*—without regular pruning, they grow gangly and mop-headed.

Be this as it may, a number of Southerners are determined to preserve the old plants. One reason is a yearning for continuity with the past, explains Steve Thomas of Waverly, Alabama. "People all remember what grew in their grandmothers' and mothers' gardens," he asserts. "I currently live in the house that my wife grew up in. Signs of her mother still grow all over the yard—althaeas, English dogwood, Grancy grey beard, and spireas."

Familiar shrubs such as althaea (*Hi-*

biscus syriacus), also known as rose of Sharon, revive fond memories for many Southerners. Sam Jones of Bishop, Georgia, remembers, "Flash Gordon and his rocket ships were the rage in the late thirties and early forties." He recalls, "I would take the withered blooms of rose of Sharon, which are shaped like rockets, and see how far they'd travel by means of my throwing arm."

The remembrances of Margaret Sanders from Columbus, Mississippi, aren't quite so joyous. "When I was a little girl and was naughty, a switch off the althaea bush administered punishment," she explains. "But I've overcome that and gotten to where I like althaeas now, even if they do always have ants all over them."

In 1991, nostalgia for old, Southern plants culminated in the publication of *Memories of Grandmother's Garden* by the Deep South Region of the National Council of State Garden Clubs. This 71-page booklet is a delightful compendium of garden reminiscences contributed by members.

Pensacola, Florida, resident Leona Venettozzi's contribution is typical.

With its graceful waterfall of bright spring blossoms, Lady Banks rose has thrilled Southerners for years.

"Cedar Lane," a magnificent rose of Sharon, features large, white blossoms with a red starburst in the center.

She writes that under a big cedar at grandma's, "there was a large Lady Banks rose, a white one. Its trunks were worn smooth with years of serving as a 'ladder' for us to climb up into the cedar tree. Then we'd pick laps full of white petals and throw them down to make it 'snow.' The cedar was so filled with branches of the rose that when it bloomed the tree was white. The rose had been given to my grandmother by a neighbor who wouldn't plant it at her house, having heard that when it got old enough to shade your grave, you'd die. Grandma

lived many years beyond that!"

A second major impetus behind the surging interest in old shrubs is their gritty constitution. "The reason I'm attracted to them, aside from their historical value, is that they're hardy," states Jane Symmes, a plantswoman from Madison, Georgia. "They've survived the vagaries of climate without watering or spraying."

Penny McHenry's French hydrangeas exemplify this tenaciousness. When she looked out at her shady backyard from an upstairs window 25 years ago, most of her azaleas and

other shrubs were struggling to hold on. "But the two hydrangeas we had been given the year before looked gorgeous," she remembers. Knowing a good thing when she saw it, she immediately began rooting hydrangea cuttings. Today her Atlanta garden overflows with the blue blossoms of more than 400 hydrangeas.

However, it takes more than public interest to restore long-neglected shrubs to Southern gardens. It also requires nurseries willing to grow these plants, as well as landscape architects, designers, and homeowners willing to use them. Fortunately, both things are starting to happen. Thomas and Symmes separately operate wholesale specialty nurseries dedicated in part to bringing the old plants back. Small mail-order nurseries are also getting into the act. And at Mississippi State University, Ed Martin, professor of Landscape Architecture, is using his classroom and private practice to spread the word about heirloom shrubs.

"I like the old plants' design qualities—colors, textures, lines, and forms," declares Martin. He suggests placing these plants in front of evergreens to emphasize their flowers, fall foliage, and winter twigs.

As Martin and other Southerners freely testify, grandma's shrubs needn't be dismissed simply because they're old. Their virtue rests in the pleasant emotions they evoke, the beauty they offer, and their having passed the test of time.

To order *Memories of Grandmother's Garden,* send $5 to Carolyn Whitmer, 12525 Ophelia Drive, Pensacola, Florida 32506. ◇

PHOTO STYLING: JULIA HAMILTON THOMASON

(**Above**) *A pair of fat bunnies rests near a supper of cabbage and pansies.*
(**Right**) *A lead-finished concrete urn with fruit is a fitting accessory for this garden room. Notice how variations in the color of the paint help accentuate the many details of the design.*

For the Look of Lead

A little paint transforms concrete ornaments into something special. Paint one, start to finish, in an afternoon.

by LINDA ASKEY WEATHERS
photography CHERYL DALTON, COLLEEN DUFFLEY

Lead garden ornaments not only endure, but they also get better with age. The metal develops a weathered appearance that enhances the ornaments' details. However, lead ornaments are costly and often hard to find. Meanwhile, you'll find a variety of reasonably priced pieces cast in concrete. The good news is that, with a little paint, you can have the look of lead for the price of concrete.

The key to this illusion is to choose an ornament that looks like it could be made of lead. Light, graceful, or formal classical or neoclassical pieces are usually best suited for a faux lead finish. Also, some concrete ornaments may have a rough surface. Look for one that is as smooth as possible for the best effect.

The techniques shown in the photographs are based on the methods of James Emmett, a decorative designer from Middleburg, Virginia. "Use a water-based exterior paint," Emmett explains. "On a warm day when it is

very dry, set the ornament out in the sun and apply the paint. It soaks into the grain, and it's dry in about 5 minutes. The reason I use latex is that oil will peel right off. Don't put polyurethane over the paint; that gives it too much sheen."

For the ornaments shown on these pages, we used two colors of flat exterior latex paint—an earthy, yellow-gray putty color called Glacier Gray by Pittsburgh Paints and a dark, charcoal shade called Gun Powder by Martin Senour.

If you are working on a container, Emmett recommends sealing the inside with a concrete water sealant or melted paraffin. Or if it's a large container, he lines it with a plastic pot and packs mulch between the two.

Statuary is not as complex because there are fewer complications from moisture. And with the finer finish, these decorative concrete pieces are as suitable for use indoors as they are outside. ◇

This planter appears to be as old and weathered as the mossy wall it adorns.

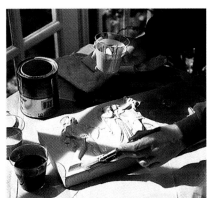

Step 1: *Mix half putty-colored paint with half water; paint liberally on the concrete. Allow it to drip, then dry.*

Step 2: *Mix half gray and half water. Paint this on, letting it puddle and run down. Let it dry.*

Step 3: *Mix equal parts putty, gray, and water. Paint and sponge this on, but before it dries completely, wipe it off. Let paint remain in the crevices of the piece. If this coat doesn't wipe off easily, use a moist rag.*

Step 4: *You can continue to refine the finish by retouching with putty or gray on a damp rag. This extra step makes the finish more complex. When paint is completely dry, use a soft rag to polish it a bit.*

APRIL

CHECKLIST
64

BEARDED IRIS, BLOOMS
WITHOUT BOTHER
66

A LITTLE LAWN INSIDE
69

QUIET ENTRY FOR
A BUSY STREET
70

PRACTICALLY PERFECT PINK
72

A BACKYARD THEY CAN USE
73

CUT FLOWERS FOR AN
EASY SPLASH OF COLOR
74

TINY FLOWERS AND
GIANT TREES
75

REDISCOVER ANTIQUE ROSES
76

CHECKLIST
for April

AZALEAS

Buy azaleas in bloom to match existing ones and to be sure that the flowers do not clash with the color of your home. Depending on the selection, mature azaleas can range from 2 to 12 feet in both height and spread. This might influence where you plant them and how far apart they need to be.

BEDDING PLANTS

An easy way to mulch beds of annuals is to prepare the soil, spread the mulch, and then set out transplants. That way you don't have to take the time to spread the mulch between all the little plants.

CALADIUMS

Gardeners whose caladiums have died because of Fusarium fungus disease or root-knot nematodes should look for new varieties from the University of Florida that tolerate these problems. Florida Cardinal has vigorous leaves about 18 inches tall with a solid-red center. It is useful for pots or the garden in sun or shade, although the red color is best in partial shade. Florida Roselight is a garden caladium (23 to 26 inches tall) with green veins and rose blotches throughout the foliage. It also will tolerate full sun.

DOGWOODS

If you are considering a dogwood for your garden, consider the differences between a seedling tree and a named selection (such as Cloud 9 or Cherokee Princess). Seedling trees are less expensive, but they may take longer to start flowering. In addition, dogwood anthracnose can be a problem in the Middle and Upper South if the tree is dug out of the woods. Be sure to buy only disease-free stock from a reputable nursery.

INSECTICIDAL SOAP

Although considered less toxic to the environment than many chemicals, insecticidal soap can injure plants if applied unwisely. If a plant is dry and stressed, a soap spray may burn the leaves. Water well, and wait several hours before spraying. Also, be careful when spraying any plant that has a lot of tender new growth. If you have any doubt, spray a small portion of the plant and wait 48 hours. If there is no injury, you can treat the rest of the plant.

LEAF DROP

Southern magnolias naturally shed older leaves at this time of year, so don't think there is something wrong with your tree if many leaves are on the ground. Gardenias may also shed leaves now, although leaf drop on them may be aggravated by dry weather or a late frost. Water and fertilize gardenias and magnolias to encourage new growth and summer blooms.

LUBBER GRASSHOPPERS

In the Lower and Coastal South, young lubbers begin reappearing in droves this time of year to strip begonias, ferns, amaryllis, and just about any other lush foliage. The best time to control them is now, while they are young. Adults are nearly impossible to kill. You can recognize the nymphs by their black bodies and red to yellow stripe right down their back. To control the pests, spray or dust plants with Sevin or rotenone. Reapply after rain or watering until all the pests are gone.

MOSQUITOES

Gardeners who grow bromeliads with cups that hold water should be aware that mosquitoes can breed in such a tiny pond. To prevent problems, apply a little *Bacillus thuringiensis var. israelensis* into the cup on a regular basis. This product is a relative of the familiar Dipel, the Bt widely used to kill cabbageworms, cabbage loopers, tomato hornworms, and other caterpillars in the vegetable garden. It is available as a spray or as briquettes. If you can't find this product at a local nursery, it may be purchased by mail order from Gardens Alive, 5100 Schenley Place, Lawrenceburg, Indiana 47025.

MOWING

The grass is growing, so remember to mow safely. Clear the area of people and pets to avoid injury from objects thrown by the mower. Never mow barefoot or in sandals or tennis shoes; wear more substantial shoes or boots. When mowing on a slope, push the mower across the slope, rather than up and down. You could easily slip on freshly mown grass. Always push the mower; never pull it toward you.

PERENNIALS

You can divide crowded plants now. Use a fork or spade to dig around the plant; then lift it out of the ground. Most clumps will just pull apart, but you may need to use a knife on others. Slice crowns into pieces, making sure there are new shoots and a clump of roots in each division. Plant at the depth they were originally growing, and water frequently.

PLANT LABELS

Keeping records of your garden plants can be very helpful, and one way is to label them in the garden. If one garden pink (*Dianthus* sp.) outperforms the other, for instance, it's helpful to know which is which. And if a perennial dies down in the winter, a label will remind you not to dig it up or walk on it by accident.

ROSES

We received a letter from a reader puzzled by the stringy, distorted growth on her climbing rose. Mike Shoup of the Antique Rose Emporium says that this problem can be caused by drifting spray of a glyphosate, such as Roundup, used to treat nearby weeds. It may take as long as six months for symptoms to disappear. In the meantime, be sure to avoid spraying any chemicals on windy days. Repeated exposure can prolong the problem.

TIP OF THE MONTH

Here's how to multiply your beets. After the beets are at least ¾ inch in diameter, pull them up without damaging the roots. Cut the tops off. Divide each beet into quarters, making sure each quarter has a piece of root. Plant the quarters in the garden 4 to 6 inches apart. Each quarter will make an odd-shaped beet. But instead of one beet, you'll have four, all of which will grow large and delicious.

Roy S. Smith
Thibodaux, Louisiana

APRIL NOTES

To Do:
- Leave bulb foliage alone until it turns yellow
- Prune dead wood out of winter-damaged trees and shrubs
- Be ready to protect newly-planted flowers from unexpected frosts
- Visit the garden center early for the best selection of flower and vegetable transplants

To Plant:
- Caladiums, glads, cannas, and other summer-flowering bulbs
- Azaleas, rhododendrons, flowering shrubs
- In the Coastal, Lower, and Middle South, tomatoes, beans, squash, cucumbers, peppers, onions, okra, eggplant, corn

To Purchase:
- Flower and vegetable transplants
- Summer-flowering bulbs
- Any necessary insecticide, fungicide, or fertilizer
- Vegetable and flower seeds

The upright flowers and foliage of bearded iris contrast nicely with the rounded shapes of boxwood and the prostrate form of garden pinks.

Bearded iris, planted here with blue phlox and pink foxgloves, can be a dramatic centerpiece in any garden.

Bearded Iris

Blooms Without Bother

BY STEVE BENDER
PHOTOGRAPHY VAN CHAPLIN

Maybe I am just a bit off the beam, but when I look at all the flashy, prize-winning bearded iris we have today, I can't help thinking of a former relief pitcher for the Boston Red Sox named Dick Radatz.

Radatz pitched during the early sixties, and for a few years literally terrorized American League batters with his monstrous fastball. Then he thought to himself, "Gee, they're all afraid of my fastball. What if I started throwing a slider, too?" A fatal mistake. In throwing the new pitch, Radatz changed his delivery and ended up hurting his arm. Shortly, he was out of baseball for good, a victim of his own tinkering.

Such pointless fiddling has also taken a toll on bearded iris. The iris that I know, the ones I grew up with, bloom beautifully spring after spring with almost no care. No spraying, no watering, no space-age fertilizers. But the newest selections seem to lack this grit. They have been bred for bigger flowers, more flowers, flowers in all sorts of exotic colors, and they look wonderful when cut and displayed at flower shows. But in your garden, most demand more attention than a toddler at the top of the stairs.

This is a shame, for good bearded iris need only admiration, never pampering. Growing from fleshy roots

Margaret Sanders doesn't know the name of these old-fashioned bearded iris in her Columbus, Mississippi, garden. But she does know to let well enough alone— they flourish without any special care.

called rhizomes, these herbaceous perennials produce truly phenomenal blossoms in April and May. Each bloom consists of three upright petals, called "standards," and three drooping sepals, called "falls." Fuzzy "beards," looking like painted caterpillars, adorn the falls, giving the plants their name. The blooms come in just about every color you've ever seen, and many are sweetly fragrant. Together with swordlike leaves, the tall flower spikes lend the garden a striking, vertical form that complements more rounded and horizontal perennials, such as peonies, pinks, candytuft, and blue phlox.

Good bearded iris aren't merely beautiful—they're also effortless to grow. No popular perennial is more drought tolerant. They need water only at planting time and during their period of active growth in the spring. Other than that, watering is optional. Water if you mind brown tips on the foliage in August; don't water if you don't. Perennial grower Andre Viette of Fishersville, Virginia, agrees. "Even in the severest drought," he states, "iris may shrivel, but they'll never die."

Most perennials that endure drought require good drainage. That's certainly the case here. You'd have better luck growing bearded iris on the center line of the interstate than in a low, soggy area with heavy clay soil. These plants actually prefer dry soil in summer, which is why you seldom see them growing in Florida and along the Gulf Coast.

Plant bearded iris in late winter, summer, or fall. Select a sunny, slightly elevated spot that sheds water quickly. Loosen the soil to a depth of about a foot and work in copious organic matter, such as compost, composted manure, sphagnum peat moss, and shredded leaves. Plant rhizomes a foot apart, but don't bury them completely. Nan Elizabeth Miles, who's been growing iris in Birmingham for 50 years, says, "Plant them so they look like ducks on a lake—with the top half of the rhizomes showing." Firm soil over the whitish feeder roots; then water thoroughly. Don't cover the rhizomes with mulch. "You can mulch between the iris," explains Viette, "but don't put mulch on top. The tops of the rhizomes should bake in the sun."

Although fancy new iris solicit frequent fertilizer and borer spray, the tried-and-true types mostly get by on their own. Given fertile soil, they beg for little extra food. But if you're feeling especially charitable, sprinkle a modicum of slow-release, organic fertilizer, such as blood meal, bone meal, or cottonseed meal, around the rhizomes in spring, just after the flowers fade. Iris borers, which hollow out rhizomes, may be a problem now and again. However, Nan claims you can control them through good sanitation. First, look for the telltale signs of borers in early spring—water-soaked, streaky leaves or leaves with ragged edges near the base. Cut off and destroy these leaves. Next, pull off and destroy all brown, shriveled leaves in late fall.

Divide iris when the rhizomes become hunched and crowded—as Nan puts it, "when they look like children all sitting on their knees." Do this in August and September. Lift the rhizomes from the ground, and divide them into sections, making sure each section has feeder roots and a fan of leaves.

I'd never pontificate about the virtues of care-free bearded iris if I didn't have selections to recommend. Iris experts from across the South recently sent me lists of selections they've found easiest to grow. You'll find 10 of their top picks listed here. Not surprisingly, a good many of these plants have been around for 20 or 30 years. For mail-order sources, send a self-addressed, stamped, business-size envelope to Bearded Iris Editor, P.O. Box 830119, Birmingham, Alabama 35283.

TEN BEARDED IRIS FOR THE SOUTH

Arctic Fury—white
Beverly Sills—coral pink
Blue Sapphire—light blue
Carolina Gold—gold
Debbie Rairdon—white and creamy yellow
Mary Frances—light orchid blue
Stepping Out—purple and white
Vanity—pink
Victoria Falls—powder blue
Winter Olympics—white

This splendid springtime combination in the Atlanta garden of Ginger Epstein blends tall white bearded iris, shorter Japanese roof iris, and peonies.

Close-cropped grass in ceramic vessels evokes a garden harvest.

Imagine the surprise when a young child finds Easter eggs nestled in a basket of real grass. Lining the basket with foil will protect it from stains and rotting.

A Little Lawn Inside

In a day and age when there are artificial substitutes for everything from foliage to fat, it's nice to stay in touch with what's real. So this Easter, why not try real grass for the basket? While it's an easy project for kids, you may find it sparks imaginative ways to incorporate living grass into your decorating ideas.

And easy it is. Select a container, add a few inches of potting soil, sprinkle ryegrass seeds on top, rake lightly with a fork, and mist or spray with water until the soil is moist. Place the container in a well-lit area, and in about 10 days you should see grass blades emerging. A week later, you'll have a "lawn" several inches tall.

If using an Easter basket or wooden container, line the container with foil or plastic. The grass will last longer if the soil can drain, however,

Two stems of nerine lilies are set into a small basket of grass and held together with a raffia bow. Concealed water picks keep the cut flowers fresh.

so you may opt for a ceramic, plaster, or terra-cotta container with drain holes. Place a thin layer of small rocks on the bottom; then add at least 2 inches of soil. Set it on a tray to catch water that runs through.

Ryegrass seed (perennial or annual) costs about 50 cents a pound and you'll only need a couple of ounces. Sow the seeds thickly but don't pile them on top of each other. Be sure the seeds are slightly covered or surrounded by the soil for good germination.

We recommend watering with a spray bottle to avoid having the seeds clump. Keep the soil moist; you will need to spray a couple of times each day until the seeds sprout. To speed up the process and reduce the frequency of watering, cover the container with plastic wrap, and punch a few holes in it so the grass can breathe. If you go this route, avoid exposure to direct sunlight to prevent burning the seed.

Once the grass is up, continue spraying daily. When it reaches the desired height, simply "mow" the lawn with a pair of scissors. You'll have a healthy stand for several weeks. Keep in mind that if you allow the grass to keep on growing it will flop over.

The possibilities of using grass in this fashion are endless, from miniature landscapes grown in wooden crates to turf around a houseplant. Or put stems of cut flowers into water picks, and set them into a container of grass for a miniature garden.

Todd A. Steadman

Quiet Entry for a Busy Street

In a garden, time brings maturity—grand old trees and cooling shade. But time can also transform a garden from a satisfactory design into an impractical one. Such change was all too evident when Cecil and Caroline Nelson purchased their home in an established Greenville, South Carolina, neighborhood.

In the original design, a long front walk led from the street to the front door of the house. That was fine when the street carried only neighborhood traffic. But it has become too busy for guests to safely pull up to the curb, park, and walk to the door.

Fortunately the Nelsons' home was built on a corner lot. Landscape Architect J. D. Martin of Arbor Engineering redirected the front walk to the quieter side street and designed a new entry. Then he made it comfortable with a curbside landing that emphasizes the entry and welcomes guests with an even, paved surface when they step out of their car.

In addition to making the entry more practical, Martin felt that the side approach was aesthetically more pleasing than the original view. Planting beds and a brick retaining wall obscure any trace of the former walk. It is obvious from the front that "you can't get there from here," so guests instinctively turn onto the side street and park near the new landing.

From the house, the plantings near the main street provide a visual buffer from the traffic, making their front yard an outdoor room, rather than a corridor to walk through.

Martin chose plants for texture, dependability, and repetition. He notes, "The yard was not designed to see how many plants you could get in, but to hold the lines [of the design] together. Although there is seasonal interest, on a day-to-day basis there is consistency."

The workhorse plants were chosen for their evergreen texture and tolerance to shade. They include pachysandra and liriope for ground

The circular landing echoes the semicircular steps and arched pediment. Caroline keeps colorful annuals blooming in the bed opposite the door.

When Cecil and Caroline bought their home, the walk went straight from the front door to the street. Unfortunately, the street was too busy for guests to comfortably park and walk to the door.

Today, passersby glimpse the house through the tree and shrub plantings. Actually, the house is more interesting because it is partially concealed.

Landscape Architect J. D. Martin relocated the walk to the side of the corner lot, where Tripp and Eleanor Gray Nelson await their carpool.

cover, carissa and hetz hollies for low-growing shrubs, and taller Japanese andromeda and Japanese cleyera for structure.

But regardless of the problems to be solved, the design needed to fit into the context of the neighborhood. Caroline explains, "Our street in spring was a mass of dogwoods, but they stopped at our yard." So Martin planted dogwoods to fit the neighborhood theme, as well as saucer magnolias, Japanese maples, and tree-form Fortunes osmanthus.

Even though the design was carefully detailed, it remains surprisingly low maintenance. All trees and shrubs were chosen to grow into their allotted space. The fescue lawn is contained by ground covers, so edging is not necessary. And with no odd mowing angles, it is easy to maintain. "Cecil doesn't like to do much in the yard," observes Caroline. "He can cut the grass in 10 to 15 minutes, and that's the end of it."

Linda A. Weathers

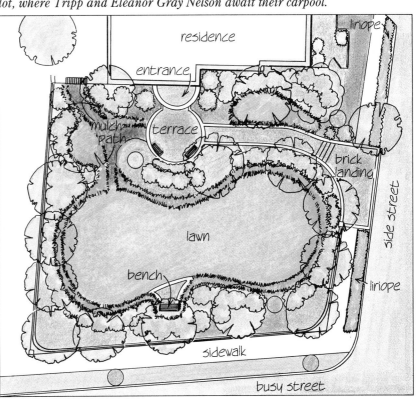

Practically Perfect Pink

Many of the plants commonly seen in our gardens, such as George Taber azalea, bear the names of people we do not know. Thus, it's exciting to discover a wonderful new plant for the South that's named for a good friend. The plant in question is Bath's pink, named for Jane Bath, a garden designer whose words and garden have graced these pages many times.

Bath's pink is a perennial form of *Dianthus* that Jane spied years ago in a neighbor's garden in Stone Mountain, Georgia. The neighbor planned to move, so Jane rescued the plant and transferred it to her own garden. Before long, it began to outshine the other pinks she was growing. Unlike them, this one didn't become woody and sparse in the center, rot in wet weather, or fall victim to winter cold. "I noticed that it was very tolerant of total abuse," she recalls. "But the nicest thing was, it looked good all the time."

Some time later, Jane gave starts of the plant to two wholesale growers

The fine-textured, blue-green leaves of Bath's pink are as handsome in winter as they are in summer.

Usually a fine choice for the foreground of a mixed border, here Bath's pink creeps over the edge of a low, stacked wall.

who admired it while touring her garden. They decided to produce it commercially, having found it much more attractive and easier to grow than other pinks. Because no one could determine the plant's original name, the two named the foundling in honor of Jane.

Given a reasonably sunny, well-drained location, Bath's pink spreads quickly to form a mat of bright blue-green foliage. It makes a fine ground cover, filler, or edging plant; you can also let it drape over a low stone wall. Sweet-smelling pink blossoms appear for two to three weeks in spring. According to *Southern Living* photographer Van Chaplin, who grows Bath's pink in his garden, the fragrance is outstanding. "You know how you can smell some flowers from 3 feet away?" asks Van. "Well, the fragrance of these flowers will fill your whole yard and your neighbor's yard, too."

Perfumed blossoms aren't this plant's foremost feature, however. That distinction belongs to its handsome evergreen foliage. As Jane explains, "I don't care what anyone says about the blooms of any plant. If the foliage looks bad, two weeks of beauty won't make up for 50 weeks of ugly." Bath's pink, on the other hand, looks good 52 weeks a year. For a striking effect, try planting it next to perennials having deep-green or yellow-green leaves.

Should fellow gardeners covet your Bath's pink and ask for a sprig, don't worry—few plants are as easy to root or divide. "You can just rip it up and give it to your friends; you don't even have to put it in a plastic bag," declares Jane. "They can stuff it in their pocket, go home, stick it in the ground, and watch it grow."

Lest you suspect that Jane might have an ulterior motive for promoting Bath's pink, be advised she receives no royalties or fees from its sale. Not that she'd mind the money—but to her, fellow gardeners enjoying her discovery is reward enough.

Steve Bender

For a list of mail-order sources, send a self-addressed, stamped, business-size envelope to Bath's Pink Editor, P.O. Box 830119, Birmingham, Alabama 35283.

PHOTOGRAPHS: VAN CHAPLIN

From an arbor, a narrow lawn rises between perennial beds. Janice Whitehead, daughter Katherine, and dog Bandit relax on a brick retaining wall.

A Backyard They Can Use

When Janice and David Whitehead moved into their Harrisonburg, Virginia, home, they could stand their new backyard, they just couldn't stand *up* in it. Although native dogwoods and oaks graced the site, the lot dropped steeply from the house to the property line. The couple wanted a level play area for their children, as well as a suitable area for growing perennials. But they didn't want to sacrifice the trees they inherited.

Charlottesville landscape architect Jack Douglas, ASLA, provided the answer. On the garden's lower end, he designed a semicircular lawn bordered by boxwoods and a handsome Chippendale fence. The fence sits atop an 8-foot retaining wall, which holds the soil added to make the lawn level. Regrading the area did force the removal of a few small trees. But in return, the family gained a wonderful play spot for the children.

Walking up a set of brick steps, you pass beneath an arbor into the garden's upper end, which is much less formal than the lower. A narrow lawn rises gently between Janice's perennial beds located in the garden's sunniest spot. An avid gardener, Janice grows flowers for cutting and also for sharing with fellow members of her garden club. A small fishpond at the apex of the lawn provides a serene focal point.

Thanks to careful, sensitive design, the garden satisfies the Whiteheads' needs without compromising the setting's natural beauty. Flowers, shrubs, bulbs, lawn, and trees coexist peacefully, to the delight of local birds, squirrels, and other assorted critters. Adds Janice proudly, "We've even had deer." *Steve Bender*

Regrading and filling produced a level, semicircular lawn on the garden's lower end. Behind the boxwoods, the lot drops off 8 feet.

PHOTOGRAPHS: VAN CHAPLIN, BRUCE ROBERTS

Cut flowers, such as these sunflowers, make excellent bouquets for indoors and out. For best results, cut them late in the afternoon and place stems in tepid water overnight before arranging.

Marigolds not only are excellent as cut flowers but also bloom very well in hot, dry weather.

Cut Flowers for an Easy Splash of Color

For most Southerners, including me, gardening is a variety of things—making the home grounds look good, planting annuals and perennials, and for some, growing vegetables. Well, it's very easy and inexpensive to add another category to this list—producing cut flowers. For only a few dollars and one row in a sunny spot, you can grow flowers to cut until the fall frost kills the plants. Annuals, such as zinnias, marigolds, and the smaller types of sunflowers, are easy to grow for a full season of cut flowers to enjoy.

Experience has taught me to wait until the soil warms up before planting. If you are a vegetable gardener and plant okra, seed your row of cut flowers at the same time. Otherwise, wait until daytime temperatures are consistently in the 70s.

Zinnias produce cut flowers all season. These were planted in a row adjacent to kale.

Before you plant, keep a couple of things in mind. First, buy seeds of flowers that will produce stems long enough for easy cutting and arranging. Marigolds, such as the Merrymum hybrids, Zenith series, Climax Hybrid series, and the Lady Hybrid series, are excellent choices. Zinnias, such as the Tetra Ruffled Jumbo series, Zenith Hybrid series, and Bouquet hybrids, have long stems and are easy to cut. Piccolo and Teddy Bear sunflowers have multiple flowers per stem and arrange easily. If you are in a store ready to buy seeds and cannot remember our recommendations, review the package. Usually, if they are good as cut flowers it will say so.

Second, and just as important in my mind, choose colors that work in your home and blend with each other. Zinnias come in a wide variety of colors; marigolds and sunflowers are generally in the yellow and orange tones.

Any location is good as long as you have full sun and a well-prepared area. Till or dig the soil deeply so roots have room to grow; then they won't require excessive watering during the dry summer periods. Sow seed according to the package directions. Once they germinate, thin to several inches apart.

Remember a few final tips. Cut where the flower will grow again—above a leaflet if possible, so that every cut will hopefully produce two more flower stalks. And, if your flowers are fertilized a couple of times and regularly watered, you should have an almost constant bouquet from early summer until frost.

John Alex Floyd, Jr.

Tiny Flowers and Giant Trees

Early on a Tennessee morning, long before the Gatlinburg shoppers and gawkers are awake, cars meander through the mountains. One by one, they nudge into the parking lot at the headquarters of the Great Smoky Mountains National Park, and the sleepy-eyed adventurers emerge, eager for a nature walk with the Smoky Mountain Field School.

The outing begins when our leader, Dr. Eugene Wofford, strides up in well-worn boots. We load up and caravan to Indian Camp Creek Trail. We leave the sunlight of a one-lane road to enter the dimly lit trail that feels like a moist sponge underfoot. It is sheltered by boughs of old rhododendrons shaded by a second-growth forest.

Our destination is Albright Grove, a stand of virgin timber that is a treasured remnant of the grand forests that once covered the Smokies. But first we enjoy the trail before us. We learn the most familiar plants along the trail—the rattlesnake plantain, galax, and partridgeberry. It doesn't take long to spot a treasure, and the keen eye does not belong to our leader. "Hey, look!" comes a call from a man from Kentucky. We gather around a tiny orchid grow-

ing in the gully at the edge of the trail. It's a three-bird-orchid, the first our leader had seen in the park.

We're instructed to steer clear of the stinging nettle. But if we should stumble into it, the wisdom is to apply the leaves of the wild touch-me-nots to relieve the pain.

Before long we're summoned by another shout, and again we see a small, rare orchid, spotted by the sharp eyes from Kentucky. Our leader attributes this abundance of orchids to the plentiful rainfall.

The sound of rushing water grows louder until we round a turn on a downhill stretch to find the perfect mountain stream—white falls around granite boulders, with rhododendron making an arbor over a narrow branch, and a log bridge spanning the wider portion. We lunch in small groups, sitting soggy on rocks and logs, shouting over the sound of the stream to talk about what's to come.

Our anticipation is too great to linger, so we hastily pack up our lunches and take again to the trail, toward the cathedral of poplar and hemlock as old as time.

It's not long before we enter the grove, a singular place with trees growing so large it takes eight of us

to reach around the girth of a single tulip poplar. Our leader suggests a silent hike, but he didn't need to prompt us. The majesty of the place stills our chatter. The magnificent scale of the trees endows them with a presence so powerful it demands whispers.

In a virgin forest it often helps to recognize trees by their bark because the leaves are too high up to identify. The binoculars we brought for birds are more often used for spotting the leaves we need to confirm the trees' identities.

This regal wood is more like a rainforest than a temperate forest. We see a yellow birch that had begun perhaps five years ago as a seed. It had germinated on a rotting stump and thrived on the ever-present moisture, sending exposed roots down the sides of the stump. After 20 more years the stump will give way to decay, leaving a tree standing up on its roots, like a man doing push-ups on his fingertips.

This is a pilgrimage of sorts for Dr. Wofford. He hadn't been to the grove this year, and we're grateful he has brought us along to this garden of ferns and moss, luminous green in the moisture and diffused light of the ancient canopy.

We pay our respects and trudge back the way we came. Back toward the cars, back through the 40-year-old forest that only hours before had been our chief delight. Now we turn back to the blacktop roads and the afternoon traffic of Gatlinburg. The stoplights are not the obstacle that they had been in the morning. Now they allow a quiet moment to reflect on the day, the trees, and the flowers.   *Linda A. Weathers*

YELLOW POPLAR

The Smoky Mountain Field School is a cooperative effort between Great Smoky Mountains National Park and the University of Tennessee, offering courses on the geology, birds, plants, and mammals found within the park. For additional information or for a brochure of programs, write the University of Tennessee Noncredit Programs, 600 Henley Street, Suite 105, Knoxville, Tennessee 37902; or call 1-800-284-8885.

Rediscover Antique Roses

BY LINDA ASKEY WEATHERS
PHOTOGRAPHY VAN CHAPLIN

Get out of the car at the Antique Rose Emporium in Independence, Texas, and you're struck at once by the seductive fragrance of roses. Roses are everywhere—climbing, cascading, and standing in hedges. But these are mostly old roses, cultivated long before the first hybrid tea rose was introduced in 1867.

"People are so intimidated by roses, but these old garden roses shouldn't even share the same name with a modern rose. They are completely different," says Mike Shoup, owner of the Emporium. In the last hundred years, rose breeders have focused on improving the flowers and strengthening the stems while sacrificing some qualities inherent in a sturdy plant, such as hardiness and fragrance.

Shoup is a member of a self-professed group of "rose rustlers." He has rescued quite a few cuttings from abandoned homesites

At Texas' Antique Rose Emporium, old roses—hardy, fragrant, and historic—are very much in demand today.

where the roses were planted by early settlers who brought a few cuttings to Texas. Those roses suited to the climate survived longer than the people who planted them. In fact, they've endured without the benefit of regular watering, pruning, or pesticides, proving their worth through generations of Texas history.

Shoup gives these foundlings names that recall the site where they were found. Examples include Natchitoches Noisette, Highway 290 Pink Buttons, or Georgetown Tea. Many have been identified later as the same old roses grown in other gardens by more recognizable names.

The rose rustlers like to grow cuttings from old roses on their own stock, rather than grafting the cutting onto a different rootstock, which is the dominant practice in modern rose production. "We grow them on their own root, and they have fantastic

Prosperity is a rose that would seem at home in an antebellum homestead.

Carol Henry greets visitors to the Emporium with a smile.

Mike Shoup and Tramp relax beneath a rustic arbor.

vigor," says Shoup, who, like any good gardener, imitates what he has observed in nature. "I haven't found any surviving roses that are grafted, so what does that tell you?"

But his reason is doubly practical. "Many modern roses that are grafted on a rootstock are fussy, and they don't like to be planted with their roots among other plantings. The old garden roses are not that particular."

Relatively low maintenance is one characteristic that sells many gardeners on old roses. "We don't really advocate heavy spray schedules at all," cautions Shoup. "That's not to say that these roses are not going to get black spot or mildew—they do. But they grow out of it, as exhibited by the fact that they are surviving out here and at abandoned homesites and places like that. They'll just go through a period where they might lose some of their leaves, but it is not debilitating."

Another appeal of old roses is that their history is often entwined with human history. For example, the parent of the Noisette class, Champney's Pink Cluster, was bred in Charleston, South Carolina, in the early 1800s. A Charleston nurseryman by the name of Noisette sent seedlings to his brother in Paris, where many more were developed. Now they have come back home, but with names like Céline Forestier and Madame Alfred Carrière. Yet, true to their heritage, they perform beautifully in the American South.

Not all old roses do. Shoup observes, "The books written in England and New England talk about tea, China, and Noisette roses they can't grow that are fabulous down here, and yet we don't do nearly as well with the gallicas, the damasks, and the mosses that they can grow so well."

Shoup's first interest, landscaping with hardier native plants, explains his philosophy of rose gardening: "We don't want to quarantine roses in a rectangle in our backyard and spray them like we do modern hybrid teas. Generally, old roses are very compatible with other garden plantings, so you can plant them with perennials or existing shrubs. Each one is distinct in their form, and each fits a niche in the garden, whether it's a climber, ground cover, or container plant. People come here to see how we have

Madame Isaac Pereire, 1881   *Will Scarlet, 1948*   *Cornelia, 1925*   *Ards Rover, 1948*

This bountiful planting of Marie Pavié sweetens the air with its fragrance.

A bounty of flowers adorns the homestead indoors and out.

incorporated them in the garden and how to use them."

To be sure, the Antique Rose Emporium is more than a collection of roses. It's a garden. What remains of the old homestead has been painstakingly restored. The picket fence encloses the kitchen cottage garden, demonstrating Shoup's ideal of roses as garden plants. There they flourish with Louisiana iris, garden pinks, columbine, phlox, petunias, and other flowers. An herb garden is planted in the shape of a wheel, with triangular beds between the "spokes." Red Gi-

ant mustard, fennel, dill, salvia, feverfew, society garlic, and more flourish there. The Mexican plum in the corner by the kitchen steps tells of Shoup's continuing interest in all types of native plants.

A windmill is original to the site, as is a barn-turned-gift shop. The log corn crib was relocated from elsewhere on the property and pressed into service as a shop. This cluster of buildings captures the nostalgia of the homestead, and arbors, beds, and containers of roses cement the image into reality.

Although the Emporium has a thriving mail-order business, there's no substitute for having the experience yourself. You have to breathe the fragrance, walk the flower-lined paths, and stand under the rose-draped arbors. And, perhaps, take an antique rose home with you.

For more information see Mike Shoup and co-author Liz Druitt's new book titled *Landscaping with Antique Roses,* published by The Taunton Press. For a personal account of rose rustling, read Thomas Christopher's remembrance in Chapter 3 of *In Search of Lost Roses,* published by Summit Books in 1989.

The Antique Rose Emporium's catalog is available for $5 by writing the Antique Rose Emporium, Route 5, Box 143, Brenham, Texas 77833; or call 1-800-441-0002.

But best of all, check your map and turn your wheels toward the town of Brenham, Texas. From there take State 105-E for 2 to 3 miles. Turn left onto State 50. Travel for 10 miles to find the Emporium on the right. The Emporium is open year-round from 9 a.m. until 6 p.m. Monday through Saturday and from 11 a.m. until 6 p.m. Sunday.

GARDEN NICHES AND ROSES TO FILL THEM

- *Climbers for arbors, fences, walls, and pillars*
  Madame Alfred Carrière
  Ards Rover
- *Cascading roses for informal borders*
  Cornelia
  Madame Isaac Pereire
- *Specimen plants for center stage*
  Duchesse de Brabant
  Marquise Boccella
- *Roses for borders or containers*
  Marie Pavié
  Cécile Brünner

MAY

CHECKLIST
84

FAVORITE, FOOLPROOF
PERENNIALS
86

GROW A COLORFUL CARPET
OF AJUGA
89

A CELEBRATION OF WHITE
90

LILIES FOR HOT
SOUTHERN SUMMERS
91

WEEDS, WEEDS, WEEDS!
92

WHO'S TO BLAME FOR
FALLING TREES
93

UPFRONT
WITH A LANDSCAPE PLAN
94

CHECKLIST
for May

APHIDS

Wilting or discolored new growth are common signs of aphids. Spraying with insecticidal soap and blasting with a jet of water from the garden hose are two safe and easy controls. The key to keeping their numbers down is persistence: Check plants every few days for signs of reinfestation and treat as soon as possible.

AZALEAS

Before cutting back an overgrown azalea, consider removing its lower limbs to create a handsome small tree. Limbs should be cut close to the trunk so as not to leave large stubs. Keep the plants green and healthy by feeding with a slow-release azalea fertilizer that contains iron as well as other minor elements.

BEDDING PLANTS

For seasonal color, set out flowering plants, such as marigolds, salvia, and impatiens. Water well after planting, and fertilize with liquid plant food.

BLACKBERRIES

After harvesting blackberries, prune established bushes to stimulate good fruit production next year. Remove fruiting canes at ground level. New canes that didn't bear fruit should be cut back to 3 to 4 feet in length.

BORERS

If a tree or shrub looks unhealthy, check the base for signs of borers. Symptoms include loose bark, sawdust, or tunnels under loose bark. Controls vary widely depending upon the plant. For specific recommendations, contact your county Extension agent.

CHRYSANTHEMUMS

Let your garden mums bloom before cutting them back for fall flower displays. Cut plants to within several inches of the ground before the first of August to ensure good fall blossoms.

CLEMATIS

For best results, plant clematis now. Find a well-drained spot with plenty of sun for the foliage and shade for the roots. Enrich poor soil with organic matter, and add several inches of organic mulch after planting. Fertilize lightly every six weeks, and water regularly. Clematis generally needs support to climb. Good selections for the South include *Clematis montana* Rubens (rosy red to pale pink), Henryi (white), Nelly Moser (mauve pink with deep-pink centers) and Jackmanii (purple).

CONTAINER PLANTS

Outdoor areas are often perfect for pots of flowers, herbs, or small ornamental shrubs. Good annuals for sunny spots include begonia, Madagascar periwinkle (*Annual vinca*), and moss rose (*Portulaca*). Coleus and impatiens are great for shade. Try adding one of the new water-absorbing polymers, such as Water Grabber, to reduce the need for frequent watering. Fertilize every 3 to 4 weeks with a water-soluble fertilizer.

EGGPLANT

Gardeners throughout the South can plant eggplant now. Space plants 2 to 3 feet apart in rows 2 to 2½ feet wide. Apply 20-20-20 liquid plant fertilizer after planting; then fertilize each plant with ¼ cup of 10-10-10 granular or equivalent organic fertilizer monthly. Water well. To keep plants producing, pick fruits when 3 to 5 inches long and still shiny.

GLADIOLUS

For blooms all summer long, stagger plantings of gladiolus two weeks apart from now through mid-June. Plant about 6 inches deep and 6 to 8 inches apart. Keep well watered. Taller selections will require staking when they reach 2 feet.

HERBS

Don't let partial shade stop you from growing herbs. Unlike most herbs, comfrey, costmary, sweet woodruff, and lovage all do well in shade.

LAWN EDGING

If you have a creeping grass lawn, use a power edger, string trimmer, spade, or other edging tool to keep borders neat. Inexpensive aluminum or plastic edging doesn't work well to control creeping grasses. Install durable edging, such as heavy-gauge metal, pressure-treated wood, or brick.

LAWNS

Fertilize lawns now for healthy growth; check with your local garden center or cooperative Extension service for recommended formulations and rates. Never apply fertilizer to wet grass, and make sure spreaders are set correctly and work properly before you use them. Flush the fertilizer hopper with plenty of water after using and then water your lawn to wash fertilizer granules into the turf. In Texas, Seville St. Augustine grass plugs should be available in garden centers from Dallas south. Now is an ideal time to establish this semi-dwarf grass. It performs well in shade, grows fast, and is resistant to disease.

MANGOES

One of our readers was kind enough to note that our February 1992 article on mangoes didn't mention a potential problem with the fruit. Contact with unripe fruit, as well as the sap (either from tree or stem), can cause irritation similar to poison ivy. Some people are more susceptible to this than others, but aloe vera gel seems to help reduce any irritation or itching. Also remember there is a two-day latent period before any symptoms appear.

MANGROVES

Mangroves provide habitats for wildlife, prevent shore erosion, and help maintain water quality by filtering runoff. In Florida, the state government has enacted regulations limiting mangrove pruning and removal to help prevent loss of mangrove wetlands. To find out how these regulations affect homeowners, contact your local offices of Sea Grant, Department of Natural Resources, or Department of Environmental Regulations.

MILDEW

Powdery mildew and downy mildew are common problems on many types of cucumbers and melons. Cucumbers resistant to both mildews include Hybrid Burpless, Slicemaster, and Hybrid Sweet Slice. Resistant cantaloupes include Aurora and Edisto 47. Tam Honeydew Improved is a resistant honeydew. There are no resistant watermelons.

MULCH

Mulching flower and shrub beds is easy insurance against dry spells and hot weather. Apply at least 2 to 3 inches of organic mulch to keep soils moist and cool.

PALMS

In warm regions of the South, this is the best time to plant palms. Small, container-grown palms may be easily planted without professional help. If you plan to install larger, single-trunk palms, be sure the contractor uses guy wires to anchor the top-heavy plant until its roots take hold.

SHRUBS

If you planted shrubs early in the spring, they probably need another feeding. Apply ½ cup of 5-10-10 or 6-12-12 per plant. Feed again in July.

SUCKERS

Remove suckers from around the base of small trees and shrubs. Small sprouts can easily be pulled by hand. If allowed to mature, they will need to be removed with pruning shears.

SUMMER ANNUALS

Some annuals do exceptionally well in the Coastal South and may behave as perennials. Pentas offer large clusters of pink, white, or red blooms that attract butterflies. They grow in partial shade or full sun. Cosmos, gomphrena, and vinca can take blazing sun. For shade, try torenia, coleus, or wax begonias. They do well under oaks, pines, and other trees whose shade is not too dense.

SUMMER FLOWERS

Bulbs, corms, and tubers can be planted now for a flower display that lasts until fall. Try calla lilies, crinum, ginger lilies, tuberose, and cannas. The new dwarf types of cannas, such as Tropical Rose, grow only 18 to 30 inches high and offer the same large, lush flowers as their taller kin.

TREES AND WIND

Trees in Florida are often subjected to high winds from sudden thunderstorms and tropical storms. Certain species fare better than others. These include pitch apple (*Clusia rosea*), Geiger tree (*Cordia sebestena*), carrotwood (*Cupaniopsis anacardioides*), live oak (*Quercus virginiana*), mahogany (*Swietenia mahogoni*), tamarind (*Tamarindus indica*), and palms.

VEGETABLES

It's planting time for most warm-season vegetables, such as cucumbers, tomatoes, pepper plants, squash, peas, and beans. If you've had a late spring, wait a few weeks until daytime temperatures are in the 70s.

MAY NOTES

To Do:
• Replace cool-weather flowers with summer flowers
• Mark gaps in spring bulb displays so you can add bulbs this fall
• Mulch trees, shrubs, and flower beds
• Sow seeds of warm season grasses
• Spray roses for black spot

To Plant:
• Summer vegetables and flowers
• Container-grown trees, shrubs, and perennials

To Purchase:
• New garden hoses and sprinklers, if needed
• Flower and vegetable transplants
• Grass seed or sod

_____

_____

_____

_____

Black-eyed Susans flourish in sun or light shade and bloom for two months in summer.

Favorite, Foolproof PERENNIALS

BY STEVE BENDER
PHOTOGRAPHY VAN CHAPLIN, BETH MAYNOR

The 1980s were the years that Southern gardeners saw the world. Whether by plane, boat, or television, we traveled in greater numbers than ever before to such places as Great Britain, Ireland, the European continent, and perhaps even below the equator to far-off Australia and New Zealand. As we trod past borders of herbaceous perennials—nonwoody plants that come back from the roots year after year—in such storied gardens as Hidcote and Sissinghurst, we naturally yearned to re-create these wonderful displays back home.

But there's a world of difference between the climates of London, England, and London, Arkansas. A plant that thrives in the former may fry in the latter. Thus, it's important that Southern gardeners concentrate on perennials well adapted to the extremes of our challenging environment. Fortunately, many exquisite perennials flourish here, needing no special care.

One of them, the super-resilient daylily, has been a particular joy to Atlanta's Barbara Stephens. Back in the fall of 1987, she ordered a "naturalizing mix" of 400 plants for a long border she had planned. "The roots came

in boxes," she recalls, "and when I opened them up, the roots looked like white asparagus. I said to myself, 'They'll never grow.' But I got out there, put them in the ground, and, incredibly, they were blooming the next spring." Since then, the plants have more than doubled in number. Composed of early, midseason, and late selections, the daylilies flower from late May until August.

Most gardeners think of ferns as finicky, delicate perennials that insist on daily rainfall and cool shade. But that's not true of the durable Southern shield fern (*Thelypteris kunthii*). As Dawn Bowman of Homewood, Alabama, discovered, if given good soil this deciduous fern will tolerate heat,

A stunning border of daylilies brings bright colors and graceful foliage to Barbara Stephens's Atlanta garden.

drought, and sun, as well as an occasional trampling from rampaging kids and dogs. A lush border of Southern shield ferns greets visitors to Dawn's home. "The thing I like about them is they're not real fussy," she comments. "When I water the impatiens nearby, the ferns get water, and I mulch the ferns thoroughly with pine straw in spring before they come up. That's about it."

Another garden stalwart that Southerners need to meet is the tenacious Goldsturm coneflower (*Rudbeckia fulgida* Goldsturm). Commonly called black-eyed Susan, this plant bears showy golden blossoms with purplish-brown centers from June into August (as does the native species that grows

TEN FOOLPROOF PERENNIALS FOR THE SOUTH

Name	Height/Light	Flower Color
Autumn Joy sedum*	18-24″ /S	Coppery-red
Balloon flower	15-24″/S	Blue, pink, white
Bearded iris*	8-36″/S	Numerous colors
Butterfly weed	18-24″/S	Orange, red, yellow
Daylily	18-36″/S,PS	Numerous colors
Goldsturm coneflower	18-24″/S,PS	Gold
Hosta	4-36″/PS,SH	Blue, purple, white
Lenten rose*	10″/PS,SH	White, rose
Purple coneflower	24-36″/S	Pink, white
Southern shield fern**	24-30″/PS,SH	None

These plants are hardy throughout the South; exceptions are
* not Coastal South or Tropical South, ** not Upper South.
Key: S = Sun, PS = Partial Shade, SH = Shade

The blossoms of Autumn Joy sedum appear in late summer and slowly change from rosy pink to brick red.

Bright orange butterfly weed combines beautifully with golden yarrow and blue veronica.

across the South). It thrives in full sun or light shade, endures summer drought, and shrugs off pests. If you can't grow this one, gardening isn't your calling.

Autumn Joy sedum (*Sedum* x *spectabile* Autumn Joy) always claims a place near the top of the list of trouble-free perennials. Few pests bother its succulent, blue-green leaves; heat and drought aren't a concern. In August, large flower clusters appear. The blooms start off pink, deepen to rose, then finish the summer coppery-red.

The list of foolproof perennials doesn't end here (see chart). While these plants are ideally suited to beginners attempting their first perennial garden, their appeal is much broader than that. As Barbara Stephens explains, "It's not necessarily people just starting out who look for the easy stuff. It's also people who have been gardening a long time and are tired of all the work. They go for something they can count on."

Of course, no perennial is truly care free. Even such lionhearted plants as the ones featured on these pages place certain demands on the gardener. Chief among them is excellent drainage. If heavy, red clay dominates your soil, supplement it with copious organic matter, or replace it entirely in the area you want to plant. To improve conditions even more, establish your border on a gentle slope or within a raised bed. Finally, determine whether prospective plants need sun or shade and if they grow well in your area.

Though many gardeners take pride in growing difficult plants, don't feel guilty if the perennials you select essentially manage by themselves. As busy as most people are nowadays, every headache headed off is a blessing. Barbara sums up the issue succinctly: "There's a time when you have to say to say to yourself, 'I want pretty, but I need to go for easy.' Fortunately, there are plants that satisfy both requirements."

If your border lacks butterfly weed (*Asclepias tuberosa*), you're missing out on one of the garden's gaudiest bloomers. Nearly incandescent blossoms cluster atop the Southern native in June and July. The blooms are typically bright orange, but may be yellow or red. They produce abundant nectar, which butterflies relish, hence the plant's common name. Butterfly weed grows 18 to 24 inches tall. It tolerates heat, drought and poor, rocky soil, thanks in large measure to deep tap roots. This feature makes an established plant difficult to transplant. However, butterfly weed is quite easy to start from seed sown in spring. Ironically, the one insect that seems to pester this plant is the monarch butterfly. You'll often see the caterpillars munching away on the leaves in summer. One or two caterpillars aren't a problem. Just pick them off and transfer them to wild milkweed, a plant they enjoy just as much.

Grow a Colorful Carpet of Ajuga

A woodland garden is a sheltered delight, but it presents the gardener with a challenge. Many handsome plants grow in the shade, but most of them offer little color except green. Ajuga comes to the rescue with spring flowers and colorful foliage.

Also called carpet bugleweed, ajuga is probably best known for its ability to spread into an attractive mat of foliage in a shaded bed. In spring its blue, white, or pink flowers make a stunning display before impatiens and caladiums are really underway. It's tough and vigorous—just what many gardeners need. Sprigging ajuga every 12 inches will allow you to cover an area quickly without a great deal of investment. And once it's started, the plants can be divided as often as once each season.

In fact ajuga is so good at being a ground cover that Nancy Goodwin of Montrose Nursery in Hillsborough, North Carolina, advises discretion when planting. "Ajuga is wonderful for an area you want carpeted. It doesn't work quite as well in a place where you are growing lots of choice little alpine plants because it can smother them."

Fortunately, ajuga is as good-looking as it is vigorous. Try underplanting with bulbs, and the blue flowers will be handsome with the white or yellow blooms of daffodils.

Only One Problem

Some gardeners have been disappointed when ajuga gets die out (a common disease) or crown rot (known in some circles as Southern wilt). Others have found that the problems are not really as serious

Try ajuga in shade for a ground cover with a bonus of spring flowers.

The tricolor foliage of variegated Burgundy Glow allows this plant to stand out even when not in bloom.

as they might seem at first.

Goodwin can attest, "Every now and then a whole patch will seem to damp off. We've found that if you just pull off all that old foliage (and don't put it in the compost), it just grows again from the roots. I don't consider it a serious disease problem because it doesn't kill the plant. It seems to happen when the weather is very hot and humid, but dry. I think that stresses the plant and makes it vulnerable. It'll come back when the conditions are better."

You Have a Choice

Not only is ajuga a boon to shade gardens, but there is also a host of selections, offering a variety of flower and foliage colors.

The most familiar species to most people is *Ajuga reptans,* which is shown blooming blue at left. However, Alba has white flowers. Silver Beauty, on the other hand, is distinctly cream-colored, rather than gray as its name implies.

Burgundy Glow is the real showoff, with tricolor foliage pictured above. Goodwin warns that Burgundy Glow will sometimes revert to the purplish form called Atropurpurea. Al-

AJUGA AT A GLANCE
Light: Shade preferred but tolerates sun if in good soil
Soil: Loose, well drained, and high in organic matter
Size: Selections ranging from 3 to 10 inches high
Growth: Moderate to fast
Problems: Crown rot

though the two look great together, the darker form is more vigorous and will overtake the variegated plants if left unchecked. You're apt to get better color from Burgundy Glow if it gets a little sun.

Ajuga pyramidalis is popular for more confined areas because it doesn't spread as quickly as *A. reptans.* It has green foliage and blue flowers, and grows a bit taller. The selection called Metallica Crispa is very different with small crinkled purplish leaves that have a metallic sheen. *Linda A. Weathers*

For mail-order sources of ajuga, send a self-addressed, stamped, business-size envelope to Ajuga Editor, *Southern Living,* P.O. Box 830119, Birmingham, Alabama 35283.

Big, bold tulips contrast nicely with the softer textures of deutzia and azaleas. Deep-green foliage in the background helps the white stand out.

A Celebration of White

On the surface, a garden composed of white-flowering plants seems about as exciting as a pot of boiled potatoes. Ah, but step into the White Garden at Ladew Topiary Gardens in Monkton, Maryland, and your opinion quickly changes. Here you witness a celebration of this most ethereal, pure, and uplifting of colors. And you come away with plenty of good ideas for combining plants in your own garden.

The show begins in April with a plethora of bulbs—Thalia daffodils, Maureen tulips, snowflakes (*Leucojum* sp.), and white Spanish bluebells (*Endymion hispanicus*). In quick suc-

cession appear the white blooms of violets, bleeding heart, viburnum, deutzia, spirea, azaleas, astilbe, and dogwood, with spring color peaking around May 15.

When summer rolls around, the tulips are replaced by white impatiens. Garden Director Lena Caron and her staff weave perennials, shrubs, and summer bulbs around their annuals, keeping white blossoms in view all the way to November. The border looks sensational in July, thanks to Iceberg roses, White Admiral and Mount Fuji perennial phlox, white calla lilies, white balloon flower (*Platycodon gran-*

diflorus Albus), Diana rose of Sharon (*Hibiscus syriacus* Diana), and summersweet (*Clethra alnifolia*). Late summer adds the delightful blossoms of Snowbank boltonia (*Boltonia asteroides* Snowbank) and Tardiva hydrangea (*Hydrangea paniculata* Tardiva). Nippon daisy (*Chrysanthemum nipponicum*) and Japanese anemones (*Anemone japonica*) dominate for weeks in fall.

White- and silver-foliaged plants echo the garden's theme. Ground covers such as Silver Mound artemisia, White Nancy spotted dead nettle (*Lamium maculatum* White Nancy), Japanese painted fern (*Athyrium filixfemina* Pictum), and snow-in-summer (*Cerastium tomentosum*) carpet the soil between flowers and shrubs, and provide needed color between peaks of bloom.

As you stroll through the garden, you realize just how many versions of white there are: silvery white, creamy white, ivory white, and blush white. Still, this all-white garden *might* be dull if its effect depended solely on shades of one color. So you're also treated to a fascinating interplay of differing shapes and textures. In spring, for instance, the solid, bold cups of tulips pierce the soft, floral sprays of deutzia. Nearby, the lax blooms of bleeding heart complement the rigid spires of astilbe.

One of the lessons this garden teaches is how white can seem to lengthen the day. Because white catches and reflects the dimmest light, at dawn and dusk the garden shines like the moon. On the other hand, blue, purple, and crimson would nearly disappear in shadow. The section of the garden that's sheltered by trees also shows how light colors aid the shady garden. White flowers and silver foliage lift the mood created by somber greens and browns.

Although Ladew devotes an entire garden to white, you'll probably prefer to implement its ideas in only a portion of your garden. Perhaps a pale corner, shaded sideyard, or wooded path cries out for a softer or lighter look. You might decide it's the perfect time to shed a little white on the matter.   *Steve Bender*

Ladew Topiary Gardens is located on State 146 about 15 miles north of the Baltimore Beltway (Route 695). It is open Tuesday through Sunday from the last week of April until October 31. For more information call (410) 557-9466.   ◇

With proper planting, lilies can enjoy success in many Southern gardens.

PHOTOGRAPH: VAN CHAPLIN

Lilies for Hot Southern Summers

Hot weather and hybrid lilies just plain don't go together. Or do they? One avid gardener, Weesie Smith of Mountain Brook, Alabama, shared her secret for planting lilies that beat the heat. It's one of the best garden tricks she has given me.

The flowerbed in my garden sits in a sunny area with red clay subsoil. Originally the ground was bricklike when dry and spongelike when wet—really not the soil for growing beautiful perennials. So I tilled it to a depth of 14 to 16 inches and amended it with compost, sand, and Pro-Mix (a commercial soil mix). While this provided a good base for growing most flowers, according to Weesie, it wasn't suited for hybrid lilies.

Using her tip, I removed the soil to a depth of 20 inches, layered new soil as shown in the illustration, and planted bulbs in spring. (It is not too late to plant now, if you can find them locally.)

The types planted range from the tried-and-true Orange Tiger Lily (*Lil-*

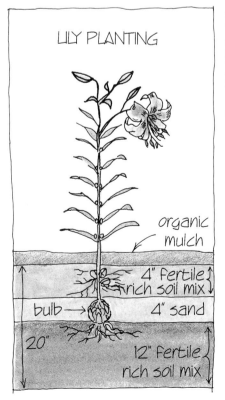

LILY PLANTING

organic mulch

4" fertile rich soil mix

bulb →

4" sand

20"

12" fertile rich soil mix

ium tigrinum) to exotic Oriental types, such as Auratum and Regale, and short-stemmed hybrids, such as Stargazer. Thanks to her advice, my lilies (shown here) have thrived for many years.

While many types of lilies grow across the South, three hybrid groups seem to like the climate in the Middle and Upper South best—Asiatic, Oriental hybrids, and Aurelians. Your best reference on a particular selection is to check with fellow gardeners—like Weesie—in your area and to experiment in your own garden. Tiger lilies (which are not hybrids, but a species) seem to thrive not only in the Upper and Middle South but also in the Lower South, where most hybrid types do not perform well.

While lilies are a royal presence in the garden, they are almost irresistible to cut and use indoors. Just remember when you cut them to leave at least half the flower stalk to ensure blooms next year.

John Alex Floyd, Jr.

Classified as a grassy weed, goose grass is a common sign of overly compacted, poorly aerated soil.

Compacted, poorly drained soil and too much shade favor the growth of common plantain.

Weeds, Weeds, Weeds!

Most of us view lawn weeds as ugly invaders, besmirchers of perfectly uniform grass. So we tirelessly seek to eradicate them using a slew of chemicals. Applying herbicides is certainly one answer but should only be the solution of last resort. A better way to control lawn weeds is to prevent them from gaining a foothold in the first place.

Weeds are opportunists and tolerate a wider range of growing conditions than turf grasses do. When you make things tough for your grass, weeds move right in. For example, if you cut the grass shorter than 1½ inches, you can expect a bumper crop of crabgrass, clover, and chickweed. Compact the soil by parking cars on it and you're asking for goose grass, common plantain, knotweed, and prostrate spurge.

Clearly, a vigorous, healthy lawn is the best defense against weeds. Cutting the grass at 2 inches or higher

will prevent most weed seeds from sprouting. Proper fertilization and watering will keep the lawn thick enough to crowd many weeds out. Yet, despite such efforts, weeds will pop up now and then. How best to go about eliminating them depends on whether they're broadleaf or grassy weeds.

Broadleaf weeds include such common pests as dandelion, plantain, clover, chickweed, buckthorn, dichondra, ground ivy, knotweed, purslane, and prostrate spurge. They're relatively easy to remove. You can spray them with a selective herbicide, such as Weed-B-Gon or 33+, or apply a weed-and-feed fertilizer. Do this when the weeds are actively growing. You can also spot treat weeds with Safer's SharpShooter, a biodegradable, soap-based herbicide. While safe for the environment, SharpShooter kills top growth only, so perennial weeds may grow back. Be sure to follow label directions.

Grassy weeds encompass such invaders as crabgrass, nutgrass, goose grass, dallis grass, and annual bluegrass (*Poa annua*). They're tougher to handle, because most weedkillers you can use on them will also kill your good grass. If you have just a few weeds, hand pull them or spot treat with Roundup, Kleenup, or SharpShooter—just keep these chemicals off your good grass. For wider applications, Ortho Crabgrass Killer will safely kill most existing grassy weeds in Zoysia, Bermuda, bluegrass, and fescue lawns. But you can't use it on St. Augustine, centipede, or carpet grass lawns. In the end, the best way to prevent grassy weeds is to cut your lawn at 2 inches or higher and apply a pre-emergence herbicide, such as Scott's Halts or Sta-Green Crabgrass Preventer, in late winter or early spring. To control annual bluegrass, apply either product in fall.

Steve Bender

Patchy, unhealthy turf opens the door to dichondra and common Bermuda grass.

Keeping the grass mowed too short will encourage the spread of white clover.

Who's To Blame for Falling Trees?

Last spring, a vicious thunderstorm ripped through my neighborhood, leaving hundreds of downed trees in its wake. As I surveyed the damage, I noticed that many of the stricken trees looked like they'd been in trouble for some time. Some had hollow centers, while others were three-quarters dead. In truth, these trees were disasters waiting to happen. And I began thinking about the legal ramifications of falling trees.

So I did some investigating—talking with insurance adjusters, lawyers, and arborists. What I discovered is this: Although laws vary somewhat from state to state, in general, if a healthy tree on your property falls in a storm and causes personal injury or property damage to a neighbor, this is considered an "act of God." You are not responsible. If, on the other hand, a *hazardous* tree on your property falls and injures someone or damages property, and it can be shown that you knew of the hazard and did nothing to correct it, then you could be held liable.

According to Alan Brook, a consulting arborist in San Antonio, most homeowners don't deliberately ignore dangerous trees on their property. They simply fail to notice telltale signs that indicate a tree may pose a hazard. Some signs are more obvious than others. For example, any tree with lots of dead branches, a hollow or rotting trunk, or numerous woodpecker holes in the trunk should be considered potentially hazardous. Other signs to look for include mushrooms or other fungal growths sprouting from the branches or trunk, or a foul-smelling seepage flowing from a crack in the trunk. Moreover, any tree whose major roots have been cut is a definite threat to blow over in a storm.

Leaning trees may look dangerous but aren't necessarily so. If they've been growing that way for years, they're probably firmly anchored. However, a leaning tree that formerly grew in the midst of other trees may become a hazard if the other trees are suddenly removed. This is because the leaning tree may have depended on the other trees to shelter it from the wind.

You can reduce your potential liability by having a consulting arborist assess your trees, evaluate their

There's no mystery why a storm toppled this sycamore. Just look at the woodpecker holes and rotten trunk.

Before it fell, this loblolly pine had been declining for years. Its trunk was hollow at the base.

condition and recommend a course of action to eliminate any problems. Arborists typically charge $50 to $60 for an hour's consultation, which is sufficient to examine the trees on most residential properties.

Correcting a hazard does not always mean removing the tree. In many cases, cabling, bracing, or pruning will remedy the situation.

To locate a trained arborist near you, call The National Arborist Association (603) 673-3311, The International Society of Arboriculture (217) 328-2032, or The American Society of Consulting Arborists (303) 466-2722. Don't wait until a disaster reminds you.   *Steve Bender*

Before, only a narrow walk led from driveway to front door.

Three guest parking spaces tuck in next to a retaining wall. Arbors offer a light, inviting way to the front door.

UPFRONT
With A Landscape Plan

The key to this major remodeling was involving the landscape architect at the beginning, not the end.

BY PHILIP MORRIS / PHOTOGRAPHY VAN CHAPLIN

The transformation of this Spartanburg, South Carolina, house took nine months, with the owners living in the basement for the duration. The new plan extended the rear of the house 7 feet. Double-hung wooden windows replaced steel-casement windows, and a spacious sunroom took the place of a small screened porch. The greatest impact, however, came from something usually considered last—the landscape.

Just about the time Architect Jack Carlisle had finished plans and contractors Vernon and Phil Griffin were set to begin on the house, they decided with owners Walter and Mabel Brice that landscape problems needed professional attention. Persistent drainage problems plagued the site, there was no easy access at grade level, and very little room for guest parking. A landscape architect and personal friend of the Brices, Shirley Carter, ASLA, then entered into the project.

Her plans dealt with these functional problems and then went on to aesthetically "lift" the house and setting with graceful wood arbors, comfortable outdoor living space, and

During a major remodeling, Mabel and Walter Brice brought in a landscape architect to help improve drainage and guest parking.

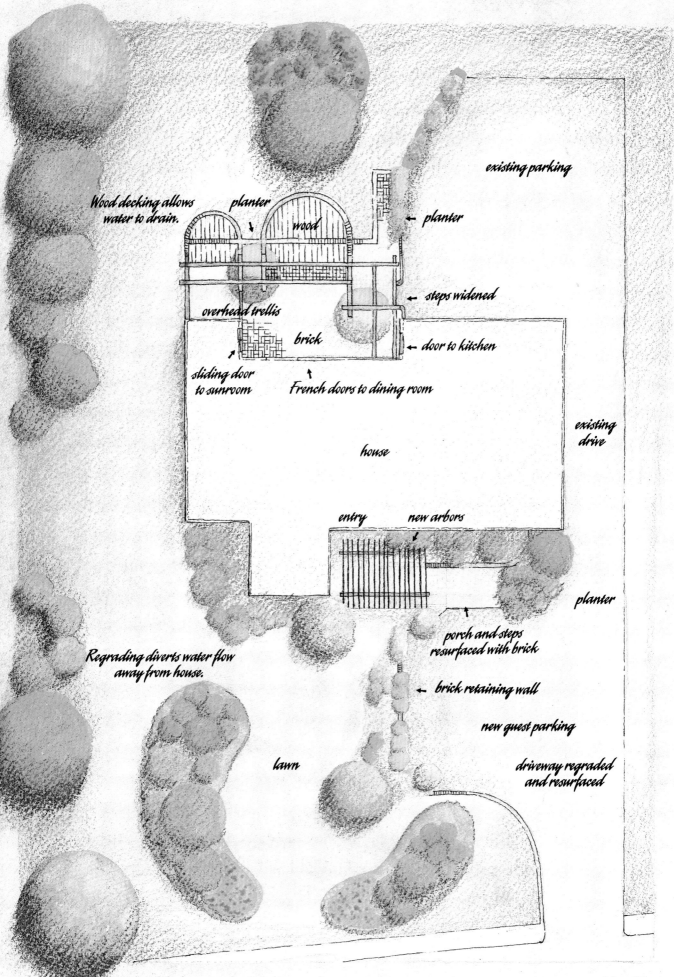

Wood decking allows water to drain.

planter

existing parking

wood

planter

steps widened

overhead trellis

brick

door to kitchen

sliding door to sunroom

French doors to dining room

house

existing drive

entry

new arbors

planter

porch and steps resurfaced with brick

Regrading diverts water flow away from house.

brick retaining wall

new guest parking

lawn

driveway regraded and resurfaced

At the rear of the house, a large arbor defines a new outdoor living space. The parking area is banked with plantings and existing stairs are wider now.

attractive but practical plantings. The owners and the re-modeling team also selected an exterior color for the house to complement the renovated setting.

"We are so thankful we brought Shirley in when we did," says Mabel. "She was so professional and easy to work with. I don't envision things very well, but I know when I like something. We let her go with it. We didn't know she was going to put the arbors in front and back, so that was a surprise, a very nice one."

Guest parking was crucial. The Brices' decision to stay in the neighborhood where they had settled and raised their children hinged partly on that. As it turned out, they now have three front parking spaces along a new retaining wall to go with four existing spaces behind the house. And there is room to turn around and leave facing the street. Stepped arbors define the entry and visually integrate the house with the parking.

"It's quite all right to take a good bit of your front yard for parking," says Shirley, "as long as you treat it as part of a landscape unit." The lawn flows between masses of shrubs and ground cover that offset the new paving.

The Brices didn't have to completely start over with new plants. Specimens they wanted to keep were stock-piled and reused in the new plan. Existing trees, including several between the parking area and the street, were also saved.

Across the expanded rear of the house, the landscape plans created adjacent large and small terraces, both sheltered by a handsome arbor like that introduced at the front. Supported by posts built up from 2 x 6s sandwiched around a 2 x 4, the arbors feature curved brackets and extended rafters with curved ends. This richness made up for the lack of architectural interest in the house itself. Standing free of the house, the rear arbors are topped by a lattice grid that softens harsh sunlight.

The terraces are flanked by brick planters containing tree-form crepe myrtles and low shrubs. Paved in brick close to the house, the terraces have rounded wooden-deck segments edged with brick extending into the lawn. Decking here permits better rain runoff and drainage. French doors open from the expanded dining room onto the large terrace. The smaller terrace has direct access from the new sunroom, and there is also a door from the kitchen to this much-used area.

"We really like that Shirley's plan allows us to be in two different areas," says Mabel. "We have a hammock in the smaller area. If there are children present they can play in that area while the adults are on the large terrace. I've always loved for children to be able to play in my yard. This plan is open with plenty of room for people to move about."

Access at grade level, especially intended for elderly parents, is across the lawn from the rearmost parking area. The landscape plan also widened steps to about 4 feet to serve this area.

All in all, this gentle and thoughtful landscape plan solved long-standing problems and gave the Brices a satisfying place to stay put. And thank heaven for the timing. "Ninety-nine times out of a hundred people think about the landscape when it's time to put in plants," says Shirley. "But things like terraces, arbors, parking, and drainage measures, need to be done during construction." ◇

On the arbor, curved brackets help unite the posts and beams.

Rear arbors stand free of the house; lattice offers dappled shade.

JUNE

CHECKLIST
100

TOMATOES TILL CHRISTMAS
102

MAKING SHADE,
ADDING STYLE
105

YARROW: LIVING SUNSHINE
FROM THE GARDEN
106

THIS PLAY AREA WILL GROW
WITH THE KIDS
107

A HARLEQUIN ROMANCE
108

SUMMER'S SHOWY PLANT
109

HANDS IN THE DIRT
110

THE LACY DAYS OF SUMMER
114

CHECKLIST
for June

ANNUAL FLOWERS

Remove faded blooms on marigolds, petunias, zinnias, and other annuals for longer flower displays. Apply a slow-release fertilizer if the plants haven't been fertilized since early spring. Pinch back petunias and other annuals that may flop or grow out-of-bounds. If you can't always tend the flowers, consider planting wax begonias, which don't need to be picked to continue blooming.

AZALEAS

Gardeners need to watch out for iron chlorosis. Yellowed leaves with dark-green veins indicate an iron deficiency. Apply liquid iron (iron chelate) at 10-day intervals until symptoms disappear.

DIVIDE BULBS

If your daffodils didn't bloom well this spring, they may be overcrowded. Dig the bulbs up after the foliage withers. Replant about 6 to 8 inches apart in a sunny, well-drained spot, or store them in a cool, dry place until fall.

FERTILIZER

Apply fertilizer to annuals and perennials now. Add about 1 cup of fertilizer per 10 square feet of annual and perennial beds. Avoid getting granules on the foliage, and water fertilizer in after application. Also, apply fertilizer to shrubs; they need about 1 tablespoon of 10-10-10 per foot of height.

FRUIT

Water plants during dry spells to ensure big, high-quality fruit. When blueberries, blackberries, and rasp-berries are ripe, they separate easily from the stem. Cover trees and bushes with netting if birds are a problem.

HARVEST TIME

Pick vegetables as soon as they ripen to keep plants producing. Snap beans, summer squash, early tomatoes, and cucumbers should be ready to harvest soon. Fertilize tomato, cucumber, and zucchini monthly with 5-10-10. Water during dry spells, and mulch to conserve moisture and reduce weeds.

HYDRANGEAS

Should your French hydrangeas need pruning, do so after they bloom. Don't wait until later, as hydrangeas will soon begin setting buds for next year's blooms.

LAWNS

Yellow and brown patches in your St. Augustine lawn indicate chinch bugs. To verify, remove both ends of a large tin can, push the can 1 inch into the ground at the edge of the damaged grass, and fill the can with water. Any chinch bugs will float to the surface. To control, water the lawn, and then apply granular Diazinon according to label directions.

MEXICAN BEAN BEETLE

Lacy, mottled leaves on snap and lima beans are signs of damage from this pest, which feeds on the underside of leaves. Larvae are yellow and covered with spines; adults are copper colored with spots. Dust or spray with rotenone or malathion according to directions.

PALMS

In Texas, this is palm planting time. Gardeners from Austin and areas south have several hardy species from which to choose. Choices include Texas palmetto, cabbage palmetto, dwarf palmetto, windmill palm, and needle palm. For best results, buy good-sized plants in 5-gallon containers or larger. Stake palms until they become established.

PERENNIALS FROM SEED

It's easy—and cheap—to grow perennials, such as Shasta daisy, coreopsis, and purple coneflower, from seed. Sow seed now in trays filled with potting soil or directly in the garden. In either case, keep the soil moist. When seedlings are 2 to 3 inches high, thin plants to about 6 to 12 inches apart. Fertilize every 4 to 6 weeks with 1 cup of liquid fertilizer.

PERSIMMON

If the leaves of persimmon trees are curling and you've eliminated aphids or other insects as the cause, then the trees are probably hungry for magnesium. To correct the leaf curl, sprinkle a couple of cups of Epsom salts evenly under the tree canopy and water in well. To prevent curl on the plants in future years, repeat this procedure every spring.

ROSE CAMPION

If you're looking for perennials that can take hot, dry locations, put rose campion (*Lychnis coronaria*) on your shopping list. Brilliant magenta flowers appear in summer on silver-gray, 18- to 24-inch plants. The variety Alba has white flowers; *L. oculata* has white flowers with pink centers.

ROSE CARE

Keep flowers picked to encourage renewed flowering on hybrid tea and floribunda roses. Spray or dust weekly with benomyl or Funginex to control powdery mildew and black spot. Fertilize monthly with 1 cup of 10-10-10 per average-size bush. When spraying for insects and disease, be sure to coat the undersides of leaves. Many of the fungi that infect roses live on the ground and splash onto the leaf underside when it rains. Mites and aphids also like the undersides of leaves. Use a sprayer with a long arm that reaches inside the shrub and has a nozzle that is easily adjusted to spray upward.

SEED ANNUALS

Try growing annuals from seed for late-summer and early-fall blooms. Sow seed at the recommended depth in loose, fertile garden soil; cover with soil, and mulch lightly. Water daily until plants emerge, thin to 4 to 6 inches apart, and then fertilize weekly with liquid 20-20-20 according to the label directions.

SHRUBS

Mulch shrubs to conserve moisture and moderate soil temperatures during the summer days ahead. Recently planted trees and shrubs are especially vulnerable to heat and drought stress. Consider installing a drip irrigation system to efficiently water shrub beds.

SUNFLOWERS

There's still plenty of time left to sow sunflower seed in the garden. Although most types grow higher than your head, there are shorter varieties, such as Sunspot, that only get

3 or 4 feet high and are a little more in scale with the rest of the garden.

TROPICAL COLOR

Gardeners throughout the South can enjoy bougainvillea, allamanda, ixora, and other tropical flowering vines and shrubs in pots or in the ground for summer color. Most tropical vines grow fast and will quickly stretch across a porch rail or climb a post. Potted shrubs, such as hibiscus and ixora, continue to bloom all summer if watered and fertilized regularly.

WEEDS

Control weeds before they have a chance to set seed. Hand pulling is best, but you may need an herbicide for large areas with lots of weeds. Follow label directions when using an herbicide, and avoid spraying on windy days. A piece of cardboard makes a good makeshift shield when spraying near desirable plants.

TIP OF THE MONTH

A carpenter's apron is extremely useful when working in the garden. You just tie it around your waist and fill the pockets with small gardening items you may need, such as nozzles, twist ties, pruning shears, and gloves. This saves many trips back to your storage area. Carpenter's aprons are available at most lumber supply stores for about $1.

Jeanette F. Benz
Atlanta, Georgia

JUNE NOTES

To Do:
- Fertilize warm-season grasses
- Prune spring-flowering trees and shrubs
- Remove faded blooms from annuals
- Divide bearded iris
- Apply post-emergence weed killer to lawn

To Plant:
- Container-grown trees and shrubs
- Glads for summer flowers
- Summer annuals
- Tomatoes for fall harvest

To Purchase:
- Lawn fertilizer
- Post-emergence weed killer
- Transplants and seeds of summer annuals

_____

_____

_____

_____

_____

_____

_____

_____

_____

_____

_____

_____

_____

Tomatoes
Till Christmas

*To discover how to enjoy
ripe garden tomatoes in winter,
we consulted the people who know
best–you, our readers.
The planning starts now.*

BY STEVE BENDER
PHOTOGRAPHY VAN CHAPLIN AND STEVE BENDER

"If we ask it, they will write."

With apologies to the movie, *Field of Dreams,* this was the premise behind a question we posed to our readers last July. "Everyone is proud to harvest the first tomato on the block," we declared. "But how can you harvest the *last* tomato?" We asked for tips on how to keep tomatoes coming from July to October, long after the neighbors' plants have pooped out. We also wanted to know how to properly store green and half-ripened tomatoes and get them to ripen over winter.

You didn't disappoint us. We received hundreds of letters from across the South, each containing homespun wisdom gleaned from years of toiling in the vegetable patch. The intriguing responses prompted us to visit some of you last fall to investigate what you were up

to firsthand. Both the letters and visits taught us a lot, and we enjoyed the education. Here are some of your expert recommendations.

First, don't count on getting fall tomatoes from plants set out in April; you need to plant a crop specifically for the fall. The exact date for planting depends on where you live. Ruby Barfield of Pearl, Mississippi, provides a good guideline for the Middle and Lower South. "To harvest the latest tomatoes," she writes, "I plant seed on the 15th of June and transplant by the second week of July." Gardeners in the Upper South need an earlier start. For example, Mrs. R. S. Henn of Louisville gets her plants in the ground by mid-June. In the Coastal South, lingering heat postpones planting until late summer. Texan Dan Loep, known locally as the "Tomato Man of Houston," plants

Allan Eddy

There are two popular methods for ripening tomatoes in winter— wrapping the fruit individually in newspaper, then placing them in a cardboard box; and (**above**) storing them on a drying rack in a cool basement. The tomatoes will ripen at different rates, so check them weekly.

Dan Loep

Allen and Julia Anderson with Pam

Alex Evashko

Homegrown tomatoes, so abundant in summer, are prized for the winter table.

in mid-August, making sure to shield his vines from hot afternoon sun.

Not everyone starts fall tomatoes from seed. Minnie J. Bailey of Eupora, Mississippi, roots suckers taken from vines planted in spring. "If there is a lot of moisture in the ground, I set suckers directly into the ground," she explains. If not, she roots them in a glass of water. In her opinion, "suckers make stronger plants than vines grown from seeds."

Some types supply better fall crops than others. Many readers sing the praises of Celebrity, a 1984 All-America winner. Others swear by Long-Keeper, an orange-ripening tomato that stores exceptionally well. Loep, who holds tomato-growing contests at his nursery each year, suggests gardeners in hot climates try heat-resistant selections that set well in high temperatures. His picks—Heat Wave and First Lady.

Now it's time to get to the "meat" of this tomato story. Assuming that you planted the right selections at the right time, how can you have ripe tomatoes in chilly fall and winter? To witness one creative solution, we traveled to Poplarville, Mississippi, which lies halfway between New Orleans and Hattiesburg, to visit garden de-

signers Allen and Julia Anderson. Outside of their 100-year-old log cabin, the Andersons devote part of their 40 acres to growing and selling cut flowers, herbs, and gourmet vegetables. When frost threatens the tomato crop, Allen piles hay bales high in the back of his pickup. Then he, Julia, and their English pointer, Pam, hop into the truck and speed to the rescue.

"We stack bales on both sides of the tomato cages and on either end, usually about three bales high," relates Julia. "And then over the very top, Allen drapes plastic sheeting or plastic and blankets, depending upon how cold it's going to get." The plastic and blankets can remain for a day or two, until the weather moderates. When it does, the Andersons remove the covering along with the top bales. This method protects plants down to about 15 degrees. Many years, Allen and Julia reach through frosted hay and pick ripe tomatoes for Christmas.

Winter gets much colder in Parkton, Maryland, a half hour north of Baltimore, where Alex and Doris Evashko live. Bales of hay alone just won't keep their tomato plants alive when freezing weather arrives. So Alex, a retired tool-and-die maker, grows tomatoes in hanging baskets inside a small greenhouse. What's so novel about that? Just this—Alex plants the vines *upside down* with stems sticking out of drainage holes that have been widened with a drill. Why? When tomatoes planted rightside up get heavy with fruit, the stems snap off at the rim of the basket. "Upside-down plants are also much easier to water," he adds. Alex uses 12-inch baskets filled with Pro-Mix potting soil, to which he adds Osmocote slow-release fertilizer. Then he mulches the top of each basket to reduce evaporation. Last winter, Alex and Doris picked ripe tomatoes on February 8.

Drive a few miles south from Parkton to the village of Jarrettsville and you might encounter the Evashkos' friend and fellow plant enthusiast, Allan Eddy. Allan, who in his own words looks like "a cross between a boat captain, Ernest Hemingway, and Santa Claus," is a retired landscape architect. He calls his strategy for preserving tomatoes over winter "The Old Cannonball Method."

"Take a tomato," he says, "throw it in a plastic bag, and freeze it. It'll turn into a rock-hard cannonball, but the skin will keep the moisture in. Then

when you want to eat it, zap it for about 20 seconds in a microwave, so it's barely thawed with ice crystals still in it. Cut it up and make yourself a salad. It's a little sloppy going, but does that taste good." Allan keeps frozen tomatoes for up to two years.

If frozen tomatoes don't warm your cockles, you can still enjoy ripe, garden tomatoes in winter. Several readers accomplish this by "hanging" their plants. Writes Robert Bolt of Pisgah Forest in western North Carolina: "When the weatherman predicts frost, pull the tomato plants up roots and all . . . then carefully take them to a cool basement, and tie them upside down from the floor joists. Let them hang there until the last green tomato turns red." William Pandak of Beverly Hills, Florida, cautions against hanging the plants too high above the floor, "in case the tomatoes . . . ripen and fall off."

No letter better explains the most popular technique for ripening tomatoes in winter than that of Fran Huddleston of Auburn, Alabama. "When we expect a damaging freeze, we pick all remaining tomatoes and wrap the green ones individually in newspaper," she writes. "Then we place them in a basket—greenest on bottom—and put the basket in a cool, preferably dark, place. They need to be checked occasionally for ripe or spoiled ones. This past season we picked in early December and ate the last one the first week in March." Of course, there are ways to refine this process. You can substitute brown paper for newspaper and a cardboard box or drying rack for the basket.

Here are a few more tips from readers. Mildred Kennedy of Yulee, Florida, advises leaving a bit of stem attached to each fruit when you store it as a hedge against rot. Also, store tomatoes stem-side up. May Bush of Pasadena, Maryland, likes to dip green and half-ripe tomatoes in a solution of 4 tablespoons of bleach to a gallon of water before storing. This kills bacteria and rot-causing fungi.

We don't have space to print more tips, but want to thank everyone who corresponded with us. We'll grant the final word to Dan Loep.

"Why bother ripening green tomatoes from the garden," we asked him, "when you can easily buy red ones at the store?"

"Because," he forthrightly replied, "I've never bought a tomato at a grocery that's as good as the *worst* home-grown tomato."

(**Left**) *This dining pavilion helps block sun from the windows and glass doors at the rear of the house—and adds an interesting focal point.* (**Below**) *The pyramidal roof of regularly spaced 2 x 2s gives a spacious, open feeling to the simple structure.*

PHOTOGRAPHS: COLLEEN DUFFLEY

Making Shade, Adding Style

Designed to provide a shady dining spot on a west-facing terrace, this open pavilion also adds architectural interest to a San Antonio house.

"The basic problem was lack of transition between the terrace and the house," notes Landscape Architect John Troy, ASLA. "And the rear of the house was plain and flat, especially with the hot sun against it."

As a solution, Troy designed a 12-foot-square pavilion with a pyramidal roof. A 4-foot-wide, flat-roofed wing connects it to the house's rear sunroom (see section). Wings on the north and south sides are about 3½ feet deep. For both openness and shade, all of the roof sections are covered with 2 x 2s spaced 2 inches apart. "Because the 2 x 2s are angled by the pitch of the pyramid, they give a lot of shade," Troy notes. To blend with the house, he suggested cedar, painted a pale taupe, for the entire structure.
Linda Hallam

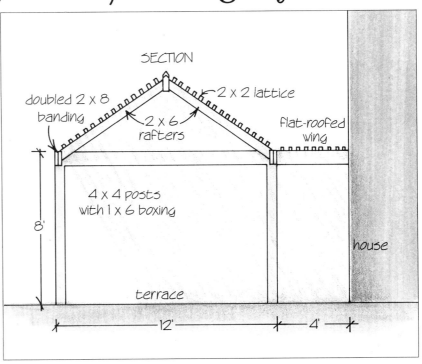

SECTION

doubled 2 x 8 banding

2 x 2 lattice

2 x 6 rafters

flat-roofed wing

4 x 4 posts with 1 x 6 boxing

house

8'

terrace

12'   4'

Yarrow beams its sunshine yellows through the garden in spring and summer. The flattened clusters contain hundreds of tiny blossoms.

PHOTOGRAPH: VAN CHAPLIN

Yarrow: Living Sunshine From the Garden

When yarrow blooms, it's as if the sun had broken through a mask of sullen clouds. The vivid yellow blossoms brighten the day and lift the spirit. This is why many a Southern flower border features yarrow.

Not all yarrows are yellow. Common yarrow (*Achillea Millefolium*), for example, sports flowers of pink, red, and white. But the yellow types, as typified by fern-leaf yarrow (*A. filipendulina*), make far superior garden plants because they stand up straight and stay where you put them. They also possess handsome foliage, which ranges from gray green to silvery. The plants' main flush of bloom is in late May or early June and lasts about a month. Sporadic blooms then appear throughout the summer.

The tallest selection of fern-leaf yarrow is Gold Plate, which reaches 4 to 5 feet tall and nearly as wide. Its flattened clusters of tiny, golden blossoms may be 6 inches across. This plant is strictly for the rear of large perennial borders. Another back-of-the-border yarrow is Parker's Variety. It grows 3 to 4 feet tall with clusters about 3 inches across.

Coronation Gold, a hybrid between fern-leaf yarrow and *A. clypeolata*, enjoys wide acceptance in the South. Growing 30 to 36 inches tall, it's ideal for the middle or rear of today's smaller flower borders. Its deep, golden clusters, about 3 inches across, appear atop fine, silvery-green foliage.

Rising fast in popularity is another hybrid called Moonshine, bred by the famous British plantsman Alan Bloom. "Moonshine—ah now, that's a neat plant,'' says Dave Bowman of Crownsville Nursery in Crownsville, Maryland. "It's much lower growing than others—about 18 to 24 inches—so you can use it up front in the border. And it's got really nice gray foliage." The softer color of its flowers is another highlight. Some gardeners call the color sulfur yellow; others call it canary or lemon yellow. But you get the idea—it's a lighter tint that's easy to blend with other flower colors.

Bowman suggests combining these yarrows with pink phlox or purple-foliaged plants. Other excellent companion plants include pink loosestrife, blue salvia, blanket flower (*Gaillardia* sp.), blue delphiniums, and red-hot-poker (*Kniphofia* sp.).

The flowers of yarrow are among the best for drying and preserving. Just cut the flowers when they're at their peak. Then use a rubberband to bind the ends of the stems together, and hang the stems upside down in a cool, dry, dark place. They will be ready for arranging in three to four weeks.

Yarrows are a snap to grow. They tolerate heat and drought and have no serious pests. "The two basic things they need are good light and good drainage," says Bowman. "Good drainage is especially important in the wintertime." Feed once in spring with a slow-release fertilizer that's sparing in nitrogen, such as cottonseed meal. Divide every three to four years to rejuvenate and prevent overcrowding. Faithful deadheading will help keep flowers coming all summer.

Steve Bender

For sources of yarrow, send a self-addressed, stamped, business-size envelope to Yarrow Editor, *Southern Living,* P.O. Box 830119, Birmingham, Alabama 35283. ◇

For safety, this 18-inch-deep pond has a removable dark-metal grill set 2 inches below the water's surface.

This Play Area Will Grow With the Kids

Children become a very important factor when deciding on a landscape plan. "A lot of people request a garden that can withstand the impact of kids. If you plan it right, once the kids are grown you can easily adapt the entire garden for adult use," explains Landscape Architect Tom Keith, ASLA.

Keith, with Arbor Engineering of Greenville, South Carolina, first sat down with clients Terri and Jesse Stafford to see what he had to work with. "There was a small deck off the back door and a steep slope that went from the house up to the property line where there was a hemlock hedge," Keith remembers.

Next, he took into account what the Staffords wanted. "We figured every kid should have a place to run, climb, swing, and slide," he says. "Plus, Terri and Jesse wanted a fountain and a place to entertain and cook outdoors."

A generous stone terrace now occupies the space near the house, with a low stone retaining wall at the foot of the slope. The terrace makes an ideal spot for Terri and Jesse to entertain and for the kids to ride their tricycles.

On the slope just above the ter-

This sliding board and sandbox, which the children enjoy now, can later be replaced by more formal features.

race, a play area with a slide and sandbox helps entertain the Staffords' young children. The play area is sited near the house so Terri can easily keep an eye on her preschoolers. As the children outgrow this area, more

formal steps can replace the sliding board and wooden steps. "We planted the rest of the slope with Parsons juniper, which should withstand the kids running up and down the hill," Keith says.

The top of a two-level fountain spills into a small garden pond about 18 inches deep. For safety, a dark-metal grill rests 2 inches below the surface to catch anything (or anyone) that falls in. "You never know it's there and, once the kids have grown, you can lift the grill out and add water plants or goldfish," Keith explains.

Near the top of the hill, a large level area, formed by cutting into the slope and building a crosstie retaining wall, provides a good spot for running and ball activities. A perennial bed hugs the base of the retaining wall. "We made it a raised bed for several reasons. It softens the impact of the retaining wall, provides the necessary drainage for perennials, and protects the plants when the kids are kicking a ball around," he says.

"What I like most about the garden is that we actually have flat areas for the kids and for us. The whole yard is useful," Terri says. And, according to plan, it will still be useful when the kids are grown.   *Todd A. Steadman*

PHOTOGRAPHS: VAN CHAPLIN

In most areas of the South, harlequin glorybower becomes a small tree or large shrub. Large clusters of sweetly fragrant flowers appear in midsummer and continue into fall.

A Harlequin Romance

Blossoms turn to bright-blue fruit attached to showy, red bracts.

With such a tongue twister for a name, it's no wonder that harlequin glory-bower languishes in obscurity. But despite the ludicrous label, this worthy plant is no joke. Fragrant blooms fill the summer, followed by colorful fruit in the fall.

Native to China and Japan, harlequin glorybower (*Clerodendrum trichotomum*), also known as Clerodendron, grows throughout the South. Winters in the Upper South can sometimes kill it to the ground, so it should be treated there as a large, herbaceous perennial.

Elsewhere, it becomes an open, spreading tree from 10 to 15 feet tall and wide. Its large, fuzzy, dark-green leaves bring a noticeably coarse texture to the garden. The leaves develop no autumn color, but drop off while still green in fall.

Leaves, however, are not the best part of this plant. That distinction belongs to the flowers and fruits. Large clusters of white, sweet-smelling blossoms appear atop the foliage in midsummer and continue their show into the fall. Each inch-wide blossom develops a bright-blue, pea-sized fruit attached to showy, red bracts. In late summer and early autumn, both flowers and fruits adorn the tree simultaneously.

You can propagate this plant by rooting cuttings, layering lower branches, detaching suckers from the "mother" plant, or sowing seed that's been refrigerated for three months. It prefers well-drained soil on the moist side, but tolerates drought. It can handle either full sun or light shade equally well. Prune, if necessary, in late winter.

Part of our region's romantic past, harlequin glorybower is found in many older gardens, especially those of the Lower and Coastal South. Unfortunately, few garden centers sell it. So we've prepared a list of mail-order sources. Just send a self-addressed, stamped, business-size envelope to Harlequin Glorybower Editor, *Southern Living,* P.O. Box 830119, Birmingham, Alabama 35283.

Steve Bender

Striking blooms and lush foliage of yellow shrimp plant decorate Richard Sacher's water garden in New Orleans.

Summer's Showy Plant

Why should a Southern gardener plant yellow shrimp plant? Let Richard Sacher, a New Orleans gardener, sum it up for you. "It's a great plant for half-day shade," he states. "It blooms freely all summer long until frost, is a fairly dense plant, and produces brilliant yellow flowers."

A small shrub native to Peru, yellow shrimp plant (*Pachystachys lutea*) is named for its showy, 6-inch flower spikes, which remind some people of shrimp. The spikes aren't really flowers themselves, but columns of overlapping bracts. The true flowers are white and emerge from between the bracts.

As Sacher mentions, two very impressive things about the plant are its extraordinarily long blooming period and its ability to bloom well in sun or light shade. Thus, yellow shrimp plant can occupy many locations in the garden, including mixed borders and planters.

The plant's true flowers are white and emerge from columns of yellow bracts.

Yellow shrimp plant is semitropical, so gardeners in the Upper, Middle, and Lower South should dig it up in fall, cut it back to 5 to 6 inches tall, pot it, and bring it indoors to a sunny window for winter. Those in Florida and the Coastal South should cut it back hard in late fall and spread a 3-inch layer of mulch around the base. Next spring, the plant will come back from the roots.

Ask for yellow shrimp plant at local greenhouses. For a list of mail-order sources, send a self-addressed, stamped, business-size envelope to Yellow Shrimp Plant Editor, *Southern Living*, P.O. Box 830119, Birmingham, Alabama 35283.

YELLOW SHRIMP PLANT

Light: Morning sun and afternoon shade or light shade all day

Soil: Moist, well-drained

Pests: Occasional mealybugs and aphids; spray with insecticidal soap

Pruning: Prune heavily in fall or early spring

Fertilizer: Feed monthly with water-soluble 20-20-20; fertilize during periods of active growth

Hardiness: Winter-hardy outdoors in Florida and Coastal South; elsewhere, keep inside in winter

HANDS
IN·THE
DIRT

*A new design helped make this modest
Atlanta backyard into a place to relax and enjoy
the view—as well as a place to garden.*

BY RITA STRICKLAND / PHOTOGRAPHY VAN CHAPLIN

Daylilies

Pat Penn's love of flower gardening got totally out of hand a few years ago when her dogwood died. "It was a huge old tree and shaded the whole backyard," she explains. The shady conditions had limited Pat to playing around with a few annuals, perennials, and bulbs in a little side area of her yard in Atlanta's Morningside neighborhood. So when the dogwood died, the garden's insidious expansion began. "Pretty soon, flowerbeds just wandered all over the backyard in little squiggles and curves with no rhyme or reason,"

she says. "It was a do-it-yourself mess."

About that time, a friend pointed out one other shortcoming of Pat's garden. "It's a good thing you like to work," he said, "because there's absolutely no place to sit down out here and enjoy what you've done."

"He was right, of course," Pat agrees. "I did just go back there and work, which I totally enjoyed. But I hadn't even considered having a place to sit down and take it all in." To bring some order to the garden and provide a private spot where she could relax after the gar-

dening chores were done, Pat called on Landscape Architect William T. Smith, ASLA.

Smith's design features three main elements: a small brick terrace, a narrow band of lawn, and naturally, an extensive flower border. The new backyard is a good model for homeowners who want lots of garden in a little space.

For example, the terrace was kept small, which prevents it from rivaling the flowers for attention. "Pat wanted just a small terrace, for no more than two or three people," Smith explains. "Because of its size, the terrace doesn't visually dominate the garden as a larger one might."

There was also room for a small

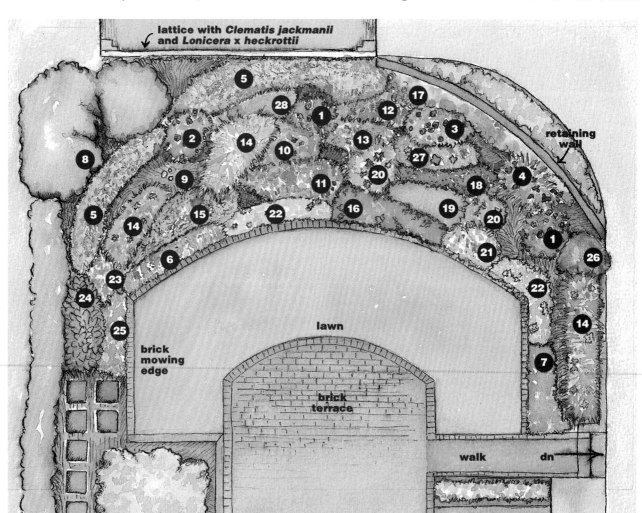

KEY TO PLANTINGS

1. *Rose Betty Prior*
2. *Rose Gruss an Aachen*
3. *Rose French Lace*
4. *Iris*
5. *Cleome*
6. *Veronica Goodness Grows*
7. *Veronica Icicle*
8. *Shrubs*

9. *Crepe myrtle*
10. *Purple coneflower*
11. *Salvia farinacea*
12. *Echinops*
13. *Solidago*
14. *Daylilies*
15. *Chrysanthemum Clara Curtis*
16. *Chrysanthemum pacificum*
17. *Hollyhocks*
18. *Salvia East Friesland*

19. *Lamb's-ears*
20. *Oxeye and Shasta daisies*
21. *Limonium*
22. *Dianthus*
23. *Astilbe*
24. *Hosta*
25. *Candytuft*
26. *Baptisia*
27. *Platycodon*
28. *Boltonia*

lawn, which repeats the shape of the terrace and wraps around it on three sides. The lawn provides overflow space if Pat entertains larger groups, and soaks up rainwater runoff from the terrace and flowerbeds. But perhaps most importantly, in contrast with the flat green lawn, the upright, gaily colored border gets even more attention. "That clear expanse of green sets off the colors of every flower in the garden," Smith says.

Of course, a garden isn't a garden without a gardener, and that's where Pat steps into the picture. Although the shape and structure of the flower border were Smith's design, the plants that flourish within it are entirely Pat's handiwork. Says Smith, "A lot of people want me to do a plan that calls for this perennial here and that one there, but I didn't do that at Pat's. She likes to experiment and learn, and has really done a wonderful job with the border."

Irish Eyes Coneflower

Modestly, Pat credits much of her success to trial and error. "I have learned to keep moving things around until I find a place where they're happy. In some cases, though, that place is 'none of the above,' " she adds with a grin.

"Most people who are really into gardening know much more about it than I do," states Pat. " I just like the feel of the sun on my back and my hands in the dirt." ◇

Pat likes to set out such annuals as petunias to keep her border colorful.

More than just a place to relax, this new terrace is also a viewing area for Pat Penn's garden.

The Lacy Days Of Summer

BY MARK G. STITH / PHOTOGRAPHY COLLEEN DUFFLEY

There's plenty for a wide-eyed child to explore in a summer field of Queen Anne's lace. The invitation is irresistible: White flower clusters atop wiry stems wave breezy hellos—like tiny starbursts floating over a sea of green. They're just tall enough to stand eye to eye with a 5-year-old.

The blooms of this impressive wildflower pop up in fields and roadsides across the South at a perfect time of year for children liberated from school. And a field of white powder puffs becomes a jungle playground for running, following the leader, playing hide-and-seek, or just plopping down in a mashed mess of foliage and flowers and kids.

This is summer to a child—a time of lemonade and laughter, fireflies and full moons, pals and all-day play. It's a time when memories are made; a time when stories are told and remembered for retelling to *their* children. The folklore surrounding many plants in the Southern landscape is often fascinating; certainly a plant with a name as majestic as Queen Anne's lace contains a fanciful tale—or two.

A field of Queen Anne's lace is a white wonderland.

According to one version of the legend, Queen Anne (a very real queen in 18th-century England) was being chased by some French soldiers through a field. She came to a barbed wire fence and, while trying to climb over it, tore her petticoat on a barb. While reaching back to free it, she pricked her finger. As testimony of m'lady's malady, fence-posts throughout the land are surrounded by

petticoat-white flowers dotted with Queen's blood, possibly the only plants that can boast a royal bloodline. Another, somewhat tamer tale has the Queen pricking her finger with a needle while making a lace doily. The accident is immortalized by a tiny, purplish-red flower (the "blood spot") in the center of the white blossoms.

Let the realists fuss over the slim chance that an English queen was hopping over barbed wire in the rural South—children are mesmerized by the tale and just as delighted to find the evidence.

It's the ageless joy of discovery, the excitement of the hunt. And part of the joy of being young—and young at heart. ◇

JULY

CHECKLIST
118

GARDEN TIMEKEEPERS
120

A CITY POOL WITH
COUNTRY CHARM
123

ORDER IN THE COURTYARD
124

SAVING THE
SOUTHERN LANDSCAPE
126

CHECKLIST
for July

ANNUALS

You can still plant impatiens, ornamental peppers, Madagascar periwinkle (*Vinca*), torenia, verbena, and other heat-tolerant annuals for bloom through fall. This late in the season, it is best to start flowers with large transplants—either grown in 4-inch pots or gallon-size containers. The bigger plants have better chances of becoming established and providing a nearly instant effect.

BULBS

It's not too late to plant caladiums, crinum, daylilies, and ginger lilies. They will have plenty of time to grow before cool weather. When planting, work compost into the bed and feed with a slow-release bulb fertilizer. Remember that bulbs need a well-drained site. Otherwise, they may rot.

CANNAS

For blooms all summer and neater plants, remove flower stalks as soon as the blooms fade. A new flower stalk should grow below the old one. Also, check the top leaves for signs of leaf roller larvae: Infested foliage will not unroll normally. If the problem is severe, dust uninfested leaves with carbaryl. Insecticides won't reach larvae protected by the leaves; hand pick and destroy them.

CENTIPEDE LAWNS

Grass that looks yellow at this time of year may simply need iron, especially if the fertilizer you use doesn't contain this element. For quick greening, spray the lawn with liquid iron in late afternoon. (Don't do this in the heat of the day as it may burn the grass.) Your lawn should be green in a couple of days.

COOL COLORS

During these hot days, flowers and foliage in cool colors can make outdoor living areas seem cooler. Consider using pastel-colored impatiens, begonias, petunias, Madagascar periwinkle (*Vinca*), and hibiscus along with the silvery foliage of dusty miller in pots, hanging baskets, or flowerbeds to "cool down" your deck or terrace.

GARDENIAS

If your gardenias should stop blooming, look for thrips or aphids. Both of these pests feed on flowerbuds and cause them to wither or fall off. Aphids feed on the outside of the buds and have tiny, pear-shaped bodies. They suck sap, causing the flowers and leaves to be deformed. They also secrete honeydew, which encourages the growth of sooty mold, a harmless but ugly black fungus on the leaves. Thrips hide in the folds of buds and flowers but will fly away when disturbed. Thrips are dark brown, torpedo shaped, and about ⅛ inch long. Control thrips with a systemic pesticide, such as Orthene; use insecticidal soap on the aphids. Be sure to spray after the sun sets because plants burn easily when sprayed in hot weather.

IRIS

Dig up and divide crowded iris now. Cut off 2- to 4-inch pieces of rhizomes with foliage. Trim the leaves back to 6 or 7 inches in an inverted V-shape, and replant the rhizomes with their top half above the soil surface and about a foot apart. Water well after planting.

LAWNS

During extended dry spells, raise the cutting height of your mower ½ to 1 inch. This will reduce moisture loss and keep roots cooler. Ideally, most lawns need about 1 inch of water a week to keep a green, healthy appearance. This should moisten the soil to a depth of 4 to 6 inches.

MULCHING

One of the easiest ways to conserve water in the garden is by mulching. Keep a 2- to 4-inch layer of mulch around shrubs, flowers, and vegetables. Pine straw, pine bark chips, and shredded hardwood bark are effective choices. As a general rule, one bale of pine straw will cover about 50 to 80 square feet of bare area. For replenishing areas covered with straw, one bale will cover about 150 square feet. One cubic yard (27 cubic feet) of bark mini-nuggets will cover about 80 square feet.

PEARS

If you notice new, upright sprouts along the scaffold limbs (the main branches growing from the trunk) of your pear trees, you need to remove them now. These sprouts can develop into branches that shade out lower, fruit-bearing limbs and make harvesting more difficult. This tender growth is easily pinched or clipped off.

PEPPERS

You can still set out these colorful, heat-tolerant plants. Space transplants 18 to 24 inches apart, and every three weeks, add 2 tablespoons of 10-10-10 fertilizer per plant. Be sure to keep the peppers well watered.

ROSES

Swollen places along the stems of rose bushes are caused by a gall infection. While there is little you can do to cure the infected rose, you can help prevent the gall disease from attacking other roses by removing the infected plant immediately. Also replace mulch in the area of the infected plant.

SLUGS

There are a variety of non-toxic methods to deal with these slimy creatures, which can wreak havoc in flower-beds and vegetable gardens. Set out pieces of cardboard in the evening; slugs will congregate under them and can be easily disposed of the next morning. Or sink shallow dishes into the soil so their rims are at ground level. Fill with beer; the slugs will be attracted to the beer and drown as they enter the container.

SOOTY MOLD

A black, sooty coating on the leaves of azaleas, gardenias, and crepe myrtles is a fungus that grows on the sticky secretions (called "honeydew") of aphids. To control the sooty mold, you'll need to use an insecticide, such as malathion, to kill the aphids.

TILLING

It is a good time to till the soil, killing weed seeds and insect larvae by exposing them to heat and dryness. Plus, you can improve the fertility and drainage of the soil by tilling in a 4- to 6-inch layer of organic matter.

VEGETABLES

Seeds of fast-growing vegetables, such as zucchini, lima beans, and bush beans, can be planted now for a late harvest. If you grew corn earlier this year, interplant pole beans within the corn rows, and let the stalks support the vines. Keep tomatoes, cucumbers, and squash picked for continued harvest.

VERBENA

Plant this tough, annual ground cover to add color to hot, sunny, and dry sites. Pink-, red-, and white-flowering selections are common, but those aren't your only choices. Peaches & Cream, a 1992 All-America Selections winner, bears multicolored clusters of salmon and apricot flowers on 8-inch-high plants. Space plants about 8 to 10 inches apart for a good massed effect, and fertilize monthly with 1 cup of 10-10-10 granular fertilizer per 10 square feet of bed.

WATER

The peak of summer is a maximum growth time for plants, so their water demands are high. Keep flower and vegetable gardens watered if it doesn't rain for three or four days. Water early in the day to achieve best results.

JULY NOTES

To Do:
- Mow lawns higher in hot weather
- Watch out for spider mites on flowers and shrubs
- Give lawns an inch of water a week
- Water shrubs and young trees deeply
- Cut back leggy annuals to encourage more blooms

To Plant:
- Replant empty areas in the vegetable garden
- Seeds of biennial and perennial flowers

To Purchase:
- A rain gauge to measure how much water the lawn and garden receives each week
- Insecticidal soap for spraying spider mites and aphids

TIP OF THE MONTH

To prevent ants from getting into your kitchen cabinets, try placing fresh mint leaves in back of your cabinet shelves. Insects aren't fond of the minty smell and will leave.

Janell Chandler
Dalton, Georgia

Moon vine

5:01 p.m.   5:03 p.m.   5:05 p.m.   5:09 p.m.

Garden Timekeepers

Some plants bloom at dawn, others at dusk.
We don't know exactly why. But we do
know why we like them.

BY STEVE BENDER / PHOTOGRAPHY VAN CHAPLIN

WAW! WAW! WAW!

The clock radio's alarm awakens me with all of the gentleness of a cattle prod. I swing wildly at the machine, like a punch-drunk fighter, vengefully smacking the alarm button to stem the racket. Bleary-eyed, I peer at the time: **5:15.** Oh great, another day at the office. Anyone besides me awake at this awful hour?

Looking out of my window at the brightening east, I have my answer. There, on the fence down below, the morning glories' vivid trumpets are splayed wide, announcing the new day. The sight quickens my circulation faster than sit-ups and French roast coffee. Great! Another day in the garden.

Four-o'clocks open in late afternoon and release a sweet scent to attract insect pollinators at night.

For those of us who relish plants, there is something fascinating about flowers that time their opening according to the light. Some, like the morning glory (*Ipomoea purpurea*), bloom at dawn. Others, including moon vine (*I. alba*), four-o'clocks (*Mirabilis jalapa*), and angel's trumpet (*Datura* sp. and *Brugmansia* sp.), blossom at dusk. Still other plants, such as the aptly named night-blooming cereus (*Hylocereus undatus*) and night-blooming jasmine (*Cestrum nocturnum*), flower near bedtime.

Why do these "garden timekeepers" behave as they do? The reason lies with the reproductive advantage that blooming at a particular time provides a plant. Many flowers require pollination by

Morning glory

(Above) *Many types of angel's trumpets bloom at dusk. The flowers open in mere minutes and remain open throughout the night.*

The scarlet flowers of cypress vine (I. quamoclit) bloom daily on its delicate annual vine.

specific insects that may be active only at certain times. So that's when plants make their blossoms available. Night-blooming flowers, for example, are typically pollinated by moths. To help moths find them, many night flowers release a sweet fragrance. Moreover, these flowers are often white, to better reflect the dim light of the moon and improve their visibility to insects.

Although botanists debate the actual triggering mechanism for the timekeepers, changes in light and temperature probably cause the opening and closing. For example, morning glories close by 11 a.m. on hot, sunny days. But on cool, overcast days, they remain open all afternoon. Likewise, night-bloomers begin closing as soon as dawn sunlight strikes them. But on cloudy days, they often stay open until mid-morning.

If you've never watched a flower open before your eyes, many timekeepers provide an opportunity you shouldn't miss. A neighbor of mine, Nelldeane Price, gardens next to an alley that I drive through to and from work every day. (Nelldeane calls us "alley friends.") Last summer, the moon vine on her fence was spectacular. I asked her to tell me about it.

She told me she'd always wanted to grow moon vine, because the one her mother grew long ago in Montgomery "smelled so wonderful." So last spring, she bought seed at a local hardware store. She soaked the hard seed, which look like corn kernels, in water overnight before planting.

Each afternoon around 5 last summer, the opening blossoms caused a commotion. "Ladies came from blocks away to see the moon vine bloom," recalls Nelldeane. "They always came at the same time, trying to time it. You could tell which blooms were going to open because they'd start to quiver. They were real quick—turn your back, and you'd miss them." Obviously, Photographer Van Chaplin didn't turn his back. The photos of the moon vine shown here were taken in Nelldeane's garden.

Gail Barton, co owner of Flowerplace Plant Farm in Meridian, Mississippi, also knows the magic of the timekeepers. She tells me that it was seeing an angel's trumpet bloom one evening when she was 10 years old that hooked her forever on gardening. "My aunt made me and my two sisters sit still and watch the angel's trumpet open," she remembers. "It

seemed to take forever, but really took about 3 minutes. By the time it opened, we were enthralled."

Garden timekeepers capture the imagination of young and old. They can revive fond memories or inspire a career. And in my case, they can even make you forget the awfulness of the hour.

This 18-foot-diameter pool features a wide border of Tennessee crab orchard stone; a built-in seat lies just under water and rims half of the pool.

A City Pool With Country Charm

A backyard pool doesn't have to be Olympic-size to offer big relief from the summer heat. That's just how Beverly Bremer feels about her small-scale pool in Atlanta.

"It isn't big enough to swim in," says Beverly, a busy career woman with grown children. "There's a seat inside the pool that goes halfway around. I sit on that, lean my head against a rock, have a little glass of wine, and read the newspaper," she says. "The pool is private and intimate, and a perfect size for a single lady to keep up."

"Beverly made it clear from the beginning that all she needed was a place to dip in and cool off," says

Landscape Architect Rick Anderson, of Daugherty/Anderson & Associates in Atlanta.

Fitted into an oddly shaped space, the pool is a perfect 18-foot-diameter circle, broken only by a mass of boulders that tumble into the water on one side. The pool deck also serves as the walkway between the front yard and the back lawn.

Although located just a short distance from her Atlanta shop, Beverly's home feels as if it's way out in the country. "It was a summer house long ago, and all the materials are very rustic," Anderson says. For that reason, he gave the pool a countrified feeling as well.

Using Tennessee crab orchard stone for the pool deck helped achieve the effect. For the coping, Anderson chose stones about 2½ inches thick. "You see that edge, so it needs to look robust and full," he explains. Farther back from the water, the paving changes imperceptibly to 1-inch-thick stones, which are more economical. To avoid the unnatural look of plastic pool skimmer covers, Anderson had removable stones fitted over the skimmer openings.

To further heighten the rustic character, Anderson added huge boulders—some overlapping the rim of the pool, some edging the deck, and others serving as steps leading down to the lawn. "These are big, heavy, chunky hunks of stone," he says, "not just little pieces cemented together."

On the eastern side, a flower border, which Beverly describes as "my wild, rustic garden," forms a backdrop for the pool. Although much smaller in scale, the border has the character and random, chaotic beauty of a country meadow.

A low hedge of Japanese boxwood runs along the edge of the paving and separates the flower border from the pool deck. Screening the pool area from neighbors on one side are huge Burford hollies, which were guarded from damage during construction. To the rear of the space, Japanese black pines serve a similar function. "I like the distinct contrast in texture between the dark, glossy foliage of the hollies and the pines," Anderson says. Rhododendrons, hemlocks, and mountain laurels add a touch of the North Georgia mountains to the pool area. "These plants had been used elsewhere on the property, so we kept that theme running through the new development."

Rita Strickland

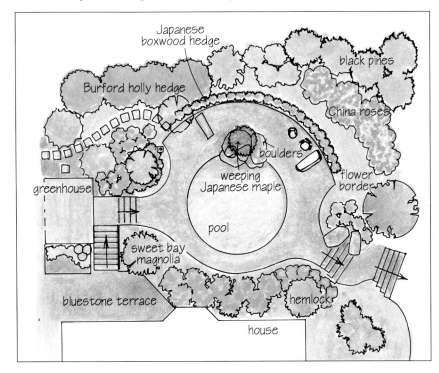

Order in The Courtyard

BY MARK G. STITH / PHOTOGRAPHY VAN CHAPLIN

When the kids grow up, the yard often needs to grow up, too. Out goes the swing set and down comes the basketball goal. That's about what happened to the small courtyard outside Bob and Mimi Cathcart's home in Charleston, South Carolina.

"The whole yard used to be paved with concrete and slate, bordered with 3-foot flowerbeds," says Mimi. "There was a basketball court for our two children, and all the neighborhood kids would come over to play in our courtyard."

As the Cathcarts' children grew, the games ended, and Bob and Mimi talked about having a garden for dabbling instead of dribbling. "I wanted to plan a garden and had some ideas, but really needed them expressed by a landscape architect," Mimi recalls.

After taking a course on landscape design offered by local landscape architects Hugh and Mary Palmer Dargan, ASLA, Mimi hired them to come up with a full design for a court-yard that catered to their needs.

The new garden plan called for tearing out the old concrete-and-slate courtyard and replacing it with a number of interesting features. Among the highlights of the new garden is a 12-foot-high latticework arbor that opens onto a bluestone terrace. The end panels of the arbor were expanded into clever storage compartments for the lawnmower and other outdoor equipment. A variety of plants, such as Lady Banks rose, and *Rosa chinensis* Mutabilis clamber up the latticework.

An oval panel of St. Augustine grass forms the center of the garden and is bordered by a brick walkway that extends in a panhandle shape to the courtyard's entrance. The middle of the "handle" was left in bare soil. This is a perfect spot for Mimi's perennials, which include sedum, dianthus, blue salvia, garden phlox, and coreopsis.

Mother Nature added some unwelcome revisions, too. Before the garden was completed, Hurricane Hugo hit Charleston in September 1989 and blew down a huge magnolia tree at the back wall, causing only minor damage. The downed tree was replaced with a smaller magnolia, and the sunlight that now pours into the courtyard allows Mimi to grow a variety of flowers and shrubs in the beds bordering the walks.

Bob and Mimi liked the new garden so much, they wanted to enjoy it even when they weren't outside. "When we were doing the garden, we also put French doors in our sunroom to bring our garden indoors all year," Mimi says. ◇

A central island filled with perennials greets visitors to this Charleston courtyard garden; the area had previously been a cement-and-slate terrace used by the Cathcart children as a basketball court.

A latticework arbor and bluestone terrace look out over a small oval of St. Augustine grass. The magnolia tree to the left of the arbor replaced a 60-foot-high magnolia blown over by Hurricane Hugo in 1989.

Concealed storage compartments were built into the lattice arbor.

SAVING THE SOUTHERN LANDSCAPE

A visit to three nature preserves reveals the value of native plants.

BY STEVE BENDER / PHOTOGRAPHY VAN CHAPLIN

To understand the people, you must first understand the place. This is a precept of Southern history. But the South we know today is not the same place Native Americans trod upon two centuries ago. Dominant plant communities that once defined whole regions have surrendered to highways, suburbs, and cities. Southern ecosystems that flourished nowhere else now flourish nowhere. Where, then, can you find the beginning South?

We found it at three very special places—places that remind us that Southern heritage isn't solely confined to museums, historic districts, and battlefields. It's also embodied in native plant preserves, where indigenous plants thrive, revealing how the Southern landscape once looked.

Crosby Arboretum— Picayune, Mississippi

Wildfire is often seen as the great destroyer. But ironically, for many plants it is the giver of life. This is particularly true for the special community of plants called piney woods. A type of savanna composed of tall grasses and wildflowers dotted with longleaf pine, piney woods once covered much of the Gulf Coast from eastern Texas to the Carolinas.

But as logging and agriculture grew in importance, wildfire became restricted and the piney woods began to disappear.

There is a place, though, where these woods still thrive, about an hour's drive northeast of New Orleans. It's the Crosby Arboretum, the first scientific and educational institution in the Gulf States devoted solely to the conservation and study of native plants and their significance to the region's environment and economy.

Established in 1979 as a family memorial to L. O. Crosby, Jr., a prominent businessman, outdoorsman, and philanthropist, Crosby Arboretum pursues several objectives. It seeks to preserve examples of the major habitats of the Pearl River Basin and educate people as to how these ecosystems work. And it strives to imbue its average of 5,000 visitors per year with a sense of place, to let them truly experience Mississippi's Gulf Coast.

Crosby's central core, a 64-acre

In Picayune, Mississippi, ground fog at dawn lends Crosby Arboretum's piney woods an ethereal, mystical quality. The tiny, white tufts among the grass are spider webs laden with dew.

interpretive site called Pinecote, contains three major habitats commonly found in South Mississippi. The first is a freshwater wetland designed to mimic the conditions of a beaver pond. Plants found here either grow in water, tolerate seasonal inundation of their roots, or require wet soil the year-round. Pond and bald cypress, golden club, and water lilies are among the inhabitants.

A second habitat demonstrates woodland succession, in which the absence of wildfire gradually transforms grassland to forest. Tree communities found here vary according to the wetness of the site. For example, drier areas encourage the growth of American beech and Southern magnolia. In wet soils, bald cypress, tupelo, red maple, and sweet bay prevail.

The third habitat is the savanna, an ecosystem dependent upon periodic burning for its survival. Under natural conditions, wildfire races through such a savanna every few years, eliminating woody undergrowth and most trees, except for fire-resistant longleaf pines. The resulting sunny meadow supplies ideal conditions for native grasses and perennial wildflowers. Crosby burns its piney woods under controlled conditions every few years to remove invading trees and shrubs. It does so in spring or early summer when lightning-started wildfires frequently appear.

According to Ed Blake, Crosby's director since 1984, the arboretum's most important function is to preserve biodiversity. An added benefit is that the natural processes at work in Crosby can make home gardening more rewarding.

"Gardens today rely on the example of the English landscape park, which is a static landscape where plants simply get older in place," he explains. "But the processes we're working on here allow for more diversity and change. If plants could be grouped together as they might grow together naturally," he continues, "then we could have gardens that don't require as much care, are easier to live with, and allow the unexpected to happen. And as our world becomes more and more the same, the unexpected becomes more important."

Regular burning of the savanna encourages growth of perennial wildflowers, such as goldenrod and narrow-leaved sunflower.

Briarwood—Saline, Louisiana

By any measure Caroline Dormon was remarkable. Botanist, horticulturist, columnist, lecturer, and author, she was also the first female forester in the United States. She painted wonderfully, specializing in watercolor illustrations of Southern wildflowers. Most significantly, she was an early and effective champion of Louisiana native plants.

After studying art at Judson College in Marion, Alabama, Caroline became a schoolteacher in northern Louisiana in 1919. The only way to reach her rural students was traveling by horse and wagon "through mile after mile of majestic longleaf pine forests." The daily sojourns impressed her with the elegance of the native flora. In her book, *Natives Preferred,* Caroline later wrote: "Nothing is more beautiful than Longleaf Pine. . . . The leaves glisten in sunlight, and young trees are fountain-like in their grace."

Caroline decided to devote her life to preserving Louisiana's forests and native plants. The site for her work would be Briarwood, a wooded, 135-acre, family-owned tract near the hamlet of Saline (located in the center of a triangle formed by Shreveport, Alexandria, and Monroe).

During her time at Briarwood, Caroline built a log house, carved trails through the woods, scooped out a "reflection" pond, and planted hundreds of wildflowers, trees, and shrubs collected during her travels throughout the South. She became one of the first breeders and promoters of Louisiana iris, a flower she described as "the queen of all native species . . . unbelievable in its range of color . . . . Never before was so gorgeous a flower brought straight from the wilds to gardens." Together with her older sister, Virginia, and sister-in-law, Ruth, she founded one

Bald cypresses and other moisture-loving plants thrive in Crosby's wetland habitat.

Louisiana iris, the signature plant of Briarwood in Saline, Louisiana, blooms in a boggy area behind the visitors center.

of the South's first native plant nurseries, which offered these new iris.

Tirelessly campaigning for native plants, Caroline almost single-handedly won the establishment of the 600,000-acre Kisatchie National Forest, located near where she used to teach. She lectured widely on native flora, and spoke often about her favorite plant, the Louisiana iris. Once, when asked how long her iris lecture would be, she replied, "Any length you desire! I can talk about these iris for 30 minutes or 30 days!"

Just before she died in 1971 at the age of 83, Caroline handed over the care of Briarwood to her longtime understudy, Richard Johnson. Born less than a mile from Briarwood, Richard had known Miss Dormon all of his life. He began working at Briarwood during the Depression. Caroline paid him 5 cents an hour to weed. Over the years, she tutored him in the lore, culture, uses, and importance of native plants, knowledge he now passes on to visitors. Richard lives with his wife, Jessie, in one wing of Briarwood's visitors center.

A born storyteller with a photographic memory, Richard can regale you with tales of the country for as long as you can listen. His

"See that plant down there with the seven leaflets?" asks Curator Richard Johnson. "It's called 'Indian peanut.'"

encyclopedic mind brims with interesting facts about the plants and animals that inhabit Briarwood. Admonishing 9-year-old grandson, Luke, to return a lizard to exactly where he found it, Richard explains, "Every lizard has his own territory. If you take him out of there, why, he'd be lost. It'd be like if we picked you up and dropped you over in Georgia."

Richard's guided tour of the preserve includes a mandatory stop at the giant, 300-year-old longleaf pine Caroline nicknamed "Grandpappy." For years, lumbermen pestered Miss Dormon to harvest the tree while it was still "good" for something. But she steadfastly refused. "My very soul lives in that old, gnarled, and weather-beaten tree," she wrote. "Oh my, the tales [Grandpappy] could tell of his rugged survival through the storms of life."

Today, Briarwood receives about 2,000 visitors a year, a sizable increase from Caroline's day. This isn't to say that Miss Dormon shunned the public. On the contrary, she was eager to teach and welcomed visitors frequently. But her woods were her sanctuary, her plants, her family, and people always came second. A journal entry, dated

January 1, 1938, she directs a prospective guest: "Bring me what you will, but leave me my wide-open view of the sky, the wind on my face, sweet clean earth to dig in, the whir of wings . . . and all my 'gift of the wild things.'"

Mount Cuba Center—Greenville, Delaware

Though similar in purpose, no two gardens could be more disparate in appearance than Briarwood and Mount Cuba. The former bears only the rough design of nature, while the latter is as soft and manicured as a woman's hand. Hardly a weed can be found throughout Mount Cuba's awesome spring displays of woodland wildflowers and native shrubs. If this place can't inspire you to garden, absolutely nothing will.

The private estate of Mrs. Lammot du Pont Copeland, Mount Cuba traces its beginnings back to 1935, when Mrs. Copeland and her husband purchased property in the rolling countryside near the village of Mount Cuba. The Copelands first developed formal gardens around their large, Georgian house. But by the 1960s,

At Briarwood, children link arms around the trunk of "Grandpappy," a mammoth longleaf pine treasured by Caroline Dormon.

Mrs. Copeland's enthusiasm for wildflowers resulted in the purchase of a large woodlot and meadow adjoining their property.

Taking advantage of a natural swale through the heart of the woodlot, the Copelands fashioned a series of four ponds descending a slope. Around these ponds and through a canopy of mature tulip poplars, they added grass paths and mulched trails lined with over 100 kinds of wildflowers and shrubs native to the Appalachian foothills.

In the early 1980s, the Copelands decided that Mount Cuba should focus its attention on education and research. Today, public access to the 250-acre estate remains limited, although Mount Cuba will be opened to the public in the future.

Richard Lighty, the center's director, guides a program with three distinct and important goals. First, foster public appreciation for the beauty and value of piedmont flora. Second, learn how to propagate native wildflowers that are threatened by overcollection, such as orchids and trilliums, and then pass this knowledge on to commercial nurseries. Third, evaluate native plants, and

It's hard to imagine a more appealing resting spot at Mount Cuba than this bench surrounded by golden ragwort, wild geraniums, and bleeding-heart.

Mulched paths lined with piedmont wildflowers meander beneath mature tulip poplars at Mount Cuba in Greenville, Delaware.

select superior forms for commercial production and garden use.

Among the program's most notable successes so far is a selection of ladies'-tresses orchid (*Spiranthes odorata*) named Chadd's Ford. This rare, fall- and winter-blooming orchid bears white, vanilla-scented blossoms on 18-inch spikes. It is now in commercial production and represents the first native, terrestrial orchid to be produced on a commercial scale. Other Mount Cuba introductions being produced include Purple Dome New England aster, Golden Fleece goldenrod, and Garnet American alumroot.

Not everyone can create a garden as heavenly as those of Mount Cuba. But because of the research being done there, nearly everyone may soon be able to grow a piece of Mount Cuba in their gardens. ◇

WHEN YOU GO

Crosby Arboretum is located on Ridge Road in Picayune, Mississippi. From I-59, take Exit 4 onto State 43 East. Turn right on Ridge Road at arboretum sign. Open year-round (except holidays), 10 a.m. to 5 p.m. Tuesday through Saturday, 2 to 5 p.m. Sunday. Admission is $2 for adults, $1 for children, and $5 for a family. For more information write P.O. Box 190, Picayune, Mississippi 39466; or call (601) 799-2311.

Briarwood is located on State 9, between Saline and Campti, Louisiana, and is open weekends in March, April, May, August, and November. Hours are 9 a.m. to 5 p.m. Saturday, noon to 5 p.m. Sunday. Admission is $5. For more detailed information write P.O. Box 226, Natchitoches, Louisiana 71457; or telephone (318) 576-3379.

Mount Cuba Center is located just outside of Wilmington, Delaware, off Route 52. Admission is by appointment only and limited to horticultural-related groups in springtime. Make reservations six months in advance. For more information write P.O. Box 3570, Greenville, Delaware 19807-0570; or call (302) 239-4244.

AUGUST

CHECKLIST
134

GETTING THEIR FEET WET
136

SELECT A RESISTANT ROSE
139

THEY ENDED THE FLOOD
140

NEW FENCE
FOR A NEW FOCUS
141

CALLAWAY'S HOME GARDEN
142

LATE-SUMMER BOUQUETS
144

CHECKLIST
for August

CONTAINER PLANTS

Summer is tough on potted plants. The soil dries out quickly, so you may need to water daily to prevent wilting. Or, you may want to incorporate a water-retaining polymer into the potting soil. Because nutrients wash through the soil, frequent watering also means frequent feeding. Use half-strength liquid fertilizer, such as 20-20-20, when you water. It's also time to cut back multiflora petunias and other annuals that overrun other plants in the pot or look unwieldy.

CUT FLOWERS

For long-lasting blooms, cut garden flowers in the morning, and place the stems in water immediately. Once you are indoors, remove the leaves from the lower third of the stems; then recut the stems at an angle, and place them in a tall container for several hours, or until you are ready to arrange.

DAYLILIES

If daylilies haven't flowered well, it's probably due to overcrowding. Dig up entire clumps; then remove soil from the roots to expose the crown. Pull plants apart by hand, or split with a sharp knife. Then replant the new divisions about 12 to 18 inches apart.

DESIGN HELP

Because fall is a good time to establish many plants in the landscape, now is a good time to work on a plan for any improvements you want to make. For best results, consider asking a registered landscape architect, garden designer, or a landscape contractor for help.

ESPALIERS

Pyracanthas, camellias, and fruit trees that have been trained to grow against a wall, fence, or trellis need to be tied back often during the growing season. Use foam-wrapped soft wire or cotton twine to tie branches to support frames; on a brick wall, use masonry nails with lead tabs.

FALL BULBS

Bulbs such as colchicum, spider lilies, and fall crocus need to be planted now. If you wait too long, these eager bulbs may flower unnoticed in a paper bag. Set the bulbs in well-drained soil at a depth twice their width; a 2-inch-wide bulb needs to be 4 inches deep. Use massed plantings (at least 40) of smaller bulbs, such as crocus, for best effect. Good choices for autumn color include baby cyclamen and white swamp lilies.

FALL FLOWERS

Fertilize late-summer and fall flowers, such as chrysanthemums, dahlias, and asters, now. Apply about 1 cup of liquid fertilizer or 1 tablespoon of granular 10-10-10 around each plant.

FALL GARDEN

Sow seeds of cool-weather vegetables, including leaf lettuce, spinach, peas, and turnips. It's also time to set out transplants of cabbage, broccoli, and kale. In the Middle South, wait until late in the month; in the Lower South, wait until September. Gardeners in the Coastal South can begin planting the fall garden late this month. Choose selections of tomatoes, snap beans, and squash that mature early (in seven to eight weeks) so they have plenty of time to produce before the weather gets too cool. Because the ground is so warm, it's best to start seeds indoors. Seedlings transplanted to the garden need shade until they become established.

FRUITS

Pick up any rotten fruit around fruit trees and shrubs to reduce disease. It's a good idea to replace old mulch, too. Prune out old raspberry canes (except fall-bearing selections) that bore fruit to stimulate strong, new canes that will produce next year's berries.

HERB ARRANGEMENT

Take advantage of the robust herb garden to create a simple welcoming badge on your door. Clip 8-inch stems of mint, rosemary, sage, oregano, thyme, or whatever is most abundant right now. Bundle tightly in a rubberband; then tie them with natural twine within a background of kraft paper. This quick-and-easy decoration lasts for only a few hours without water, but you can enjoy the chopped herbs with a special dinner.

SEEDS

It's time to mail-order seeds of flowers and vegetables for the fall garden. Allow at least two or more weeks for delivery. Order cool-weather flowers that are easy to start from seed sown in the garden and that will bloom early next spring; good examples are poppies and bachelor's buttons. Also order an ample supply of vegetables that you can seed through fall and winter; these include lettuce, radishes, and greens.

SUMMER PRUNING

Now's your last chance to prune overgrown hollies and other woody evergreen shrubs. Otherwise fall freezes may damage any new growth that results. Trim shrubs at an angle to allow sunlight to reach lower branches. Avoid pruning azaleas, forsythia, and other spring-flowering shrubs now because they are forming flowerbuds for next spring's displays.

SWISS CHARD

Sow seeds now for a fall harvest. For variety, try the selections Rhubarb (pictured) and Vulcan, which have red veins and stalks. Soak seeds overnight for better germination; then set about 4 inches apart and about ½ inch deep. Seedlings come in clusters, so when they sprout remove all but one. Thin again to about a foot apart when plants are large enough to grow together. Florida gardeners should sow seeds late this month for a fall harvest. You may need to lay a board over the seedbed to help keep the soil cool until the seeds germinate, which may take as long as 14 days.

TRANSPLANTS

When you begin setting out fall transplants late this month, remember they have been growing in a highly organic soil mix quite different from your native soil. Help transplants make the transition to native soil by gently loosening some of the roots at the bottom of the root ball. Otherwise, they may continue growing in a circle and never root into the native soil.

WATERING

Dry spells can injure even established trees and shrubs, so be prepared to water them in times of drought conditions. Use a soaker hose or drip irrigation system to minimize runoff as well as evaporation

YELLOW JACKETS

Keep yellow jackets away from seating areas by making sure that there is no food or drink around. Yellow jackets will gather around soft drinks and other sugary fluids spilled on pool decks, patio floors, and outdoor furniture. Remove pet food dishes as soon as kitty or pooch has finished eating. Yellow jackets are particularly fond of pet foods containing tuna or mackerel. Finally, keep garbage can lids tightly sealed.

TIP OF THE MONTH

Every year I grow lima beans in my vegetable garden. When the plants quit bearing and start to lose their leaves, I trim them back to about 6 inches and water them well. They quickly put out new growth and bear a second crop that I can harvest till frost.

Clara Mathews
Murfreesboro, Tennessee

AUGUST NOTES

To Do:
- Continue to give extra water to shrubs, trees, flowers, and lawn to make up for summer drought
- Control fleas in the lawn
- Continue to remove faded blooms from annuals
- Replace vegetables already harvested with vegetables for fall—cabbage, broccoli, Brussels sprouts, collards, and kale
- Watch out for bagworms on evergreens; handpick and discard
- Put out a hummingbird feeder

To Plant:
- Colchicums, autumn crocus, and other fall-blooming bulbs
- Cool-weather vegetables for fall

To Purchase:
- Pesticide to control fleas in the lawn
- Transplants of cool-weather vegetables
- Fall-blooming bulbs
- Hummingbird feeder

_____

_____

_____

_____

_____

_____

_____

_____

_____

_____

_____

Getting Their Feet Wet

Not all plants need good drainage. Some of the most fascinating thrive with water all around.

BY STEVE BENDER

For most plants, water is a bit like wine—fine consumed in moderation, but toxic in excessive amounts. There are plants, however, for whom too much water is a good thing. They thrive with their roots in water, their stems in water, and sometimes totally immersed in water. Plants this different are bound to stir up interest among Southern gardeners. Indeed, where there's a pond,

stream, spring, bog, or just mucky soil, somebody is probably experimenting with water plants.

Water plants fall into three broad groups. The first one is **submerged plants.** These plants are rooted to the bottom and completely covered by water. Although they can grow in moving water, they're usually planted in the still water of a pond. This is because a fast-flowing stream oxygen-

ates itself, while a pond depends largely on submerged and other plants within it to manufacture life-giving oxygen. Submerged plants also purify water by absorbing mineral salts and carbon dioxide produced by animal wastes and decaying plants.

Submerged plants should be the first plants to add to a backyard pond or small water garden. You'll need one plant for each square foot of pond suras those that are rooted to the bottom, but whose leaves float upon the surface. Water lily, lotus, water hyacinth, floating-heart, water clover, and duckweed are all floaters. Floaters thrive in still water, so they're reserved for ponds and water gardens.

Like submerged plants, floaters purify water by filtering wastes, absorbing nutrients, and adding oxygen. And as Yolande Giannelloni, a water gardener in Metairie, Louisiana, points out, their roots and leaves also provide fish with ready places to hide and spawn. Water hyacinth is particularly good for this, she says. But perhaps the greatest contribution floaters make is shading the water, thereby depriving algae of sunlight. Allowing floaters to cover 60% to 70% of the water's surface significantly reduces algae. If algae are unrestricted, they could turn the water green.

The largest and most varied group of water plants is called **marginal plants**—not because they're iffy to grow, but because they live near the edges, or margins, of water. They typically grow in water from 3 to 6 inches deep and hold leaves and flowers high above the surface. However, they'll also grow in moist, well-drained soil on the bank of a stream or pond.

Marginal plants are primarily aesthetic. They soften the edges of ponds and streams, forming a natural buffer. In addition, their characteristically vertical forms contrast nicely with the horizontal shapes of floaters. Most importantly, they offer colorful flowers and foliage.

You'd be hard-pressed to locate more striking features than the azure spikes of pickerel rush, the gilded spears of golden-club, or the incandescent leaves of variegated sweet

flag. If such lesser known plants as these don't intrigue you, then you may be surprised to learn that old-fashioned cannas grow quite well in wet soil, as do elephant's-ears and all sorts of iris—such as Japanese iris, Louisiana iris, and yellow flag.

Getting Started

In most areas, you can plant submerged and floating plants from April through September. However, water lilies and lotus take time to get established, so it's best to plant them in spring. The planting of marginal plants depends on whether they're going to be in or out of water. Those in water can be planted at the same times as submerged and floating plants. Plant those targeted for drier soil in spring or fall.

Don't expect a large selection of water plants at your local garden center. For an extensive offering, contact a mail-order, specialty nursery (see the note at the end of this article). Most water plant catalogs furnish detailed instructions on how to design and build a water garden. They also supply liners, pumps, filters, fish, snails, chemicals, fertilizers, and containers.

When constructing a backyard pond, it's much better to plant submerged, marginal, and rooted floating plants in containers than in the actual pond bottom. Containers are usually black or brown, either plastic or pressed pulp, and hold from 5 to 30 quarts of soil. Never use ordinary potting soil for water plants, as organic matter and other soil amendments float in water. Instead, fill the container halfway with a mixture of two parts heavy topsoil to one part coarse sand, to which you've added the appropriate amount of slow-release fertilizer. Then press plants into the soil, cover the soil with a half

Growing 12 to 18 inches tall, golden-club offers velvety green leaves and numerous yellow-tipped flower spikes.

Tropical water lilies hold their fragrant blossoms well above the surface. Variegated sweet flag streaks skyward in the upper left corner.

face. Most of them prefer water 18 to 24 inches deep. Don't plant deeper than 3 to 4 feet or the decreased amount of sunlight reaching them may inhibit cleansing of the water. Popular submerged plants include anacharis—if you have an aquarium, you know this as "seaweed"— lacy-leaved cabomba, and grasslike vallisneria.

The second group, known as **floaters,** includes plants that float freely upon the water surface, as well

inch of clean pea gravel, and lower the pot into the water. Situate pots in the pond according to the depth of water the plants require.

Flowering water plants, such as water lilies, need at least 5 to 6 hours of sun per day. But don't be discouraged if your yard is shady. Most nonflowering water plants do fine in light shade. And don't think that water plants need lots of space. Miniature versions make it possible to create a beautiful water garden in a container no larger than an old iron kettle.

If water plants have one problem, says Yolande, it's that they're *too* easy to grow. They need yearly dividing to keep them under control. For most, summer is the time to do this. Winter care is also less challenging than you might think. During cold months, take tropical plants indoors to a bright window and store in moist sand. Let the hardy plants fend for themselves. "People always ask me what I do for my plants in winter," remarks Hal Reiss of the Pond Doctor in Kingston, Arkansas. "I tell them I just go in the house and watch TV."

WHERE TO FIND IT

Mail order sources for plants and equipment are listed below. Most catalog costs are refundable with the first order.
1) Aquatic Garden & Koi Company, P.O. Box 57, Hwy.537, Jobstown, NJ 08041. Telephone: 609/723-4220. Catalog: $1
2) Lilypons Water Gardens, 6800 Lilypons Rd., Lilypons, MD 21717-0010. Telephone: 301/874-5133. Catalog: $5
3) Pond Doctor, HC65, Box 265, Kingston, AR 72742. Telephone: 501/665-2232. Catalog: $2
4) Van Ness Water Gardens, 2460 N. Euclid, Upland, CA 91786. Telephone: 714/982-2425. Catalog: $3
5. Trees by Touliatos, 2020 Brooks Rd., Memphis, TN 38116. Telephone: 901/346-8065. No charge for plant listing and price list.

Pickerel rush lends bright color to Barbara Robinson's water garden in Atlanta.

Dainty water poppies bloom at the foot of variegated sweet flag.

Olympiad *Iceberg* *Tournament of Roses*

Select a Resistant Rose

If you want to bring a smile to the face of a pesticide salesman, mention the word "roses." Probably more pesticides have been sold to treat the ailments of modern roses than any other group of ornamental plants.

Although dozens of pests attack roses, the two most serious are both diseases—black spot and powdery mildew. Black spot appears as roughly circular, purplish-black spots on the leaves. The spots gradually enlarge and coalesce, causing leaves to yellow and drop. Severe cases of black spot may completely defoliate a plant, greatly reducing the number of flowers. Powdery mildew, on the other hand, looks like grayish-white powder on leaves, twigs, and flowerbuds. It often distorts and defoliates young shoots and prevents flowerbuds from opening.

Areas having long growing seasons, high humidity, and ample rainfall are often hotbeds of rose disease. Thus, the Lower, Coastal, and Tropical South see the worst outbreaks, although the Upper and Middle South experience trouble, too. Moreover, enclosing rose beds behind walls, fences, and hedges can promote disease because they may restrict airflow and prevent foliage from drying.

Another factor in spreading diseases is the proximity of a rose to disease-prone roses. Previously healthy roses often develop disease when planted near infected ones.

When you buy a rose bush from the garden center, the standard recommendation to prevent disease is to spray the plant every 7 to 10 days throughout the growing season with an appropriate fungicide, such as Funginex, benomyl, or Daconil 2787. But if you're like many gardeners, you're looking for ways to reduce spraying. Planting roses in areas with good air circulation and isolating them from infested plants will certainly help. But it's even more important to select roses that have the genetic makeup to resist disease. Improving disease resistance is a major goal of rose breeders today.

To find the most disease-resistant hybrid tea, grandiflora, floribunda, shrub, and climbing roses, we polled rose experts from across the South. Their recommendations are listed in the chart. Keep in mind that none of these roses are immune to disease. In most cases, you'll still need to spray. But you'll spray much less often than you would for highly susceptible roses.

Steve Bender

DISEASE-RESISTANT ROSES

SHRUB
Bonica
Carefree Beauty
Graham Thomas
Rugosa

HYBRID TEA
First Prize
Mr. Lincoln
Olympiad
Pristine
Tiffany
Touch of Class

GRANDIFLORA
Gold Medal
Pink Parfait
Queen Elizabeth
Shreveport
Tournament of Roses

CLIMBING
America
Golden Showers
Lady Banks
New Dawn

FLORIBUNDA
Cherish
Europeana
French Lace
Gene Boerner
Iceberg
Sunsprite

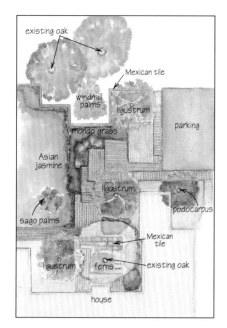

existing oak

Mexican tile

windmill palms

ligustrum

parking

mondo grass

Asian jasmine

ligustrum

podocarpus

sago palms

Mexican tile

ligustrum   ferns   existing oak

house

They Ended The Flood

For Michael and Diane Koontz of Ocala, Florida, the Great Flood didn't occur just in biblical times. It also occurred every time there was a hard rain. Rainwater would gather at their parking area, rush down a slope, and run smack against the house—and sometimes through it. "Once during a bad storm, the water came in under one door and went out under another," Michael recalls. To stem this unwelcome tide, the Koontzes called upon Landscape Architect John Adams, ASLA.

The soil around the house is quite sandy, so poor drainage wasn't the problem. "It was just that the slope was so steep, the water never had a chance to sink in," says Adams. Accordingly, he devised a three-fold strategy to manage runoff. First, he built a swale near the parking area to carry runoff from the street around the property. A low retaining wall at the top of the lot serves as a backup. Second, he and Michael decided to terrace the slope with wooden decks and planting beds to slow the water and allow it to percolate. Finally, Adams installed subsurface drainage in front of the house.

The Koontzes wanted their entry garden to do more than solve the water problem; they also wanted it to

A series of decks terraces this slope, slowing runoff. Large oaks and evergreen ground covers foster a lush look.

PHOTOGRAPHS: VAN CHAPLIN

project a lush, natural look. Adams retained the existing canopy of large oaks then planted a mixture of evergreen shrubs and ground covers beneath it. To encourage closer looks at the plants, the decks make several turns that slow the approach. For seasonal color, the Koontzes set pots of bromeliads and caladiums at the corners of the decks.

Mexican tiles mortared to concrete blocks add a luxurious touch to the steps and retaining wall. Though designed primarily for indoor use, the tiles have held up well for six years.

Thanks to the decks and massed plantings, the garden requires remarkably little maintenance. "It's just amazing," declares Michael. "All we have to do is sweep the decks and everyone comments on how beautiful the yard looks, like we've been working at it all day."   *Steve Bender*

A low retaining wall of Mexican tiles mortared to concrete blocks helps direct excess water.

A picket fence screens the entry garden and is in scale with the house.

New Fence For a New Focus

A small change can make a big difference. For proof, take a look at the entry garden in front of Johnny and Gwynn Naylor's home in Baton Rouge. The builder's original plans called for a stuccoed wall to enclose a New Orleans-style courtyard. But a solid wall would have overpowered the house. So the builder, Steve Plauché, decided to try a picket fence.

Plauché's fence idea proved to be a gem. Six feet high at the posts with panels 10 feet wide, the picket fence is in scale with the house and in character with the neighborhood. For added interest, Plauché cut the pickets nearly even with the stringer in the center of each panel and progressively longer toward each post.

"Instead of a monotonous straight line across the top, now the fence sways up and down," explains Johnny.

Inside the fence rests a charming garden, approximately 35 feet long and 30 feet wide, designed by Baton Rouge landscape architect Philip Moser, ASLA. Crepe myrtles, a windmill palm, small shrubs, and a variety of annuals and perennials surround an exposed aggregate terrace edged in brick. Johnny, who owns a local garden center, changes the annuals seasonally to fill the garden with color and also to "test new plants we get in." Other than transplanting flowers, this tiny retreat requires little maintenance.

Whether greeting guests or just puttering with the flowers, Johnny and Gwynn enjoy the garden year-round. The fence is open and airy enough to let in sun and air, but still provides necessary privacy. A bubbling fountain in one corner supplies the comforting sound of flowing water. Low-voltage lamps light up the fence panels at night, permitting the family to relax in the garden after dark.

Like most gardeners, Johnny is an experimenter and has changes planned for the courtyard. He's thinking about replacing the fountain with a different type, or planting perennials he's never tried before. Nonetheless, he's pleased with his garden so far. "An entry should please both the eye and ear," he comments. "And that's what we tried to accomplish."

Steve Bender

Viewed from the balcony, the garden contains a variety of trees, small shrubs, and flowers, all within easy reach from the terrace.

Black-eyed Susans and other flowers add bright color throughout the seasons.

PHOTOGRAPHS: VAN CHAPLIN

Callaway's Home Garden

The Southern set for the PBS series "The Victory Garden" lies at the center of Callaway's 7½-acre vegetable display garden.

BY LINDA ASKEY WEATHERS
PHOTOGRAPHY VAN CHAPLIN, SYLVIA MARTIN

"It's the best kept secret in Callaway Gardens," remarks Barrie Crawford, a volunteer. She was talking about Victory Garden South, located in the middle of a 7½-acre plain of vegetables at Georgia's Pine Mountain resort. The compound of rustic buildings—surrounded by plantings and bounded by a picket fence—was built to serve as the Southern set of the PBS series "The Victory Garden." However, it fills a dual purpose.

Curator Lucinda Mays explains, "This is the home demonstration garden for Callaway's guests, and it's our only one designed on a residential scale. My wish is that visitors will come in and find a corner or a border or some idea that they can carry home and use—how to trellis a particular plant, what perennials perform in the shade, or which selections make successful color combinations. I don't have anything that takes an unusual amount of care; that's not what this garden is for."

Walk into the garden and, indeed, it feels like home. In fact it is home to birds, butterflies, and anyone who shares a passion for nature. Throughout the garden are birdhouses, feeders, and water features.

Last fall the entrance was lined with purple and pink cosmos. Walking through them was like being with Dorothy in the poppy field on her way to Oz; they were so pretty you just wanted to lie down in them. They were planted not just for gardeners, but also to nourish migrating monarch butterflies on their way to Mexico. They came, first one, then a couple. Soon the garden was teeming with them. The idea was so successful Lucinda is growing another floral way station this year with yellow and orange cosmos.

Even if local residents return several times in the same season, they always find new ideas here. Series producer John Pelrine explains, "The garden needs to change constantly to be a source of fresh ideas for

The complex feels like a rural homeplace surrounded by gardens.

Throughout the Victory Garden set is a variety of plants grown by methods amateurs can imitate in their own gardens.

the show, and it does. Besides, the changes give visitors more of a reason to come back."

If you watch the show, chances are you saw the moss garden that was planted last season. It's sure to get even better this year. And there is always an assortment of vines—from luffa and jicama to climbing nasturtium and cypress vine—and all fit into the overall design. Lucinda is growing at

least 12 kinds of tomatoes for visitors to compare, and she designed an entire section of vegetables that Native Americans were growing when Christopher Columbus arrived 500 years ago. Flower enthusiasts will enjoy the late-summer and fall-flowering salvias, joe-pye weed, sunflowers, and chrysanthemums in the perennial border.

Visitors are invited to watch as Lucinda and Executive Producer/Director Russ Morash, discuss a segment, rehearse the dialog, and then capture it on videotape. It's fun to see the taping in person and then catch it on TV.

Callaway Gardens is located southwest of Atlanta and east of Montgomery, Alabama, a short drive off I-85. If you are planning to visit, call ahead and check the dates that are scheduled for taping.

Victory Garden South is at its best from mid-March through mid-October. For reservations telephone 1-800-282-8181; for information telephone (404) 663-5187.   ◇

Curator and host of Victory Garden South, Lucinda Mays emphasizes the garden's features and explains how the visitor can duplicate her results.

Late-Summer Bouquets

The broad faces of sunflowers first catch your eye. Then an instant later, you discover the surprise of spiky okra and a graceful branch of quince.

PHOTO STYLING: MARJORIE JOHNSTON
ARRANGEMENTS: NAOMI THOMASON

BY KATHERINE PEARSON
PHOTOGRAPHY COLLEEN DUFFLEY

Celebrate harvest time with a special arrangement. The effect is both downright earthy and delightfully sophisticated.

Perhaps the best arrangements capture a moment in time within the growing season. The casual bouquets shown here reflect the late-summer garden, where both flowers and vegetables make their last grand show.

This late in the summer, it's no sin to yank an entire stalk from the vegetable garden for the sake of a striking arrangement indoors. Experienced flower arrangers, always looking for interesting materials to include, treasure fruit-laden stalks for drama and surprise. In addition to the possibilities in our arrangements, look for clusters of beans and small squash still on the vine. What might be an upright line another time of year becomes a graceful hanging bough shaped by the weight of the harvest.

And what about those who are not experienced at arranging? The random, casual character of these bouquets eliminates the need for professional skills. Selecting a tall container with a narrow mouth also helps make arranging easier. The narrow opening tends to do the arranging for you. Concentrate on three different heights and shapes: some upright lines; mass to fill the center; and a naturally trailing form that will droop below the lip of the container.

Compare the easier, upright arrangements of sunflowers and hyacinth beans with the tomato and red pepper bouquet arranged in a broad, shallow basket. In the basket, six different plant materials combine in a skillful and graceful way that admittedly takes more practice. ◇

(**Top**) *Hyacinth beans twist energetically from within a simple pairing of marigolds and cosmos.* (**Above**) *Flaming red peppers and miniature tomatoes spark this arrangement of grass heads, geranium, and winged elm.*

SEPTEMBER

CHECKLIST
148

**SALVIAS THAT THRIVE
IN THE FALL**
150

**THEY WENT WILD
OUT FRONT**
152

LUSHNESS WITHOUT LABOR
153

**THROWING THE DRIVEWAY
A CURVE**
154

**MUMS AND MARIGOLDS
TOGETHER**
155

THIS GAZEBO IS A CLASSIC
156

CHECKLIST
for September

ANNUALS

Warm-weather annuals that do well in mild fall temperatures can be planted now. Marigolds, candytuft, cleome, begonia, and petunias will thrive during the cooler months ahead. It's also time to order seeds of winter annuals, such as stock, sweet pea, bachelor's button, lupine, delphinium, and larkspur. Gardeners from the Upper South may know lupine and delphinium as perennials, but in the rest of the South they grow as winter annuals. Sow seeds in flats now and transplant in late October.

BAGWORMS

Silken, needle-covered bags hanging on pines, junipers, hemlocks, arborvitae, and other evergreens are homes for bagworm caterpillars. These insects live in the bags and feed on the foliage as they move about. To lessen their damage, handpick as many bags as you can; you can also spray them with Bacillus thuringiensis (such as Dipel and Thuricide), acephate, or Diazinon. Follow the label directions carefully.

CITRUS

In the Coastal South, plant citrus trees now so they can establish their roots before cold weather arrives. If possible, locate the trees on the south side of the house to provide extra protection from northern winds. It might make the difference whether the tree survives a cold snap, especially in North Florida. The most cold-hardy varieties are kumquats and satsumas. They will tolerate temperatures to about 20 degrees or lower if they've had a chance to harden off properly before the cold strikes.

COMPOST

Build or buy a compost bin to prepare for the onslaught of leaves and other plant debris this fall. Choose a sturdy, well-built bin that is large enough to handle the load. Remember to turn the pile every three months, moving uncomposted material into the center of the pile.

DRIED FLOWERS

Many flowers in bloom now can be picked and dried for use in arrangements. Some of the best include celosia, gomphrena, Mexican bush sage, and goldenrod. To dry, bundle the flowers together with a rubberband; then hang them upside down in a dry, sheltered area.

FALL FLOWERS

Plant some fall-blooming perennials and shrubs in your garden for colorful displays in autumn. Asters, Japanese anemone, showy sedum, and sasanqua camellia are just a few choices available at local garden centers and nurseries.

GARLIC

Plant individual cloves of garlic now for a harvest next summer. Choose a sunny spot in the garden; space cloves 4 to 6 inches apart and 3 inches deep in rows a foot wide. Set cloves with their tip ends up. The leaves that sprout will stay green through winter.

HARDY ANNUALS

Sow seeds of hardy annuals, such as sweet alyssum, calendula, candytuft, annual pinks, sweet peas, and snapdragons. Gardeners in the Upper South can start seeds in flats indoors and transplant in spring. In the Middle and Lower South, sow seeds directly in the ground later in the month.

INDOOR HERBS

Take cuttings or buy small plants of rosemary, oregano, sage, and other herbs to grow indoors for fresh use. Pot them in 6-inch containers, and place in a sunny window. Keep plants well watered; if possible, set the pots in a shallow tray filled with pebbles and water to increase humidity. Even opening the window on mild days can help.

LAWNS

Once the night temperatures are consistently below 60 degrees, fertilize cool-season grasses, such as tall fescue and bluegrass, with 6 pounds of 16-4-8 or 8 pounds of 12-4-8 per 1,000 square feet of lawn. Water the grass thoroughly after applying fertilizer. Your lawn needs just enough water to keep it healthy. Too much water runs up your bill and causes the grass to grow faster so you mow more. In areas with watering restrictions, irrigation also becomes a legal concern. A lawn needs water if it has a dry, bluish cast, it doesn't spring back when you walk on it, or the leaf blades begin to curl from the sides. In Florida, the state Water Management District recommends ⅔ inch of water per application (the old recommendation was 1 inch). You can measure how much water is being applied by setting out empty containers in different spots about the lawn. Run the sprinkler until the containers hold ⅔ of an inch of water. Make note of how long it took; that's how long you'll need to water. Overseed warm-season lawns, such as Bermuda and centipede, with perennial ryegrass for a green lawn this winter. Mow the grass about an inch high; then rake the soil deeply. Use a seed spreader for even distribution of the seed; apply 7 to 15 pounds per 1,000 square feet. Water regularly to achieve best germination.

PERENNIALS

Dig and divide perennials, such as coneflowers (left), garden phlox, foxgloves, and Shasta daisies. Transplant them soon to enable their roots to become established before winter. Label plants so you'll know what is coming up next spring.

STRAWBERRIES

Plant strawberries now in full sun and fertile, well-drained soil. Dig 8 to 10 inches deep, and add compost or peat moss to improve the soil. Space plants 18 to 24 inches apart in beds 2 feet wide. Allow 3½ to 4 feet between the rows.

VEGETABLES

Sow seeds of lettuce, turnip, mustard, spinach, radish, carrot, Chinese cabbage, and kale for a fall crop. Keep soil damp until germination occurs. It's getting cool enough in the Middle and Lower South to set out kohlrabi, cabbage, broccoli, and cauliflower transplants now. Gardeners in South Florida and South Texas can plant beans, cucumbers, corn, squash, to-

matoes, basil, and other vegetables and herbs that like warm weather. In the Coastal South, you can plant fall tomatoes (early-maturing varieties only), bush beans, pole beans, squash, and cucumbers. It is also time to begin sowing seeds of cool-season crops for the fall garden. Suggestions include collards, mustard, radishes, and turnips. Lettuce is best started from transplants now because the seeds have trouble germinating in the hot soil.

SEPTEMBER NOTES

To Do:
- Replace summer annuals with cool-weather annuals, such as pansies
- Apply pre-emergence weed killer to lawn to control annual bluegrass
- Sow seed of cool-weather grasses
- Fertilize cool-weather lawns
- Sod warm-weather lawns

To Plant:
- Cool-weather annuals and vegetables
- Spring bulbs
- Perennials

To Purchase:
- Spring bulbs
- Annual and vegetable transplants
- Grass seed and sod
- Lawn fertilizer
- Pre-emergence weed killer
- Perennials
- Potted mums

Salvias
That Thrive In The Fall

*Many perennial salvias come into full glory
when cool weather arrives. Here are some of the
best ones for the South.*

BY MARK STITH
PHOTOGRAPHY VAN CHAPLIN, SYLVIA MARTIN

Many summer-flowering annuals and perennials hit bottom in autumn. The reasons are numerous, but the effect is the same: Yuck.

Not so with perennial salvias. Fall is when many of them come into full-color glory, with spikes of blue, purple, and red flowers so brilliant you'd swear they were plugged into something.

You've probably used the popular annual salvia (*Salvia splendens,* also called scarlet sage) as a bedding plant for summer color, or you may have grown sage (*S. officinalis*) in your herb garden. But you might not be as familiar with the perennial flowering salvias.

The Fall Lineup

Mexican bush or velvet sage (*S. leucantha*) is a "true fall salvia," says Lucinda Mays, of Callaway Gardens in Pine Mountain, Georgia. Mexican bush sage produces scads of purple flowers from late summer to the first frost atop 3- to 4-foot-high plants (don't be surprised if they get higher than that in warmer areas of the South). Experts suggest two forms of Mexican bush sage: Emerald is a selection with purple spikes and white centers; All Purple has—you guessed it—all purple flowers.

Another great salvia for fall is *S. guaranitica*. It doesn't have a common name, but is certainly worth

Salvia guaranitica *has some of the largest blooms of any salvia. Its azure flowers can be 2 inches long.*

Autumn sage is brilliant in fall with bright magenta flowers. White and pale-red selections are also available.

The purple racemes of Indigo Spires get longer and more intensely colored as autumn progresses.

In fall, Mexican bush sage mixes well with yellow swamp sunflowers and the burgundy foliage of Red Shield hibiscus.

learning a little Latin for. Another late bloomer, it boasts some of the biggest flowers in the bunch. Wisps of 1½ to 2-inch-long bluish-purple flowers appear on 3- to 5-foot-high plants. It's best used as an annual in all but the Lower and Coastal South and does well in light shade.

Indigo Spires, a hybrid salvia of debated parenthood, gets rave reviews from Sheila Goss of Crosspoint Farm in Durham, North Carolina. "The flowers are a rich, deep blue that stands out in fall," she notes. Plants get 3 to 6 feet high; the flower stalks elongate (about 18 to 20 inches) and deepen in color as fall approaches.

Other great salvias for fall include *S. uliginosa,* with azure flowers atop 4- to 6-foot-high plants, and mealy-cup sage (*S. farinacea*). Forsythia sage (*S. madrensis*) bears bright-yellow flowers and is reportedly winter hardy as far north as Raleigh.

Tips for Growing

Zealots may debate the best salvia in the bunch, but there's one thing they all agree on: Providing good drainage is a must. If you have heavy clay soils, add sand, fine gravel, or rich, loamy soil mixes.

Another essential requirement is providing plenty of water during summer, especially in August. Use a slow-release fertilizer, such as Osmocote (about a teaspoon around each plant), at planting and again in mid-summer.

Most salvias need full sun for best performance. Pests and disease problems are minimal, although whiteflies can be a problem on large-flowered types such as *S. guaranitica.* Lucinda Mays recommends using insecticidal soap instead of strong pesticides that might harm insects and hummingbirds that feed on the nectar.

Many salvias are tender perennials, so gardeners in the Upper and Middle South should take 4- to 6-inch cuttings of plants (remove the flower stalks), set them in containers filled with moist sand, and overwinter them in a greenhouse or cold frame.

If you don't want to go to the trouble of rooting cuttings, treat the plants as annuals. Or mulch heavily, and hope for a mild winter. If your gamble doesn't pay off, salvias are such vigorous growers that you'll get full-size specimens from 1-gallon plants set out in spring.

Where most expect an expanse of trimmed lawn, this home boasts a meadow of native grasses and wildflowers that truly reflect the Hill Country of Texas.

They Went Wild Out Front

Phlox and blue-eyed grass are flowers that come and go through the growing seasons.

At the home of Georgia and Mike Dunn, compromise resulted in a delightful blend of traditional and natural. "My husband is a manufacturing manager, and I'm a photographer," Georgia explains. "He wanted a more traditional landscape and I wanted an outdoor stage for flowers, butterflies, and wildlife." The result is a typical planting at the foundation and a front-yard meadow.

Having moved to Austin from Minnesota, the Dunns knew they would need some advice on developing a landscape that not only fit the house and lot but also would survive the challenges of Texas weather. They got that advice from Stephen K. Domigan, ASLA, a local landscape architect who specializes in ecological landscapes.

"The Dunns involved me in the project from the very beginning," says Domigan. "A lot of times I have to talk a homeowner into trying a meadow, but Georgia wanted one from the start. And by having a stretch of St. Augustine lawn and more traditional plants, such as dwarf yaupon and cherry laurels, along the foundation, Mike was happy too."

There are two important considerations to keep in mind when taking on a project like this. First, learn the fine art of maintaining a meadow. "It's not that a meadow requires more work—in fact, this probably requires less time than a lawn. It's more a matter of learning *what* to do and *when* to do it," Domigan explains. With wildflower meadows, you have to let flowers set seed before you cut them. On the other hand, you don't want spring flowers crowding out emerging summer flowers. "It's largely a matter of timing," Georgia says, "and there are times when it looks a little scruffy.

"And let's be realistic," she adds. "There is a lot of weeding required to get a meadow started. I've been taking notes so I can learn from year to year." But part of the proliferation of weeds can be attributed to the fact that topsoil from elsewhere was introduced over the drain field, as was required by the county health department. "It had a lot of weed seed in it," Domigan says bluntly.

If you live in a subdivision, you need to consider how a meadow garden will fit in. "We live in a formal neighborhood, and there is a definite contrast between my front yard and my neighbors'," Georgia acknowledges. "We have a traditional planting along the street to help tie into the neighborhood, and we keep the foundation planting neat."

While this approach is probably not suited for every setting, the Dunns feel good about what they are doing and have found rewards. "I love the colors: the Texas bluebonnets, Indian paintbrush, evening primrose, and the *Salvia greggii*. But my favorite is the wine cup," Georgia says. And, as Domigan points out, "None of the native areas are ever irrigated or fertilized. They truly survive on what nature provides." *Todd A. Steadman*

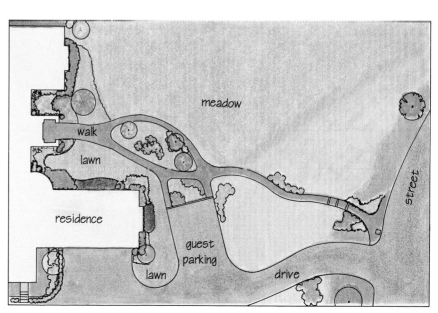

A simple palette of evergreens—wax myrtles, azaleas, and dwarf mondo grass—provides a lush look without much maintenance, while a privacy wall screens the garden from other homes close by.

Lushness Without Labor

Many people enjoy the random, cluttered appearance of a cottage garden. But not Jim Welch of Alexandria, Louisiana. Jim wanted his small backyard to express a simple, straightforward look. He also wanted it to be lush and inviting year-round. To fulfill this wish list, Jim called on Landscape Architect Jeffery Carbo of Patrick Moore Landscape Architects.

Because of the close proximity of other homes, adding privacy was a must. So Carbo designed a handsome wall of wooden panels and brick columns to enclose the area and transform it into a courtyard. For extra screening, limbed-up wax myrtles rise above the wall.

Jim's career as an ophthalmologist leaves him little time for garden maintenance. So you won't find a fussy lawn in this garden. In its place, Carbo covered the ground with Fashion azaleas and dwarf mondo grass, a wooden deck, a brick terrace and stepping pads. Automatic sprinklers keep the garden green. About the only upkeep required is filling small beds with seasonal annuals and pruning occasionally.

Chances are, though, if you visit Jim, you won't find him busy with either job. More likely, he'll be relaxing in the spa on the deck, surrounded by verdant, well-ordered serenity. You might say his garden is beautifully simple. Or simply beautiful.

Steve Bender

Tucked amid tall pines, a pair of new parking spaces directs guests to the front door of this Jackson, Mississippi, home.

Throwing the Driveway a Curve

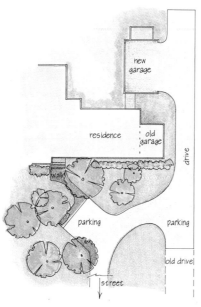

Jack and Betty Love McLarty had a problem that plagues many homeowners. Though the front entry to their Jackson, Mississippi, home was attractive, visitors rarely used it, opting instead for the entrance at the kitchen door around back. In addition, the growing family had more cars than places to put them. The McLartys called on the local landscape firm of Griffin and Egger to help find some solutions.

"The original drive reminded me of an airport runway," says Clifton Egger of the firm. "It ran straight down the property line and back to the garage." As part of a remodeling, the McLartys enclosed the garage to gain some interior space and then built a new one behind the house. But that change alone did nothing to solve the circulation problem.

The answer lay in bringing the drive in nearer to the middle of the lot, putting a bend in it, and providing two spots for parking out front. "First, we put two places in line with the front door," says Egger, "just to encourage visitors to come in that way." A new front walk, as well as improved plantings, deliver guests to the doorway in style.

For family use, or when the McLartys entertain, two more spaces are tucked off the drive near the edge of the property. And a wide area of paving adjacent to the new garage serves both as a turnaround and as space for two more cars.

As a bonus, this work allowed improvement in drainage on the site. "We added a slight swale to the middle of the drive," Egger says. "Before, it was too flat. Now the water can drain out to the street."   *Bill McDougald*

Marigolds and mums offer spectacular color in the Southern Living *area of the Birmingham Botanical Gardens.*

Mums and Marigolds Together

For many Southerners, it's a reflex—when fall rolls around, fill your garden with mums. But are mums your only choice? Not according to wholesale grower Carole Barton of Barton's Greenhouse & Nursery in Alabaster, Alabama. Many annuals traditionally planted for summer should be planted for autumn as well, she says. The familiar French marigold is a good example.

Marigolds in fall enjoy several advantages over mums. For one thing, they bloom from the time you plant them right up until a hard frost. Mums, however, flower only three to four weeks. Marigolds also have the upper hand with regard to cost—you can probably buy three or four potted marigolds for the price of a single potted mum. Pests are another consideration. Marigolds suffer less from insects and disease in autumn than they do in summer. But rainy spells in fall make mums susceptible to several diseases, including botrytis bud rot.

Of course, marigolds have their

Although mums finish blooming in three to four weeks, marigolds bloom from fall until a hard frost.

own shortcomings. "They don't have the pretty pink or lavender flowers some mums do," Carole points out. An easy way to circumvent this is by planting mums and marigolds to-

gether. Granted, such a combination risks looking a bit flashy, particularly if you place yellows next to reds or pinks next to oranges. But then again, a brief seasonal display is allowed to be gaudier than one that lasts all summer. For a few short weeks, it's fun to relax the rules.

Don't think of fall marigolds only as alternatives or companions to mums. You can also use them to replace beds of tired summer annuals that have been battered by heat, drought, and insects.

Although it is too late to start your own marigolds from seed, fall transplants are available from some nurseries. But remember, planting marigolds this time of year is still a relatively new idea, so not every garden center may carry these plants now. If yours doesn't, don't be discouraged. Garden centers stock what customers ask for. As more and more gardeners request fall marigolds, retailers will get the word.

Steve Bender

Stately columns and a pitched roof give this gazebo grand proportions.

THIS GAZEBO IS A CLASSIC

Here's a handsome structure that adds a touch of elegance to any garden. Our complete plans show you how to build one yourself.

BY MARK G. STITH / PHOTOGRAPHY VAN CHAPLIN

A gazebo can bring a certain spirit to almost any garden setting. Whether plain or fancy, it can transform a simple garden into someplace special. This attractive example serves a number of functions—practical as well as decorative.

"We use our gazebo as a gateway to the rest of the garden rather than a destination," says Linda Weathers. In the Weathers's backyard, the structure separates a patterned vegetable, flower, and herb garden from the rest of the yard. It's also a wonderful vantage point, as well as a convenient retreat for taking a quick break from gardening chores or dodging a sudden rain shower.

Built with stock lumber, the gazebo sits on a 7- x 9-foot poured-concrete pad. It's just large enough for an intimate seating area, yet is in proportion to the rest of the garden. Although constructing this gazebo from our plans is within the skill level of the advanced do-it-yourselfer, the Weatherses hired a contractor, the Kerf Company of Birmingham.

Three columns at each corner add architectural emphasis and are in scale with the impressive, steeply pitched (12 in 12) roof. The four large columns are 6 x 6, pressure-treated wood posts enclosed with 1 x 8s; the eight smaller columns are built up from 1 x 6s boxed together.

The notched molding at the base of the columns allows air to circulate inside them. Angled metal braces bolted into the concrete pad anchor each column. Laid in a herringbone pattern on the concrete, brick pavers add a finished appearance, and coping brick hides the edge of the slab.

The roof, 12 feet high at its apex, is substantial enough to hold a ceiling fan or light fixture underneath; it would be easy to run wiring through one of the smaller, hollow columns to provide electricity. The gazebo's asphalt shingles match those on the house. Latex enamel paint, a shade lighter than the house's exterior, gives the wood a matte finish.

To order working drawings for this gazebo (please indicate plan number 207SLP when ordering), send $50 to *Southern Living,* P.O. Box 830349, Birmingham, Alabama 35283-0349. Credit card orders call toll free 1-800-755-1122. ◇

Brick coping dresses up the edge of the flooring and helps hide the concrete slab underneath.

OCTOBER

CHECKLIST
160

FALL COLOR WITHOUT FAIL
162

A COLORFUL SPRING COMBO
166

THIS WATERFALL BELONGS
167

MAGNOLIA TOPIARIES
168

PILE UP PUMPKINS
170

SPICEBUSH SEASONS
THE FALL
171

A MAJOR LOOK
AT MINOR BULBS
172

CHECKLIST
for October

AMBERSWEET ORANGE

This new orange developed by the USDA has been publicized as being exceptionally cold hardy, but that is not necessarily so, according to Dr. Larry Jackson, professor of horticulture at the University of Florida Citrus Research and Education Center at Lake Alfred. Ambersweet is at least as hardy as Hamlin and other popular sweet oranges, but plantings haven't been subjected to hard freezes, such as those of the 1980s, to give it a proper test.

BIRD FEEDERS

Now that winter is just around the corner, set out a feeder to help birds through the harsh months ahead. Check with local wildlife experts to determine the best seeds for birds in your area (oiled sunflower seeds are a popular choice). Keep the feeder well stocked, and clean it regularly.

CALADIUMS

Gardeners in the Upper and Middle South need to dig up frost-tender bulbs, such as caladiums and gladioli. Remove any soil clinging to the bulbs, and keep them in an old onion or potato bag in a cool, dark area. Make sure the bulbs are dry before storing.

CAMELLIA SCALE

Yellow splotches on the foliage are good clues to an infestation of this insect; the undersides of leaves will have crusty, white deposits. Spray according to label directions with a systemic insecticide, such as Orthene or Cygon, or apply a dormant oil spray to the underside of the foliage. The oil coats the pests so they suffocate.

CLEOME SEED

Saving seeds of cleome is easy. To harvest, simply open the slender, beanlike pods, and brush the seeds into an envelope (or an old 35mm film canister). Store in a cool, dry location for sowing next spring.

FLOWERBEDS

The dormant season ahead would be a good time to establish or expand a flower or vegetable garden. Adding soil amendments or taking soil samples now will allow plenty of time for planning — as well as planting — the garden next spring.

HERBS

Fall is an ideal time for herbs in the Coastal South. Those sensitive to the heat and humidity — sage, lavender, and French tarragon — will do well from now until next summer. Rosemary, Greek oregano, bay, and mint don't mind heat and humidity and will live for several years. In frost-free areas, add basil and dill to the list. Be sure all your herbs are planted in well-drained soil or grow them in raised beds.

HOUSEPLANTS

Before freezing weather hits, bring in houseplants you had set outside for the summer. Many indoor plants are tropical in origin and could be injured by cool temperatures (in the 40s) even before freezing weather comes. Fall and winter bring reduced light and cooler temperatures. This means your houseplants won't need as much water. Always check the moisture by poking your finger about an inch into the soil; water when the soil feels dry.

PANSIES

Set out pansies now for blooms throughout the cool months. Try some of the newer, heat-resistant types, such as the Maxim series or Padparadja, a bright-orange pansy that is a 1991 Fleuroselect Gold and All-America Selections winner. Space plants about 6 inches apart; apply about 1 teaspoon of a slow-release fertilizer around each plant. Wait until hard freezes are forecast to mulch heavily; remove faded blooms for continued flowering.

PYRACANTHAS

The heavy load of berries produced by healthy pyracanthas grown as espaliers can be a strain on their supports. Make sure that support wires, cables, or other fasteners, as well as the trellis frame, are in good condition.

PINE STRAW

Collect fallen pine needles to use as mulch throughout the year. Use them around azaleas and other shrubs, and in flower and vegetable beds. Because of their waxy coating, pine needles generally last longer than shredded bark mulches. Store the unused portion in trash bags or in a pile covered with plastic to keep it dry.

SPANISH MOSS

Clear excessive amounts of Spanish moss from small trees and the lower branches of large trees using a long pole with a hook on the end to grab the moss and yank it down. For limbs out of reach, use a trombone-type sprayer to apply a copper spray mixed with a few drops of liquid detergent to help the spray stick. Be careful however: copper is lethal to fish and marine invertebrates.

TOMATOES

Autumn frosts can spell doom for tomato plants in the garden, but it doesn't mean you have to stop enjoying homegrown tomatoes (see "Tomatoes Till Christmas," page 102). One method is to pick all the tomatoes, wrap them in tissue paper, and place in a cardboard box in a cool, dark area indoors. Be sure to check them often for ripeness.

VEGETABLES

In frost-free regions of the Coastal South, it's time to plant fall and winter tomatoes, corn, beans, and most cool-weather vegetables. Elsewhere, limit plantings to cool-weather vegetables. Those that tolerate frosts—spinach, onions, cabbage, some lettuces, collards, and kale—will yield through winter. Gardeners in the Lower South can still sow seeds of cool-weather vegetables, such as lettuce, carrots, edible-pod peas, spinach, radishes, and turnips. In the Middle South, fast-maturing vegetables, such as garden cress, turnips (for greens), and radishes, can be sown. Frost comes this month to the Upper South; remember that the flavor of turnips, kale, and parsnips is improved if you wait to harvest until after the first frost.

TIP OF THE MONTH

Here's a foolproof way for starting roses in fall. When the weather starts to cool, simply snip off a 3- to 4-inch section of a branch. Dig a hole, and plant the section. Water it thoroughly; then place a fruit jar over it until spring. After the threat of cold weather has passed and the cutting starts to sprout, tilt the jar just a bit to let in outside air. Leave the jar like this for several days, until the cutting gets used to the environment. Then remove the jar, water the rose, and watch for the blooms.

Linda Elgin
Belton, Missouri

OCTOBER NOTES

To Do:
- Clean plant debris from vegetable and flower gardens
- Rake and compost leaves
- Dig and store tender bulbs
- Divide perennials
- Fertilize cool-weather lawns
- Transplant trees and shrubs
- Bring tender potted plants indoors
- Overseed warm-weather lawns with annual or perennial rye

To Plant:
- In the Upper South, spring bulbs
- Trees, shrubs, perennials
- Cool-weather annuals

To Purchase:
- Spring bulbs
- Lawn fertilizer
- Compost bin for leaves
- Cool-weather annuals
- Potted mums
- Annual or perennial ryegrass seed

You can't beat the dramatic coloration of flowering dogwood in autumn.

FALL COLOR
Without Fail

Trees are often dependable signals of the season. Here are several that won't let you down.

BY MARK G. STITH / PHOTOGRAPHY VAN CHAPLIN

Okay, class. We're going to play "word association." So close your eyes, and say "autumn." What comes to mind? Football games? Back to school? County fairs? Whatever scene you conjured up, brightly colored trees were probably in the picture.

That's just the way it is. Fall and the leaves that light its fire are inseparable. More than any other phenomenon, the turning leaves are nature's signal flags for a change in season.

So it's no small disappointment when trees don't provide the foliar

fireworks we expect from them.

But here are some trees with never-fail color in fall, the kind of trees that you depend on year in and year out for colorful displays. Most of them are commonly available in local garden centers and nurseries. And now is an ideal time to plant them.

No tree says Southern better—or

The fan-shaped foliage of ginkgo turns a pure butter yellow in fall. Don't be in a hurry to rake up the leaves—they look great even when they've fallen.

The deep, golden yellow of hickory is among the grandest sights of the season.

Sugar maple captures the afternoon, autumn sun with its glowing yellow foliage.

prettier—than the **flowering dogwood** (*Cornus florida*). Frankly, the tiers of white flowers that clothe the branches in spring are quite enough to sell anyone on this tree. But then comes the second show in fall, with drooping red leaves and bright-red berries. New variegated selections, such as Cherokee Sunset, offer even more color, but there's nothing wrong with just plain old dogwood. Remember it prefers light shade rather than full sun. And be sure to water this shallow-rooted tree during summer droughts, or scorched leaves may ruin the fall show.

Another great tree for late-season sparkle is the **ginkgo** (*Ginkgo biloba*). Although native to China, ginkgo is right at home in the South. We're glad because there is nothing quite like this hardy and durable tree. Its unusual, fan-shaped leaves look like little fishtails that suddenly turn

the purest yellow. Unfortunately, the effect doesn't last long—the leaves shed quickly and completely—but they look almost as beautiful lying on the ground. One caution: There are male and female ginkgo trees. The females produce foul-smelling fruit, so plant only male selections, such as Saratoga and Shangri-la. Don't count on this tree for quick shade—young ginkgoes grow slowly.

Crepe myrtle (*Lagerstroemia indica*) is a small tree with a big impact for much of the year. Not only does it get your attention in summer, with bright, frilly clusters of flowers, but the foliage grabs the microphone about now, broadcasting colors that range from a soft yellow to muted or-

Crepe myrtle, ornamental cabbage, and garden mums are a great color combination for fall.

Japanese maples are perfect accent trees for small spaces. Many selections have outstanding fall color.

The native sourwood tree is among the first to turn red, often beginning in late summer. Bees visit the white summer blooms to make the delicious sourwood honey we enjoy in autumn.

ange and deep, wine red. Powdery mildew on the leaves can really spoil the show, so if you're planting a new crepe myrtle—or two—or a bunch, try to go with one of the mildew-resistant selections, such as Muskogee (lavender-pink flowers), Natchez (white), or Tuscarora (coral-pink). Plant crepe myrtles in full sun for the best color.

Saying that **sourwood** (*Oxydendrum arboreum*) turns red in autumn is like saying Hank Aaron played a little ball. Many people rank this small native tree right up there with the dogwood for almost year-round beauty, and sourwood certainly doesn't lose any points for fall performance. However, it can be difficult to transplant, so choose a container-grown tree if possible.

The golden yellow leaves of **hickory** (*Carya* sp.) surely signal that the times are a-changin'. The sight of one

of these stately trees against a backdrop of pines is one of the grandest spectacles of autumn. Most are big fellas—from 60 to 100 feet tall or more, depending on the species. Nurseries seldom offer them, because long taproots make the trees hard to transplant. So enjoy hickories by conserving majestic specimens wherever they grow or nurturing chance seedlings that volunteer in your yard.

Sugar maple (*Acer saccharum*) is another tree that's fabulous in fall. Leaf color varies, but most often you'll see it turn a sunny yellow. For the most consistent color, choose a named selection such as Legacy, Sweet Shadow, Newton Sentry, Seneca Chief, or Endowment. **Japanese maples** (*A. palmatum*) also have excellent fall foliage, and are perfect if you're looking for an accent tree near the front door—or any-

where it can be admired up close. Although many Japanese maples feature red summer foliage, the fieriest autumn colors come from selections whose leaves are green in summer, such as Osakazuki. The leaves of Sango Kaku are tinged with red in spring, turn green in summer, and mature to gold in fall when the young stems turn coral for color into winter.

Is there a clear favorite in the bunch? I can't help but recall a comment Horticulturist Charles Bruce once made about a totally different group of plants, hibiscus, that are his passion. We were walking past a long row of them, all showing pieplate blooms in nearly every color of the crayon box. When I asked him if he had a favorite, he replied without hesitation, "Oh, whichever is the last one I look at."

Ain't it the truth.

A Colorful Spring Combo

The pastel spires of foxgloves combine with sweet William in the foreground for a perfect spring display. Set out year-old plants now for blooms next year.

You've heard of investment banking, no doubt. The idea goes something like this: You put a little in now, you get a lot back later. Well, here's a little investment gardening you can do now for some great returns this coming spring.

The goal is to get this great collage of color using sweet William (*Dianthus barbatus*) and foxgloves (*Digitalis purpurea*). It's a perfect and reliable plant combination that has worked well for many years in the *Southern Living* garden, located in the Birmingham Botanical Gardens. "You'll get a month or month and a half's worth of blooms out of them," says Horticulturist Charlie Thigpen, who plants and maintains our displays. Here are some tips for attaining the colorful combination, which blooms in late spring in the Lower South.

First, make sure you're working with rich, well-prepared soil in a mostly sunny spot. The size of the garden is up to you (and your budget), but you need a space that's big enough to make an impact—a 16-square-foot area is about the smallest you should work with.

Set out the foxgloves (to save money, buy the smaller plants available in flats) this fall, spacing them about 12 to 18 inches apart in the back of the flowerbed. Sprinkle a small handful of slow-release fertilizer into the hole before planting. To assure good-size plants, Charlie sets out 1-gallon containers of sweet William. Space them about a foot apart in front of the foxgloves; give them the slow-release fertilizer treatment also. Keep the plants well watered over the winter months; no additional fertilizer is necessary.

When the show begins next spring, remove the spent blooms on the sweet William for more prolific flowers (or snip them earlier; they make great cut flowers). After the main flower spike on the foxglove fades, cut it off to encourage additional blooms. The resulting spikes won't be as large as the original one, but will extend the blooming period.

Although the sweet William can bloom for several seasons to come, the foxglove will usually fade and flop, so it's better to treat the combination as an annual spring display. Even so, the long-lasting parade of flowers will be one of the best investments that you've ever made—outside of the stock market.

This waterfall could have looked out of place, but lush foliage helps soften its lines for a more natural appearance.

This Waterfall Belongs

People love water—its look, its feel, its sound. So it's no surprise that many want to add a water feature to their garden. The key to a satisfying result is making the feature look like it belongs. That was the challenge facing Jim and Bette Leeward of Ocala, Florida, when they called in Landscape Architect John Adams, ASLA.

The Leewards had asked Adams to design a small deck that they could use for dining and entertaining at the back of their house. But when Jim suggested adding a waterfall next to the deck, Adams balked. "John didn't think it would seem natural," recalls Bette. "He thought it was going to look like it was placed there for no reason." Jim, however, remained adamant. So Adams did his best to make this feature fit right in.

First, he selected a native stone, chert, for the waterfall. Spraying the chert with buttermilk encouraged algae to grow for an aged, natural-looking surface. Next, Adams had the pool's bottom and sides painted black to darken the water, making it appear deeper. He then surrounded the waterfall with lush evergreens, such as philodendrons and Mexican heather, to soften its lines and hide the water source. Finally, he placed the water-fall in front of a background of existing shade trees.

Even without the accompanying waterfall, the deck deserves mention, especially for the wood used in its construction—not pressure-treated pine, but Alaskan white cedar. Bette selected this particular wood because its natural gray color matched the stain used on the house. To keep the boards from warping and drawing apart as they dried, Adams insisted that they be screwed down rather than nailed. The wood has held up surprisingly well—six years so far—in Central Florida's wet, humid climate.

When Jim and Bette entertain, the deck serves as an outdoor room. Two sets of French doors open from the living room onto the deck, making it easy for guests to circulate. And for quiet dining in mornings or evenings, splashing sounds from the waterfall set a relaxing mood.   *Steve Bender*

On cool mornings, Bette Leeward enjoys breakfast out on the deck.

Magnolia Topiaries

To create fine, all-season arrangements, just select a pretty container and gather greenery and flowers from your garden.

BY JULIA HAMILTON THOMASON
PHOTOGRAPHY COLLEEN DUFFLEY

Imagine having elegant magnolia topiaries like these, any time you want. Even better, you don't have to wait for them to grow because they are assembled like any other floral arrangement, by building up from the container and adding one flower or piece of greenery at a time.

These topiaries are the work of Joe Gordy, AIFA, of Evergreen, Alabama. Joe, a talented floral designer, finds that the lustrous foliage of Southern magnolia works best for topiaries such as these. For long-lasting arrangements, he uses magnolia leaves that have been treated with a preservative. He also creates topiaries with fresh magnolia leaves, and sometimes adds garden flowers at the base of the arrangement.

Joe uses a variety of containers, including urns, clay pots, and porcelain jars and planters. If he selects one that's fragile or valuable, he first assembles the topiary in a plastic pot or papier-mâché liner, and then sets the topiary in the more decorative container.

For the trunk, Joe selects a tree branch with good shape, color, and texture. If fresh leaves are used, the trunk should have three prongs at the top, where a block of moistened florist foam can be wedged in place. When preserved or dried leaves are used, the trunk should be cut to a point at the top, so that a dry polyurethane foam ball can be attached (see sketches).

By varying the height of the topiaries and the foliage and flowers he

A topiary of preserved, dyed magnolia leaves becomes a permanent decoration for a home. Ribbons can be changed with the season to vary the accent color. Flowers with the stems placed in water picks can also be inserted into the foliage.

These topiaries of fresh magnolia leaves give the effect of miniature living trees with flowers growing underneath.

uses, Joe achieves a variety of effects. And these arrangements are not restricted to tabletop use. For example, a pair of tall topiaries may be used to flank an interior doorway.

Using Preserved or Dried Magnolia

It is not difficult to preserve magnolia leaves yourself, using either glycerine or a floral preservative. If you use a floral preservative, follow product directions. You can buy these supplies, or have preserved magnolia

Joe Gordy arranges magnolia cuttings in florist foam at the top of the topiary.

leaves ordered for you at a craft shop or a florist.

To preserve magnolia leaves in glycerine, lightly crush the stems of the foliage. Mix 2 parts glycerine to 1 part water. Let the leaves stand, either immersed or with the stems in a few inches of the glycerine solution, until they are dry (usually two to three weeks). Whether you use floral preservative or glycerine, it should take one to three weeks to treat the leaves.

Preserved leaves will turn a dark, rich brown suitable for many arrangements or you can apply a light coat of green spray paint. You may be able to locate a commercial preservative that contains green dye; such preserva-

tives will simultaneously color and preserve the foliage.

Fresh, untreated magnolia leaves may also be used but undoubtedly will curl as they dry. To prevent curling, lay the leaves face down and weight them down with bricks or boards until dry. Then use dark-green spray paint to add color.

Cut a block of polyurethane foam to fit snugly inside the liner or decorative container you have chosen. Glue the foam in place using a hot-glue gun.

Select a tree branch, and cut both ends to a point. Cut a hole in the foam. Apply hot glue to one end of the branch, and insert it in the foam. Next, cut a hole in a 4-inch diameter

polyurethane foam ball. Apply glue to the other end of the branch and press the ball on the end of the branch. Insert cuttings of preserved magnolia in the foam ball so that they radiate evenly from the center.

If you are using a liner, place it in the more ornamental container. You can cover the foam at the base of the topiary with sheet moss, dried leaves, or potpourri.

Using Fresh Magnolia

Shape a block of polyurethane foam to fit within a widemouthed container or liner, leaving approximately 3 to 4 inches between the top of the container and the foam. Glue the foam in place with a hot-glue gun.

Select a tree branch that has three 4-inch-long prongs at the top. Cut the bottom end of the branch to a point. Cut a hole in the foam. Apply hot glue to the pointed end of the branch, and insert it into the foam.

Condition cut magnolia leaves and fresh garden flowers by letting them stand in slightly warm water for several hours.

Place one block of florist foam in water until saturated. Trim corners from foam. To make the arrangement last longer, wrap the wet foam with plastic wrap to keep water from evaporating. Insert magnolia stems into the florist foam, using enough leaves all around to keep foam from showing. If you are using a liner, place it in the decorative container.

Soak three or four blocks of florist foam in water. Lay the wet foam in the container on top of the polyurethane foam. Then insert stems of garden flowers and foliage cuttings, completing the arrangement and covering the foam. ◇

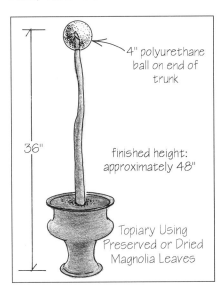

36"

4" polyurethane ball on end of trunk

finished height: approximately 48"

Topiary Using Preserved or Dried Magnolia Leaves

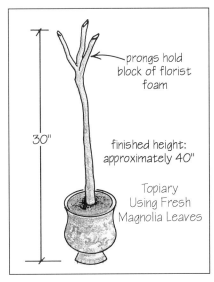

30"

prongs hold block of florist foam

finished height: approximately 40"

Topiary Using Fresh Magnolia Leaves

Carefully stacked fresh pumpkins provide a unique autumn composition; grapevines looped around them add to the seasonal look. If the skins aren't broken, the pumpkins should look good for a month.

Pile Up
PUMPKINS

Why not try your hand at creating these whimsical pumpkin arrangements to greet guests? It's as easy as—well—pumpkin pie.

All you need to make this variation on the typical "pumpkin at the door" are three of graduated sizes, a large container, and about 15 feet of grapevine for draping. If you can't get grapevine, honeysuckle or kudzu vine would work just as well. Make sure the largest pumpkin will perch atop the container without plopping down too far or balancing precariously—just measure the rim of the container before you head out to buy the pumpkins.

It's a good idea to stack them on site before you take them home, just to make sure that they are well matched and balance in a straight line. Although urns were used for these topiaries, clay pots or large baskets protected by a sheltered entry would work just as well.

Once you've got all the materials, simply stack the pumpkins atop each other. Don't poke any holes in them for added support; they will last a lot longer if the skins aren't broken. If you're concerned about trick or treaters toppling the pumpkins over, you could apply clear silicone sealant between them for added stability. For even more of an autumn look, loosely circle the pumpkins with loops of grapevine.

You could try all sorts of variations on this theme, from carving or painting the pumpkins for a totem pole effect to making an October snowman. Whatever look you choose, it will be a delightful way to celebrate the harvest season.

THE PICK OF THE PATCH

When you head down to the produce department, roadside stand, or neighborhood pumpkin patch, keep in mind a few tips for picking the best ones.

In general, choose a pumpkin with unbroken skin and good color. If you're going to try your hand at making an arrangement, make sure you've got a compatible bunch of pumpkins with fairly level bases and no obvious discolorations.

If a jack-o'-lantern is the objective, go ahead and buy the pumpkin while the selection is still good, but don't carve the face until you're ready to display it—pumpkins deteriorate quickly once the skin has been cut.

Pumpkins grown in the home vegetable garden should be harvested when the vines die and the pumpkins begin to color up. Leave about 3 inches of stem when cutting them off the vine; handle carefully to avoid bruising or tearing the skin. And by all means, get the children involved in the whole process—planting, harvesting, and decorating—it's a fun way to teach them about plants and folklore.

Spicebush is right at home in a woodland setting with ferns carpeting the ground.

Spicebush Seasons the Fall

Spicebush yields neither nutmeg nor cinnamon, but it isn't hard to figure out its name. Just hold a crushed leaf or a broken twig to your nose, and you'll discover a spicy scent reminiscent of sassafras. Indeed, it's close kin to sassafras, and people have used the bark of both plants to flavor tea.

Native to the woods of the Eastern United States, spicebush (*Lindera benzoin*) is a large, deciduous shrub that grows 6 to 12 feet tall and wide. In a sunny spot, it becomes dense and rounded; while in shade, it stretches and opens up. The light-green leaves, 3 to 5 inches long and 1 to 2 inches wide, turn bright gold in fall. It's no exaggeration to say that spicebush is among the finest plants for yellow fall color.

Wildlife enjoys this plant just as much as the gardener. The tiny, yellow flowers that appear in spring give rise to scarlet fruits on female plants. Initially, the fruits are hidden by foliage, but when the leaves drop in fall, birds and other animals rush in for a

The leaves slowly change from light green to bright gold in fall.

feast. Among the birds that dine on spicebush are robins, catbirds, thrushes, and cardinals.

In the garden, this uncommon plant makes a serviceable addition to the shrub border. It's also a fine under-story plant for a naturalized area because its fall leaves blend well with the autumn colors of dogwoods, maples, sumac, and sassafras. If it's in a moist, shady spot, try underplanting it with ferns, hostas, and woodland wildflowers. In a sunny location, combine it with plants such as daylilies, ornamental grasses, and hydrangeas.

Spicebush needs no coddling. It has no significant pests, grows in sun or shade, and tolerates just about any well-drained soil. However, it grows most rapidly in moist soil that contains plenty of organic matter. Once established, this shrub can be hard to transplant, so start with a small, container-grown plant purchased from a nursery and choose your location carefully.

Like many native plants, spicebush may not be available at local garden centers. If you'd like a list of mail-order sources, send a self-addressed, stamped business-size envelope to Spicebush Editor, *Southern Living,* P.O. Box 830119, Birmingham, Alabama 35283.　　　*Steve Bender*

*Tête-à-Tête dwarf narcissi stand half the height of the Ice Follies daffodils
behind them. Each Tête-à-Tête flower stalk bears multiple blooms.*

A Major Look At Minor Bulbs

BY STEVE BENDER / PHOTOGRAPHY VAN CHAPLIN

If your knowledge of bulbs ends with tulips and daffodils, read on. The big world of little bulbs is about to open for you.

Americans in general, and Southerners in particular, like things big—big cars, big houses, big ranches, big boats. The bigger something is, the more attention it commands and the more value we place upon it. This fascination with bigness extends to the garden. Think back to all the bulbs you planted last fall. Chances are, the lion's share consisted of tulips, daffodils, and Dutch hyacinths, all chosen for big, bold blooms you could spot a block away.

Seasoned gardeners know, however, that bigger isn't always better. For proof, just examine the array of small, flowering plants grouped under the unfortunate heading of "minor bulbs." Sure, their blooms may seem miniscule when compared with the overblown trumpets of King Alfred daffodils. But minor bulbs offer numerous advantages over their bigger brothers.

To begin with, many little bulbs begin flowering in winter, a time when the garden cries out for color. They also multiply freely and naturalize; a few eventually form a drift. In addition, their foliage, often thin and grasslike, doesn't become an eyesore when it dies down in late spring. Finally, buying minor bulbs this fall won't threaten your budget. Large-flowered daffodils can frequently cost as much as $1 apiece while 50 starflowers will set you back a mere $5 or so.

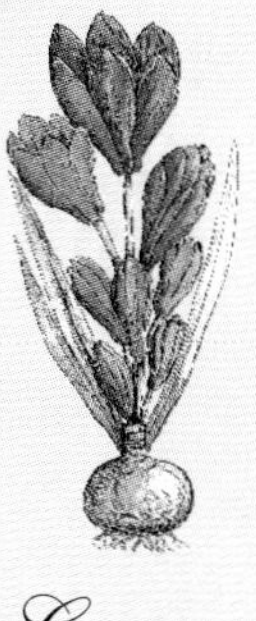

Crocus

Among the earliest blooming and most popular of the minor bulbs are **crocuses** (which actually grow from

(**Above**) *Planting grape hyacinths in a ground cover of common periwinkle helps to hide the bulbs' yellowing foliage in late spring.* (**Right**) *Many minor bulbs, such as these crocuses, naturalize freely on the woods' edge, blooming in filtered shade.*

corms). As you might expect, people typically prefer the large-flowered, hybrid Dutch crocuses, such as Yellow Mammouth. But some opt for the many species known as snow crocuses, which may have smaller blooms, but flower more freely and offer a wide range of colors and bloom times. Two species I particularly recommend are *Crocus sieberi* and *C. tomansinianus*. The former is truly the earliest spring bloomer, displaying its lilac-blue flowers and red stigmata by January 15 in my Birmingham garden. The latter is a little bit sleepier, holding back its amethyst blooms until the first few days of February.

Close on the heels of snow crocuses comes the nodding, green-tipped bells of that old Southern standby, the **snowflake.** In my neck of the woods, blossoms appear anytime from Valentine's Day until the beginning of March. According to experts, there are actually two types of snowflakes out there—spring snowflake (*Leucojum vernum*) and summer snowflake (*L. aestivum*). But it

Snowflake

doesn't make a whit of difference. The two look similar and bloom at nearly the same time, but spring snowflake is hardly ever sold.

For some strange reason, snowflakes have lost favor in recent times, so that today you mostly spy them poking up in older gardens. Indeed, as I walked through an antebellum neighborhood in Columbus, Mississippi, last winter, borders of dainty snowflakes lining front walks seemed the rule. Had I been a resident there decades ago, I'm sure I would have witnessed members of a garden club sharing bulbs with one another. Nowadays, plenty of nurseries offer snowflake bulbs, but plant swapping remains a Southern tradition.

Dwarf narcissi have become favorites of mine lately for very good reasons. There are dozens of kinds providing a bloom season that extends from late winter to mid-spring.

They're easy to grow and reproduce rapidly. Their short stature suits the confines of my small garden. And unlike big daffodils, their foliage is rather inconspicuous.

So many wonderful forms exist that I hesitate to single out any. But here are three selections you're sure to enjoy: Tête-à-Tête, featuring buttercup-yellow petals and a promi-

Narcissus

(**Above**) *The stately spears of Spanish bluebells bring welcome blue to the mid-spring garden.*

Spanish Bluebell

nent, central cup; lemon-yellow Hawera, a super naturalizer that's made for mixing with blue phlox; and Baby Moon, whose dainty, golden blossoms bestow an intensely sweet scent.

A garden can never have too much blue in it, as far as I'm concerned. Fortunately, among minor bulbs blue flowers abound. Perhaps the most graceful of these, and certainly the tallest, is mid-spring's **Spanish bluebells** (*Hyacinthoides hispanicus*), also

Grape Hyacinth

known as scilla and wood hyacinth. True, Spanish bluebells can bear pink or white blossoms atop its foot-tall stems. But blue is the color to have, especially when pink azaleas or tulips reside nearby. For earlier blue, count on **grape hyacinths** (*Muscari* sp.), which are classic bulbs for massing despite the fact that they average only 6 inches in height. *Muscari armeniacum* sports deep royal-blue blooms, while those of *M. azureum* show off a refreshing sky blue. ◇

IN THE GARDEN

If you wonder why you're reading about minor bulbs now, it's because fall is the time to plant. All of the ones mentioned are simple to grow. Set them 3 to 4 inches deep and apart into loose, well-drained soil that contains a good bit of organic matter. Either sun or light shade is fine. Some minor bulbs sprout foliage in late fall. Don't worry if it freezes; this won't harm them. But don't cut leaves back until they turn yellow in late spring. Be warned that crocus corms are a favorite dish of chipmunks, mice, and squirrels. So if rodents run amuck in your garden, don't plant crocuses, unless you're willing to bury the corms inside cages of chicken wire.

You'll find that little bulbs lend themselves admirably to many situations in the garden, including rock gardens, the woods' edge, mixed borders, formal displays, and naturalizing in ground cover. When planting a display, remember that strength lies in numbers—to make an impact, always plant in multiples of 25 and keep colors together.

Don't be surprised if you find yourself planting five kinds this fall and twice as many the next. Little bulbs, I've long suspected, are addictive. If that's true, it's a fine addiction.

NOVEMBER

CHECKLIST
178

LOSE YOUR WINTER BLUES
WITH YELLOWS
180

PLANTS AS
PERFECT ACCESSORIES
182

AMARYLLIS HERALDS
THE HOLIDAYS
185

POPPIES *PARR EXCELLENCE*
186

CHECKLIST
for November

ANNUALS

Plant cool-weather annuals now for continued blooming until early spring. Favorites to start from transplants include dianthus, pansies, petunias, and snapdragons. When choosing snapdragons, be sure to check the label for height. Dwarf selections stay low, behaving more like a ground cover, while standard selections form high-reaching spikes. Sow seeds of fragrant sweet peas at the base of a fence or trellis to give the vines a place to climb. Other annuals easy to start from seed include Shirley poppies and bachelor's buttons. Larkspur, forget-me-nots, bachelor's buttons, and Shirley and California poppies. Pick a sunny spot, and till the soil thoroughly. Cover the seed with a light cover of mulch after sowing, and water.

ASPARAGUS

Set out asparagus anytime from now until early spring. They will take up a fairly permanent spot in your garden, so prepare the soil well by tilling deeply — at least 12 inches — and work in about one-third organic matter to two-thirds soil. Plant the crowns about 3 inches deep and 18 inches apart in rows 4 feet apart. Apply 3 inches of mulch over the crowns.

BULBS

Set out spring-flowering bulbs across the South. As a general rule, set large bulbs, such as daffodils and tulips, 8 inches deep; set smaller bulbs 1 to 2 inches deep. Drainage is essential; avoid spots where water collects. Bulbs that can be planted through winter in the Coastal South include amaryllis, calla, crinum, paperwhites, spider lily, watsonia, and zephyr lily.

CITRUS

In areas where citrus is hardy, remove thorny shoots that may appear at the base of satsuma and other grafted citrus trees. These are shoots from the rootstock onto which the citrus variety is grafted. This rootstock is used because of its resistance to soilborne pests and cold. Simply remove the suckers by cutting them off at their base using a pair of sharp pruning shears.

CALADIUMS

Dig up caladium tubers before the first freeze and as soon as the foliage starts to decline. Brush off remaining soil, and let the tubers dry in the sun; then cut off the dead leaves. Dust with a powdered fungicide, such as captan; then store the tubers in mesh bags in a cool, dry place.

FALL COLOR

For colorful fall foliage in the years ahead, plant trees now. Shumard oak, Chinese pistachio, green ash, and Western soapberry are several trees that will do well in Texas. In areas to the East, plant flowering dogwood, red maple, Southern sugar maple, scarlet oak, hickory, ginkgo, or sourwood.

FRUIT

Plant fruit trees and shrubs, including blueberries, blackberries, bunch grapes, apple and pear trees, now. For best results, follow local recommendations for the most suitable selections in your area. Check with an established garden center or your county Extension office for planting advice.

HIBISCUS

Gardeners in the Coastal South where freezes are light can try overwintering hibiscus by the following method: Cut the plant back to about one-fourth its height, and bank sand around the stump until it is completely covered. Then mulch with leaves or straw. Water on days that a freeze is predicted. In spring, remove the mulch and sand from the hibiscus, and apply a slow-release shrub or 6-6-6 fertilizer.

ORNAMENTAL KALE

It's not too late to plant ornamental kale and cabbage for color. Buy good-sized (at least 4-inch pots) plants that will fill beds quickly. Peacock Hybrid kale has feathery leaves that deepen in color as the temperature drops. While they can take frost, they won't survive a hard freeze. Space plants about a foot apart in well-prepared beds; mulch heavily when light freezes are forecast.

PEONIES

Plant peonies now in the Middle and Upper South. It's important not to plant them too deeply. Set the tubers no more than 2 inches below the surface in rich, well-drained soil in a sunny location. For best results, choose a variety that blooms in early to mid-season.

PRIVET

Watch for leaf spot on waxleaf privet (*Ligustrum japonicum*). This fungal disease causes large brown spots with circular rings inside the spot. You can prevent the problem by applying a copper spray through winter and early spring. You may also need to apply a shrub fertilizer that contains extra iron and manganese to bring out the deepest green.

SALAD VEGETABLES

Gardener's in the Coastal South can sow seeds of looseleaf, Bibb, and romaine lettuces every couple of weeks through winter for a continual supply of salad greens. Choose selections for their different colors and textures. Red Sails is a looseleaf variety whose leaves develop a bright-red color, especially in winter. Oakleaf is another looseleaf type whose interesting green leaves are lobed, like those of some oaks. Bibb types, such as Buttercrunch, are a nice medium green with a more chewy texture. Cos and other romaine types develop dark-green, extra crispy leaves. In colder areas, grow lettuce in a cold frame.

SOIL TEST

The dormant months ahead would be a good time to have your soil analyzed for major nutrients and pH, a measure of the soil's acidity or alkalinity. By testing the soil now, you have time to make the necessary adjustments for ideal growing conditions next spring. Soil test kits are available at garden centers; your county Extension office also offers a soil analysis service.

WINTER MOWING

Raise the cutting height of your mower a notch when cutting newly seeded fescue or bluegrass lawns. The grass will have more leaf area and produce more food for next spring. Make sure the new lawn gets ample water during this critical stage.

YARD DEBRIS

It's that time of year—leaves and limbs can cover the yard in no time. Use a chipper to grind up fallen branches and a leaf shredder to make soil-enriching compost or mulch. If such equipment isn't in your budget, consider renting, or share the cost with a couple of neighbors.

NOVEMBER NOTES

To Do:
- Continue garden clean-up
- Rake and compost leaves
- If necessary, lime lawn and planting beds
- Dig and store tender bulbs
- Clean and store garden tools and lawn mower
- Collect and store seeds from summer annuals
- In Lower and Coastal South, purchase and refrigerate spring bulbs at least eight weeks

To Plant:
- Trees and shrubs
- Spring bulbs

To Purchase:
- Spring bulbs
- Trees and shrubs
- Lime
- Soil test kit

Lose Your Winter Blues *With* Yellows

So you think nothing much blooms in winter? Think again. These plants brighten with blossoms of sunshine yellow.

BY STEVE BENDER/PHOTOGRAPHY VAN CHAPLIN

Yellow is the color of the sun, so it's not too much of a stretch to imagine that yellow flowers in the garden bring the sun in with them. Depending on the season, this can be good or bad. In the blistering summer, for example, too many yellows simply reinforce the idea that it's awfully hot. But when winter's gray and gloomy, the garden needs all the sun it can get. That's when yellow flowers truly lift the spirit.

It's not winter yet, so there is still plenty of time to plant for the upcoming season. The following plants will give you good reason to explore the yard in January and February.

Wintersweet (*Chimonanthus praecox*) is always a surprise. Related to the much more familiar sweet shrub (*Calycanthus floridus*), this plant greets the New Year with pale-yellow, sweetly scented blossoms. On sunny, relatively mild winter days, the fragrance is surprisingly powerful—you'll probably smell the perfume long before you spot the translucent flowers.

A large shrub growing 8 to 12 feet tall and wide, wintersweet enjoys full sun or light shade and well-drained soil. For best flowering, prune out the old canes after they bloom; new canes will grow 5 to 6 feet in a single year. The plant's glossy green leaves often hang on well into winter, sometimes obscuring the flowers. So after a hard freeze, run a closed hand over each branch and strip the dried foliage from the stem.

String four or five temperate days together in late January and you'll see the curious, eyelash blossoms of **hybrid witchhazel** (*Hamamelis* x *in-termedia*) unfurl. Some selections feature orange and red flowers, but the most popular, Arnold Promise, sports clear-yellow petals. Smelling of sweet spice, the blossoms seem immune to winter cold. Once open, they make their minds up to stay, and frost won't kill them. Marvelous autumn foliage in colors of yellow, orange-red, and burgundy is an added bonus.

Upright and spreading, most witchhazels become very large shrubs, reaching 15 feet tall and wide. They'll grow in either sun or light shade and like moist, acid, well-drained soil that contains lots of organic matter. Unfortunately, as with wintersweet, the leaves often persist into the winter, long after turning brown. They're not easy to strip by hand, as their petioles (leaf stalks) cling stubbornly to the branches. Clipping the petioles with a small pair of scissors is an effective, if tedious, remedy.

If you've ever wondered why that strange forsythia down the street has green stems, the answer is it isn't a forsythia. It's **winter jasmine** (*Jasminum nudiflorum*), a mounding or cascading shrub that grows 3 to 4 feet high and often twice as wide. Usually blooming about 10 days earlier than forsythia, winter jasmine isn't as showy because it never opens all of its flowers at once. However, winter jasmine remains in bloom for several weeks, whereas forsythia fades after a week or so.

This vigorous grower, often used to cover slopes, prefers full sun and moist, fertile soil. But it also tolerates dry, poor soil. You'll find winter jasmine easy to propagate, as its stems quickly root wherever they touch the soil. Periodic pruning keeps the shrub tidy.

Nobody would put flowering dogwood (*Cornus florida*) high on a list of underused trees. But one type of dogwood, **cornelian cherry** (*C. mas*), merits much more acclaim. Named for its bright-red fruits, this 20-foot-tall tree bears clouds of yellow blossoms in late February and early March. For two weeks or more, its shaggy-barked limbs appear dusted with sulfur.

Similar in shape to flowering dogwood, cornelian cherry accepts a wider range of growing conditions, enduring both drought and poor,

Straplike petals of hybrid witchhazel appear well before the leaves. This selection is Arnold Promise.

Many people confuse winter jasmine with forsythia, but the jasmine's green stems are a dead giveaway.

A cousin of the better known flowering dogwood, cornelian cherry bears clusters of bright-yellow blooms as late winter warms.

slightly alkaline soil. But given its druthers, it opts for moist, fertile, well-drained soil and light shade. For a particularly handsome winter combination, try underplanting cornelian cherry with a sweep of Lenten rose (*Helleborus orientalis*), an evergreen ground cover. The white and rose blossoms of the latter open at roughly the same time as the tree's.

Plants don't bloom to please you and me. They do so to reproduce. So you may wonder why any plant would bloom in winter, considering that insect pollinators are absent then. The answer is that insects aren't absent. Many lie dormant through the cold, waiting for a mild spell to provide a midwinter meal. On a sunny January day, they awaken briefly and head for the blooms that await them. Insects appreciate the yellows of winter. For different reasons, so do we.

OTHER YELLOWS OF WINTER

Leatherleaf Mahonia (*Mahonia bealei*)—shrub
Winter Aconite (*Eranthis* sp.)—bulb
Pansy (*Viola* x *wittrockiana*)—annual
Crocus (*Crocus* sp.)—bulb
Forsythia (*Forsythia* sp.)—shrub

In a casual setting, schefflera and a corn plant grow in wooden baskets that mix with the wicker furniture.

Plants as Perfect ACCESSORIES

Just the right houseplant makes all the difference in many decorating situations. Here are some designer favorites with hints for keeping them alive and well.

BY MARY MCWILLIAMS
PHOTOGRAPHY
COLLEEN DUFFLEY

Can houseplants be an investment? Well, maybe that's a bit of a stretch. But there's no reason a perfectly placed one can't become a prized accessory. The key to your investment is in assembling a collection of plants that will work well in your design and also survive in your home. We asked a few of our favorite interior designers what they choose to complete beautiful settings.

One general feeling among designers is that the choices do not have to be intimidating. Interior Designer Lynn DeYoung, ASID, of Huntsville, Alabama, says, "Houseplants should be the finishing touch to a room. When selecting containers, I choose those that repeat the colors in the room or a particular motif in the wall-covering." For example, using a porcelain jardiniere that repeats the colors in rugs and fabrics brings harmony to the overall design. In a more casual setting, such as a bright, cheerful sunroom, assorted baskets repeat the feel of wicker furniture.

A bird-of-paradise, planted in a large, copper container, blends with some of the Southwestern furnishings in this sunroom.

Fresh blends of foliage planted in innovative containers make appealing decorating alternatives. Your budget will appreciate the savings, too.

"I love to garden as an outlet and an escape from professional challenges," says Designer James Essary, ASID, of Charlotte. "A room is completed with plants—just like treasured accessories," the designer explains. He has a passion for plants and the impact they can have. A favorite of Essary's is the large lady palm. "The hearty, fuzzy trunk sprouts leaves that are large, like the palm of your hand. Remember to trim the berries from the plant or they will leave black droppings on the floor." Large houseplants can act almost as furniture in a room, anchoring the overall design. Essary applies this rule in his own home by using a variety of palms. "They are worth the initial expense when their longevity of growth is considered," he says. The key is to think

Underplanting the Ficus alii *with bromeliads provides a blooming composition with longevity and easy care. The mixture of succulents planted in the earthenware bowl lends a Southwestern appeal.*

A lady palm adds fullness and dimension to this handsome living room. It fills an empty corner, eliminating the need for another piece of furniture.

(many species of *Rhapis*) is a few feet from a sunny south window. A plant in a 12-inch container will need about a quart of water every four or five days.

They just don't come any more durable than **Chinese evergreen** (*Aglaonema* sp.). It's a good plant for a room with a north-facing exposure out of direct sunlight. Water it once a week. **English ivy** (*Hedera helix*) is another hardy houseplant; place it near a window and don't let the soil dry out.

Bromeliads (many different species) are quite tolerant of neglect. Simply fill the central cup with water; locate the plant near a south-facing window in winter. **Boston fern** (most kinds of *Nephrolepsis*) needs moist soil and more light than you might think—a few feet from a sunny spot is ideal.

Bird-of-paradise (*Strelitzia reginae*) likes to be near a window, too. Try to keep the soil evenly moist, but letting it dry out won't hurt. **Succulents** include a wide range of heat- and sun-loving plants. In general, the more you can provide of both, the better the specimens will be. Water about half as often as you do your other houseplants.

For ease when watering, place a plastic liner in the base of the basket to catch overflow. Most stores that sell plants will have a variety of sizes available. It is best to buy a liner that is slightly larger than the base of your pot to provide more room for the excess water. ◇

of the return on your investment. "My palm, for example, is five years old and growing strong."

Houston designer Trisha Dodson uses plants creatively. A Boston fern, positioned high on a wall with a wooden bracket, attains greater importance and dimension. Dodson also recommends underplanting potted trees. "This adds fullness and color to indoor trees, which is a nice alternative to just topping the exposed soil with moss," she advises. Regional houseplants are among her favorites. "The authentic Southwestern succulents and bird-of-paradise work well with many Texas designs," she says.

Dennis Carola, who owns Tall Plants, a Houston nursery specializing in a variety of trees and plants, offers several suggestions for using indoor plants successfully. "Bromeliads are very popular and require virtually no maintenance," says Carola. They make wonderful choices for underplanting when the container size allows. He also recommends a newer type of ficus tree called *Ficus alii.* "The great plus to this plant is that it only drops, on the average, 3 leaves

for every 30 that a regular ficus drops, and there is very little sap, too," he explains.

Keeping Them Growing

To be great looking, houseplants need to be alive and healthy. Here are some quick tips on keeping these plants looking their best.

Benjamin fig (*Ficus benjamina*) does best near a sunny, south-facing window but away from drafts or air vents. Keep the soil evenly moist. A related indoor tree, *F. alii,* has thinner, longer leaves and can tolerate lower light levels. Leaf shedding, a common occurrence with Benjamin fig, is less of a problem with this tree. In most cases it's a better choice.

Corn plant (many selections of *Dracaena* are sold as corn plants) is more forgiving of neglect and missed waterings, and can flourish in bright rooms away from windows.

Schefflera, another common houseplant, prefers bright light— even some direct sunlight in winter. Keep the plant well watered and out of cold drafts.

The ideal spot for a **lady palm**

Set up on a bracket, this Boston fern emphasizes the height of a Texas sunroom.

PHOTOGRAPH: VAN CHAPLIN

Amaryllis, with its flamboyant, trumpetlike flowers, is an easy indoor plant whose blooms add a touch of the unexpected to the season.

Amaryllis Heralds The Holidays

Holidays are heydays for festive plants like amaryllis (actually selections of the plant genus Hippeastrum). Its bright, almost hand-sized blooms fit right in with the gleam and glow of the season. Like any plant, it has certain needs for top performance. Amaryllis could just about come with the following instructions: Add water, and stand back. But here are a few more tips for getting the most from your amaryllis bulbs for this season and beyond.

Bulbs are usually sold either loose or in prepackaged kits with plastic or ceramic containers and potting soil.

Some garden centers and florists sell prepotted plants either in bloom or nearly so. They cost more, but you are relatively assured of flowers during prime holiday time. Plan ahead if buying a kit or loose bulb: It may take as long as four to eight weeks for a bulb to bloom after planting—the warmer the room, the faster it grows.

Your choice of colors? You can go with all shades and not-so-subtleties of red, pink, and white. There's even a new yellow selection called Yellow Pioneer, with sunny, 5-inch blooms. For a big red, it's hard to beat Sun Dance; Star of Holland is red with a white star in the center.

If you bought a loose bulb, choose a container that is only slightly larger than the bulb's diameter and preferably has holes for drainage. You'll need to line the bottom inch of the container with fine gravel if there are no holes in the bottom. Tamp quality potting soil firmly around the bulb; take care not to damage the tender, fleshy roots. Leave the top half of the bulb exposed. For a different look, glass bulb vases especially designed to accommodate large bulbs are available.

Place the bulb near a sunny window, and allow the soil to dry out slightly between waterings. Avoid getting water on the neck of the bulb, where it can get in the old leaf scars and cause rot. You don't need to mist the foliage or fertilize. If most of the light comes from a single window, rotate the pot about a quarter turn every few days to ensure that the flower stalk elongates in a more or less straight-up manner. You may need to insert a stake alongside the bulb to support the stalk as it develops.

Getting it to rebloom isn't all that hard, but it is a test of your gardening follow-through. After the blooms are finished, cut off the flower stalk. Water and feed it as you would any houseplant; then stop watering it in late summer. After the leaves have wilted and yellowed, cut them off several inches above the neck. Store the bulb, pot and all, in a cool, dark place (a basement or a cool closet) for about a month. After this period, place the bulb in a room with moderate light and 70-degree daytime temperatures for about three weeks—you can also begin watering again.

In early November you can relocate the pot to a sunny spot, keep watering, and get ready to watch one of the greatest holiday reruns you'll see this side of the television set.

Mark G. Stith

Poppies
Parr Excellence

by STEVE BENDER / photography VAN CHAPLIN, TINA EVANS

Sometimes the best stories are those you just stumble upon. Take the case of David Parr and his poppies. Senior Photographer Van Chaplin and I were returning from a trip to South Carolina, driving down Birmingham's Montevallo Road, when we spotted a field of flowers. Pinks, scarlets, oranges, and whites beamed by the hundreds in the late-spring sun. "Now, *that* looks like a story," declared Van. I made a mental note to investigate the next morning.

I discovered that the flowers were the handiwork of David Parr, a learn-by-doing gardener if ever there was one. More than 10 years ago, David admired Shirley poppies growing in a neighbor's garden and decided to try his hand. He ordered seed, then obtained permission to cultivate an empty lot by the roadside. His poppies were a hit, to say the least. "Hundreds of people stop every year and ask me how I grow them," David says proudly. For those of you who can't visit, here's how he does it.

Following a hard frost in November, David tills the soil. Because Shirley poppy seeds are tiny, almost dust-like, he mixes them with coarse builder's sand to facilitate an even distribution. For extra color, he mixes in bachelor's-button seeds too. Then, just before a rain, he broadcasts the seeds across the ground, not covering or fertilizing them. "They come up almost immediately," notes David, "and I've never had cold weather kill them." Thinning the seedlings is optional. "There will be a carpet of seedlings," he admits, "but the stronger ones will outgrow the others."

When the weather warms in late February, the seedlings begin a growth spurt. David feeds them by broadcasting 10-10-10 or 13-13-13 fertilizer over the ground, again just before a rain. Weeks of spectacular bloom ensue in about a month. By mid-May, most of the plants are going to seed.

David collects the brown seedheads in a glass jar and saves them for sowing next fall; each seedhead contains hundreds of seeds. Then he mows the withered plants and tills them under.

Aside from public ovations, the thing that keeps David planting poppies every year is the simple beauty they supply. "The flowers themselves are sort of translucent," he observes. "When the sun shines through them, it's a whole new color. It's like turning on a light."

Shirley poppy seed is available from Porter & Son, P.O. Box 104, Stephenville, Texas 76401-0104; and Thompson & Morgan, P.O. Box 1308, Jackson, New Jersey 08527. ◇

David Parr gathers seedheads in late spring and stores them in a glass jar for fall sowing.

DECEMBER

CHECKLIST
190

RED BERRIES
BRING WINTER CHEER
192

ALONG THE WOODEN PATH
194

TRY A LIVE TREE
196

ORNAMENTS
BEYOND THE TREE
197

A MASTERFUL MIXTURE
OF LEAVES
198

A LEISURELY DAY
AT LEU GARDENS
199

CHECKLIST
for December

CHEMICAL STORAGE

Make sure powdered or granular chemicals are protected from moisture; keep the labels intact for proper identification. Keep liquid chemicals sealed tightly and stored in a cool, dry place that's protected from freezing temperatures and excessive heat. Be sure all such materials are out-of-reach of children and pets.

CHRISTMAS TREES

Here are a few quick tests for freshness. Bend the needles back to see how pliable they are. Hold the tree by the trunk, and give it a firm shake to see if it retains its needles. Once you've got the tree home, cut at least 2 inches off the base and place in a bucket of warm water. When it's in the stand, check the water level daily, and never allow it to fall below the base of the trunk.

COLD FRAMES

In the Middle and Lower South, sow seeds of lettuce and other cool-weather greens now for a regular harvest. Rainfall can't reach the plants, so don't forget to water as needed; vent the frame on warm days by propping the lid open a couple of inches, or invest in an automatic frame opener.

COMPOST

Turn your compost pile at least once this month to ensure even decomposition. Continue to add discarded fruit and vegetable matter, eggshells, and coffee and tea grounds to the pile. Spread about a cup of fertilizer over the pile and water lightly to speed up the process.

EVERGREENS

Use evergreens to fill voids after leaves drop. Good choices include wax myrtle, Indian hawthorn, dwarf yaupon, nandina, pittosporum, Japan cleyera, sweet viburnum, waxleaf privet, and abelia.

FERNS

Winter is a good time to divide and separate existing ferns. Dig up a good-sized specimen, split it into four equal parts, and replant in a spot with similar light and moisture. Apply generous amounts of compost to help their performance in poor soils. Water during dry periods until regrowth begins in the spring.

FIRE BLIGHT

This bacterial disease causes branches to look as if they've been torched, leaving crispy brown leaves hanging from dead stems. To protect fruit trees, spray with fire blight spray (contains streptomycin) when blooms begin to open. Fruit trees most susceptible include loquat, pyracantha, apple, quince, pear, and crabapple. Prune off the infected portion, and spray the rest of the plant.

FIREPLACE ASHES

Wood ashes contain potassium, a valuable element for root development. Make sure ashes are cool; then sprinkle them lightly in your vegetable or flower garden, or in your compost pile.

GIFTS FOR GARDENERS

A nice garden tool, such as a sturdy trowel, digging fork, or spade, is always welcome. Knee pads, a straw hat, or other accessories can ease the strain of working outside.

LOQUATS

These popular ornamental trees are sensitive to hard freezes, so try to plant them in a protected area on the south side of the house in the Lower and Coastal South. Established plants should be protected from extreme temperatures with a light blanket or black plastic. Be sure to remove covers the next morning.

POINSETTIA

Buy plants with the center yellow flowers not quite open; the display will last a lot longer. Place the plants near a sunny window and away from forced air vents. Poke a few holes in the foil wrapper to allow water to drain freely (use a saucer to catch the overflow water); keep the soil evenly moist but not soggy.

Transplanting

When moving a young tree or shrub, preserve as much of the root ball as possible. Dig a trench around the plant; then cut the roots underneath with a sharp spade or shovel. Work a burlap bag under the root ball to move it. When replanting, set the plant at the same depth as it grew before, and water thoroughly after planting.

Tree bark

Now is a good time to plant trees with attractive bark and branches, including beech, crepe myrtle, river birch, coral bark maple (*Acer palmatum Sango Kaku*), and paperbark maple (*A. griseum*), and lacebark pine (*pinus bungeana*).

Vegetables

Beets, radishes, and turnips can overwinter in the garden if extra mulch is added. A 6- to 8-inch layer of leaves, straw, or other mulch can protect them from freezes, allowing you to harvest them when you're ready. Plant seeds of turnip, mustard, lettuce, radish, and spinach now in the Lower and Coastal South.

Watering

Evergreens and other plants still need watering during dry spells, even in winter. Watering well before hard freezes increases their chances of survival.

Tip of the Month

A good way to keep potting soil from escaping through the drainage hole of a potted plant is to place a standard drip coffee filter in the bottom of the pot. The filter acts as an effective soil barrier, while permitting drainage. For large pots, you'll need to use a commercial-size filter or three standard-size filters. But try not to overlap filters over the drainage holes.

Janet A. Barbour
Smithfield, North Carolina

December Notes

To Do:
- Buy Christmas tree early for best selection
- Gather greens for holiday decorations
- Rake and compost leaves
- Mulch trees, shrubs, and perennials after the first hard freeze
- Water evergreens thoroughly
- In Coastal South, continue to refrigerate spring bulbs

To Plant:
- In Middle, Lower, and Coastal South, trees and shrubs
- In Lower South, spring bulbs

To Purchase:
- Live and cut Christmas trees
- Christmas tree lights and stand
- Poinsettias, kalanchoes, Christmas cactus, and other seasonal flowers
- Tools and garden equipment to give as presents

_____

_____

_____

_____

_____

_____

_____

_____

_____

_____

_____

_____

_____

_____

_____

Lusterleaf holly

Red Berries
Bring Winter Cheer

One thing is for certain—there's no such thing as just a plain, old, red berry. Take a look at some of our favorites.

BY MARK STITH / PHOTOGRAPHY VAN CHAPLIN

Wonder why we get so excited about colorful baubles and bangles this time of year? Maybe we come by it naturally. This is the season when red berries are at their brightest and best. They cluster, cascade, or cling tightly to their parent plants in so many alluring variations on a common theme.

Even if no other group of plants berried up, hollies

Aucuba

would make plenty to go around. One of the most reliable and prolific is Burford holly (*Ilex cornuta* Burfordii). Clumps of brilliant-red fruit sit among the glossy, deep-green leaves, which struggle for room on crowded branches. If that isn't Christmas-on-a-stick, then Santa doesn't ho-ho-ho. Unlike most hollies, Burford holly doesn't need a male plant to set

fruit, but it's a good idea to have one to help produce abundant berries year-after-year. Willowleaf holly (*I. cornuta* Willowleaf) is similar but smaller in size, with narrower leaves and blood-red fruit.

Other hollies are not to be outdone, however. Deciduous hollies, such as winterberry (*I. verticillata*) and the similar possumhaw (*I. decidua*), appear to have been absolutely pelted with red gumballs stuck tight on otherwise barren branches. For good berry production, you need to buy a male pollinator plant for winterberry and possumhaw.

There's no such thing as a red pearl, but the shiny, translucent berries of the native yaupon holly (*I. vomitoria*) resemble strands of precious beads among the thin, light-gray branches and light-green foliage. Lusterleaf holly (*I. latifolia*) is a dead ringer for a magnolia with its big, deep-green leaves. Come winter, dense clumps of intensely red fruit hold close to the green stems, cluing you in to the fact that this plant is something very unlike magnolia and very special. Yaupon and lusterleaf holly need a male pollinator plant, too.

Hollies may have an edge on other plants when it comes to berries, but they by no means have a monopoly. Two stalwarts of the Southern garden, pyracantha (*Pyracantha coccinea,* also called scarlet firethorn), which is a favorite to espalier in sunny spots, and nandina (*Nandina domestica*) can match them berry for berry. And not many people realize that the common aucuba (*Aucuba japonica*) can produce berries, too, though not as prolifically as the above-mentioned plants. But what it lacks in number it makes up for in size: The ½-inch oblong berries are borne about one to five in a cluster.

We would surely be remiss to leave other berry-laden plants out of the parade, from the well known to the unusual. Flowering dogwood (*Cornus florida*) and tea viburnum (*Viburnum setigerum*) come to mind as respective examples. But with so many different plants that offer red fruit this time of year, you should have the very berriest of holidays.

Pyracantha

Burford holly

Along The Wooden Path

Winding its way through a subtropical garden,

Path

*a simple deck
defines spaces
and creates
places.*

BY
BILL MCDOUGALD
PHOTOGRAPHY
VAN CHAPLIN

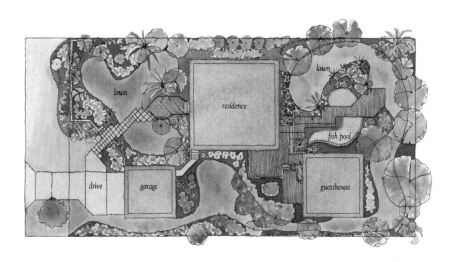

Is it a deck? Is it a porch? Or maybe a pathway?

For Diana and Trevor Bond of Naples, Florida, the wooden structure that drifts just above ground level through their lush garden is all of these and more.

The style of the Bonds' home is known as Key West Victorian, Diana notes. "It has a porch on all four sides, with a wide overhang like older Florida homes," she says. The deck, designed by Naples landscape architect Christian Busk, works as an extension of the porch and a pathway into the densely planted landscape. "When we sited the buildings, we raised everything up to be above the flood stage," says Busk. "That's one reason we used decking for the pathways throughout the garden."

"In front, the deck comes up and joins the porch," Diana says. An arbor welcomes you into the garden and guides the approach to the deck.

The end of the deck at the rear of the lot serves as a garden destination near a small fish pool. "It's so close to nature that even animals find it an oasis. There's a big turtle that's made his home in the pond," Diana says. "And sometimes we have heron fly in to fish—we have to run *them* off."

Casual plantings help keep garden maintenance to a minimum. "We cut everything back heavily once a year," says Busk. "It helps let light and air in and helps hold down the population of insects."

A painted finish on the deck also serves to reduce upkeep. "Our only problem is mildew," Diana says. "We were advised to use a garden sprayer to apply a mix of bleach and water (about ¼ cup bleach to a gallon), but I've found that a sponge mop works better. Once in a while I just put on my rubber gloves and sponge off the deck. The mop makes it easy to keep the mixture off the plants."

Busk's natural plan for the landscape leaves the Bonds with confidence to mix and mingle new plantings with the original scheme. "Over the years we've moved a few things around, cut a few things back," Diana recalls, "but a garden is a continuous thing, especially one that is lush like this."

In fact, that lush, natural feel is one of the garden's most attractive qualities. "Though our lot isn't actually very big, the plants really block out any traffic noise," Diana concludes. "You just don't feel like you're on a street with any other houses." ◇

PHOTOGRAPH: VAN CHAPLIN

Live Christmas trees are usually smaller than cut trees because the root ball's weight makes bigger trees impractical. This Norway spruce sits in a galvanized tub so it can be easily watered.

Try a Live Tree

Do you have a Scrooge-like aversion to spending 50 bucks on anything you're going to toss out two weeks later? Or would you like to beautify your yard with a living memento of this holiday season? If either answer is "yes," buy a live tree this Christmas. Then to greatly increase your tree's life expectancy, follow these guidelines.

■ Select a tree that will grow well in your area (see box). When buying a tree, look for fresh, healthy foliage, a straight trunk, and well-spaced branches. Avoid one-sided trees and those with lots of yellowing and dropping needles. Make sure balled-and-burlapped trees have firm, unbroken root balls. If possible, select a tree growing in a container.

■ Water the root ball every three days until you're ready to bring the tree inside. Water from the top. Don't soak the root ball in water or it may fall apart when you lift the tree.

■ Keep the tree indoors for no more than 10 days; 7 days is better. If you keep it inside any longer, it may break dormancy and die when it is

LIVE CHRISTMAS TREES FOR THE SOUTH

Upper and Middle South— Colorado spruce, Norway spruce, Douglas fir, white fir (*Abies concolor*), red cedar (*Juniperus virginiana*), white pine, Scotch pine, Afghan pine (*Pinus eldarica*)
Lower and Coastal South— Red cedar, deodar cedar, Virginia pine, Afghan pine, Leyland cypress
Tropical South—Deodar cedar, Southern red cedar (*Juniperus silicicola*), Norfolk Island pine, sand pine, slash pine, Arizona cypress, Leyland cypress

taken back to the cold.

■ Place the root ball in a large, galvanized tub so you can water the tree without wetting the floor.

■ Use small, twinkle-type lights instead of larger, hotter lights. The tree won't dry out as fast.

■ When you're ready to plant outside, select a sunny, well-drained spot where the tree has plenty of room to grow. If the spot is some distance from the house, use a wheelbarrow or garden cart to transport the tree. It usually takes two strong people to lift the root ball.

■ Dig a hole as deep as the root ball and twice as wide. Place the tree in the bottom of the hole, stand it up straight, and fill in around the root ball with soil; then use your foot to firm the soil. Water thoroughly; then mulch the tree with several inches of shredded bark or pine straw.

Steve Bender

196 *December*

Ornaments Beyond The Tree

While shopping for your holiday dinner, add unshelled nuts to your market order. They can take on a whole new purpose this season as special ornaments and memorable gifts. Make these easy, natural decorations from walnuts, as we did, or from whole pecans, almonds, or other nuts.

Use nut ornaments as party favors at each place setting of a holiday dinner party. Later your guests can hang a remembrance of the evening on their trees. Place the decoration at the top of the plate and alternate place settings with varying ornaments.

A large bowl or platter atop an entry chest, console, or fireside coffee table is the perfect cradle for these items. It's best to use florist moss as a bed for arranging them. Ribbon and strands of beads swirling between the ornaments give the collection a festive touch, or you can simply garnish with sprigs of greenery clipped from the tree.

If you have a more casual setting, such as your kitchen countertop, mix a few candy canes between the balls. The candy canes are simple to position because of the spaces between the nuts.

Follow our easy instructions and it will take about 30 minutes to assemble each ornament. The finished size depends on the nuts and plastic foam balls you choose (those shown here are about 6 inches in diameter). Note that because of their weight the ornaments require sturdy branches for hanging.

Mary McWilliams

Let nut ornaments set the theme at your holiday table. After dinner, guests can take the party favors home to add a natural touch to their trees.

STEPS FOR EASY ASSEMBLY

■ Take a 3-inch plastic foam ball, and apply Spanish moss (purchased at your local crafts store) to its sides using a hot-glue gun. Be careful; the glue gets very hot. Spread the moss around evenly so that the foam does not show through.

■ Using about 14 inches of ribbon, make a loop for hanging. If you want a bow at the base of the loop, take another piece of ribbon about 45 inches in length, and overlap it two times allowing for extra ribbon to provide the tails. Ribbon with wired edges works best for bows because it keeps its form. Use hot glue to at-

To make the ornaments, include on your shopping list plastic foam balls, glue gun, Spanish moss, tape measure, ribbon, thumbtacks, and nuts.

tach the ribbon to the top of the ball, and insert a thumbtack through the ribbon and into the ball. Apply glue around the thumbtack for extra support. Then spread out the loops of the bow.

■ Glue and position nuts with the points facing outward to give the ornament more definition and fullness. Nestle the nuts closely on top of the moss.

■ For a more elegant ornament, lightly spray metallic gold or silver paint on random parts of the ornament after assembling. Let dry completely for several hours, and enjoy your creations.

PHOTOGRAPH: CHERYL DALTON

A great combination for shady gardens—the deep-green, spear-shaped leaves of nipponlily contrasted with Southern maidenhair fern's light-green, lacy foliage and variegated caladiums

A Masterful Mixture of Leaves

Coarse leaves, delicate leaves. Long leaves, wide leaves. Light-green leaves, dark-green leaves. One of the most enjoyable aspects of gardening is combining foliage of different sizes, colors, and textures. A successful composition has a life of its own—it surpasses the sum of its parts. Here's such a combination that you can grow in a shady garden. It's composed of two plants that you probably know and one you may not.

First, the familiar. The lacy, light-green foliage in the foreground belongs to our native Southern maidenhair fern (*Adiantum capillus-veneris*). Few plants contribute such soft texture to the garden. Dark, wiry, almost hair-thin stems hold scalloped leaflets the size of your fingertip. Southern maidenhair grows from 15 to 18 inches tall and spreads slowly.

Of course, you recognize the large, variegated leaves in the back—caladiums. Only impatiens exceed them in popularity for adding color to shady borders. Caladiums come in red-, pink-, and white-leaved selections and range in size from 8 to 24 inches tall. The selection shown is called Candidum.

Now for the dark-green mystery plant, the one whose identity will separate expert gardeners from beginners. If you guessed that it's cast-iron plant, turn in your trowel. The correct answer is nipponlily (*Rohdea japonica*), a smaller, look-alike evergreen. Native to China and Japan, nipponlily grows 15 to 18 inches tall and features glossy, spear-shaped leaves. Showy red fruit in the fall helps atone for its inconspicuous flowers.

One key to any successful combination is using plants that enjoy similar growing conditions. That's certainly the case here. All three prefer moist, well-drained soil that contains plenty of organic matter. Hardiness varies from plant to plant, however. Caladiums must be dug and stored over winter in all but the Tropical South. Nipponlily and Southern maidenhair are questionable in the coldest parts of the Upper South, but should do well elsewhere.   *Steve Bender*

If you would like a list of mail-order sources, send a self-addressed, stamped, business-size envelope to Foliage Combination Editor, *Southern Living*, P.O. Box 830119, Birmingham, Alabama 35283.   ◇

Mary Jane's Rose Garden at Orlando's Leu Gardens contains more than 1,000 roses in 75 varieties.

A Leisurely Day at Leu Gardens

When most people visit Orlando, the last thing they do is relax. Rather than unwinding amid placid lakes and moss-draped trees, they streak from theme park to theme park like hummingbirds among flowers. But if you want a change from the breakneck pace, there is one place in this bustling city where you can literally stop to smell the roses—Leu Gardens.

Leu Gardens began as the estate of Harry P. Leu, a successful Orlando businessman, who purchased the property in 1936. Leu and his wife, Mary Jane, spent much of the next 25 years collecting plants from around the world to build fabulous gardens. In 1961, Leu donated his estate to the city of Orlando to be developed as a municipal botanical garden. Today, in the words of Executive Director Janet Alford, "Leu Gardens gives visitors an opportunity to see the true beauty of Orlando.

"Orlando originally was famous for its natural beauty," Alford explains. "Many winter tourists came here for our beautiful lakes and scenery. But with all the attractions Orlando has developed, sometimes the natural beauty is overlooked." Fortunately, with its green, rolling hills, blue water, avenues of giant camphors, and thousands of blossoms, there's no eluding the natural splendor of Leu Gardens.

According to Alford, the gardens' main mission is "to teach people about the kinds of plants that will grow successfully in Central Florida." To that end, the gardens include a native plant collection, as well as collections of azaleas, orchids, palms and cycads, cacti and succulents, aquatic plants, flowering trees, annuals, and perennials. The camellia collection, composed of more than 2,000 plants in 50 species, ranks among the largest in the world. Mary Jane's Rose Garden (the rose was Mrs. Leu's favorite flower) contains more than 1,000 plants in 75 varieties.

Approximately 60,000 people visited Leu Gardens last year. Many of them took part in one or more of the 30 gardening classes and workshops taught throughout the year by the gardens' staff and plant experts from the community. The 1992 schedule features adult education classes on growing daylilies, orchids, grapes, camellias, and wildflowers. There are also courses geared toward children.

If you're visiting Central Florida and find your heartbeat racing, a leisurely day at Leu Gardens may be the perfect tonic.

The gardens are located at 1730 North Forest Avenue in Orlando. They're open from 9 a.m. to 5 p.m. daily (except Christmas). Admission is $3 for adults and $1 for children 6 to 16. For additional information call (407) 246-2620.   *Steve Bender*

The gazebo in the Rose Garden frames a splendid view of the original farmhouse, which has been restored as a museum.

PHOTOGRAPHS: VAN CHAPLIN

LETTERS TO OUR GARDEN EDITORS

Acorns: Could you please tell me how to germinate acorns?

Barbara Mayfield
Quitaque, Texas

Acorns are quite easy to germinate, as long as they're fresh and not damaged by insects. Unfortunately, a good percentage of acorns you find on the ground have already been chewed on by weevils. When you do find good ones in the fall, sow them immediately or store them in the refrigerator for spring planting. To sow, barely cover the acorns with moist soil and place them in a warm, sunny spot. They will sprout soon.

African violet: Could you give me some advice about how to grow African violets?

Glenda Atkinson
Wilson, Arkansas

Caring for African violets isn't difficult. They like bright, indirect light, the kind you find coming through a northern window. You can also grow them under fluorescent lights. Give them fertile, well-drained soil. Let the top inch of soil go barely dry between thorough waterings, but never let the soil become soggy. Use tepid water, never cold, and don't wet the foliage. Feed once a month with a general-purpose houseplant fertilizer or a special African violet fertilizer.

Azaleas: We have azaleas growing under large pines. Over the years, a lot of pine straw has accumulated around the shrubs. Is this good or bad for azaleas?

Barbara Budemer
Georgetown, Louisiana

Pine straw makes an excellent mulch for azaleas because it conserves moisture, keeps the soil cool, and inhibits the growth of weeds. And, as it breaks down, it acidifies the soil and adds organic matter. For most gardens, pine straw is a blessing, not a curse.

Barbecue ashes: I've heard that barbecue ashes could be added to a compost pile or flowerbed. Is this safe if a petroleum-based charcoal starter has been used?

Jackie Wiegand
Oakdale, Louisiana

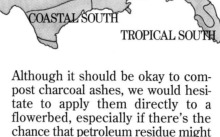

Although it should be okay to compost charcoal ashes, we would hesitate to apply them directly to a flowerbed, especially if there's the chance that petroleum residue might still be present.

Bermuda grass: I would like to know if Bermuda grass will grow in my area.

G. D. Holman
Knoxville, Tennessee

Bermuda grass is hardy in Knoxville, although it may be injured during severe winters. Tall fescue is probably a better choice. If you decide to go with Bermuda, select one of the improved Bermudas, such as Tifway, Tifgreen, and Tufcote. They have a finer texture and better color than common Bermuda. However, they also need more frequent watering, mowing, and fertilizing. Spring is a good time to install a Bermuda lawn. You can use either seed (common Bermuda only), sprigs, plugs, or sod.

Cactus query: Please help me identify a particular cactus. It is smooth and green with no thorns and has beautiful flowers that look like starfish when they unfurl.

Katherine Haskins
Madisonville, Louisiana

The plant you describe is a starfish plant (*Stapelia* sp.), which resembles a cactus, but is actually a succulent. Starfish plant is quite easy to grow indoors. Just give it bright, indirect light and well-drained soil. Let the soil dry between waterings.

Chinese chestnut: I have several tall Chinese chestnut trees in my

yard. They bear nuts by the gallon, but they have worms. Because the trees are too tall to spray, are there any other methods for controlling these pests?

Don Amburgey
Jenkins, Kentucky

It appears that your trees are infested with weevils. To kill newly hatched weevils, spray the trees according to label directions with methoxychlor in July. If you can't spray them, do the next best thing and drench the soil beneath them with either Diazinon or Dursban this April. This will kill the weevil larvae. Also be sure to pick up and destroy any infested nuts on the ground.

Common periwinkle: The common periwinkle in my yard has failed to thrive. I would appreciate your advice.

Lucian L. Tatum
Griffin, Georgia

Common periwinkle (*Vinca minor*) prefers moist, well-drained, slightly acid soil that contains plenty of organic matter, such as compost, leaf mold, or sphagnum peat moss. It also needs light shade. Fertilize in spring, sprinkling one handful of 5-10-5 fertilizer per 10 square feet of bed. Do this when the foliage is dry, and brush off any granules that get on the leaves.

Compost: Last week, I noticed ants and roaches in some soil I was adding to my compost. Can you give me some tips on how to control these insects?

Betty M. McConkey
Birmingham, Alabama

Ants and roaches may use the compost for shelter temporarily, but will quickly leave it, unless you add such "tasty" items as rotting fruit, banana pccls, and other food scraps. By keeping the compost moist, turning it frequently, and adding plenty of organic matter, you can raise its internal temperature to well over 100 degrees, sufficient to drive insects out. Don't spray the compost with an insecticide, as this may prevent earthworms and soil microbes from doing their jobs.

Confederate rose: Little green worms eat the leaves and buds of our Confederate rose. We sprayed the plant with bug spray and ended up killing it. Can you tell me a little bit about this plant and what to spray it with?
Mrs. J. F. Rogers
Fort Walton Beach, Florida
Confederate rose (*Hibiscus mutabilis*) is a large, multistemmed shrub that is prized for its stunning flowers. Its single or double blossoms open white, change to rose, then finally deepen to blood red. Often, all three colors are present at the same time. The plant is winter-hardy in the Lower, Coastal, and Tropical South. The spray you used was either the wrong chemical, improperly applied, or both. To rid Confederate rose of the green worms, spray it according to label directions with carbaryl, malathion, Diazinon, or Dipel (*Bacillus thuringiensis*).

Crown-of-thorns: The leaves of my crown-of-thorns plant periodically turn yellow and fall. What causes this?
Eloise Wallace
Charleston, West Virginia
Crown-of-thorns (*Euphorbia milii*), a spiny succulent grown for its showy red or yellow flowers, needs bright light to keep its foliage. Leaves quickly drop when the light gets too dim. Another possible cause of the problem is insufficient watering during spring and summer. Although the plant likes the top inch of soil to dry between thorough waterings, if the soil dries completely during these months, the plant will drop leaves.

Daffodils: An entire bed of King Alfred daffodils on the side of my house failed to bloom this spring. The flower stems were about 30 inches long and the buds on top were dry and brown. What is the problem?
Leo B. Schemmel, Jr.
Owensboro, Kentucky
Brent Heath of the Daffodil Mart in Gloucester, Virginia, suggests the following possibilities. First, the excessive length of the flower stems may indicate too much shade. Daffodils bloom best in full sun. Second, the drying of the flowerbud is a condition known as "blasting." This occurs most often with double-flowering selections, but some of the old-fashioned singles, such as King Alfred, will do it too. Blasting often follows either an unusually warm, dry spring or a normal spring in which a sudden cold snap dries the bud. The best way to avoid blasting is to plant daffodils in protected spots out of cold, dry winds and also to give them ample moisture in springtime before they begin to bloom.

Dogwood: I have a dogwood "volunteer" about 2 feet tall growing 6 inches away from the foundation of my house. I would like to move it out into the yard. Can you tell me how to do this so I won't kill it?
Pam Puckett
Troy, Tennessee
Move your tree in February or, at the latest, March, while it's still dormant.

EDITORS' NOTEBOOK

Last week I discovered a black, yellow, and green caterpillar munching away on the dill out back. My initial impulse was to stomp and squash. But then I recognized the critter for what he was—the offspring of a black swallowtail butterfly—and stayed my foot. One reason we see fewer butterflies in gardens nowadays is that we're too quick to dispatch their progeny. Unlike the larvae of pests such as gypsy moth, butterfly larvae seldom operate in sufficient numbers to cause serious damage. In addition, most are quite specific about what they eat. Monarch caterpillars consume milkweed and butterfly weed. Large orange sulfurs insist on cassias and mimosas. Black swallowtails prefer dill, celery, parsley, and Queen Anne's lace. By allowing caterpillars to dine on a few leaves here and there, we can keep the adult populations up without sacrificing the garden. To learn to identify different kinds of caterpillars, look for field guides and books about butterflies in the nature section of your bookstore.
Steve Bender

PHOTOGRAPH: TINA EVANS

The key to successful transplanting is taking as many roots with the tree as possible. For a tree under 3 feet tall, sink a spade into the ground about 1 foot out from the trunk and make a circle around the tree; this would give you a rootball about 2 feet wide. In your case, however, the nearby foundation will make the root ball slightly smaller and a bit one-sided. Reach under the root ball with your hands, and lift it gently from the ground. Take the tree to its new location, and plant it at the same depth it had been growing previously. Make the hole at least twice as wide as the root ball. Use your foot to firm soil around the tree; then water thoroughly. Be sure to water the tree well during summer droughts, especially during the first year of growth.

Fairy ring: Our lawn service recently told us that our centipede lawn has a problem called "fairy ring." Can you tell me what it is, how we got it, and what we can do about it?
Gwen Mettlen
Aiken, South Carolina
Fairy ring is caused by a fungus that consumes organic matter in the soil. The name comes from the fruiting bodies of the fungus—mushrooms—which often form rings on the lawn during rainy weather. The grass on the edge of the ring appears darker because the fungus releases nitrates, which fertilize the grass. However, the grass in the center of the ring often looks stunted. Unfortunately, there is no good way to control fairy ring. If the dark-green ring in the lawn bothers you, try giving the grass inside the ring a little extra nitrogen fertilizer to even up the color.

Galax: I'd like some information about a plant called galax. Will it grow in my area?
Katherine R. Fix
Staunton, Virginia
Galax (*Galax urceolata*) is a woodland wildflower native to the Southeast. Although it bears spikes of small, white flowers, this perennial is primarily prized for its glossy, round, evergreen leaves, which change from deep green in summer to rich burgundy in winter. Galax prefers full shade and cool, moist, acid soil containing plenty of organic matter. If you can supply these conditions, it should do well in Staunton. Just be sure that any plants you purchase were propagated by the nursery and not collected from the wild. Over collection decimates native populations.

Gerberas: The leaves of my gerbera daisies frequently turn brown and crisp along the edges. Does this result from too much sun or not enough water? Also, as long as the plants put out new growth, is there any reason why they should not continue to bloom?
Mary Cupstid
Vicksburg, Mississippi
Gerberas need a lot of water during the summer. So the reason the leaves of your plants turn brown along the edges is probably that the plants dry out. Although gerberas produce very showy blooms, they typically don't bear great numbers of them at any one time, and often rest between flushes of blooms. Feeding your plants monthly throughout the growing season with water-soluble 20-20-20 fertilizer should encourage blooming.

Gnats: We live in a rural, forested area. Every time we walk out into the garden from spring until frost, we're attacked by clouds of gnats. A wide-brimmed hat and "Skin-So-Soft" helps, but the insects still drive us crazy. Would putting up some purple martin houses help? *Janice Graves*
Blountsville, Alabama
Your gnat problem probably does have something to do with the dense vegetation around your house. The purple martin house may help. You might also consider putting up a bat house. Contrary to popular belief, bats don't spread disease. But they do consume huge quantities of insects every day. You may order either a bat or purple martin house from Gardener's Supply, 128 Intervale Road, Burlington, Vermont 05401.

Ground cover for shade: Help! I need a low-growing ground cover that will thrive in the shade of a 100-year-old oak. Any suggestions?
Shawn Murphy Hitchcock
Decatur, Georgia
There are a number of shade-tolerant ground covers you might try. Among them are carpet bugleweed (*Ajuga reptans*), English ivy (*Hedera helix*), common periwinkle (*Vinca minor*), Japanese pachysandra (*Pachysandra terminalis*), mondo grass (*Ophiopogon japonicus*), and Lenten rose (*Helleborus orientalis*). All of these are easy to grow and readily available at most garden centers.

Growing impatiens: I've been collecting seeds from my impatiens and would like to start plants in a differ-ent area of my yard next year. Should I plant the seeds in pots or sow them right into the garden? *Laurie Jones*
Birmingham, Alabama
You can do either. If you prefer the first method, fill a pot with moist, finely milled potting soil. Sprinkle seeds atop the soil; don't cover them. Place the pot in a warm, sunny window. Be sure there's good air circulation around the seedlings. They may take 12 weeks before they're ready to go outside. If you'd rather sow the seeds outside, just sprinkle them over the surface of an empty, unmulched flowerbed. Sow seeds now or in spring.

Heat pump: I just installed two heat pumps for my duplex. The contractor says that the hot airflow will de-

EDITORS' NOTEBOOK

Plants don't bloom to please you and me. They live according to their own schedules. That's why it sometimes pays to be patient. Case in point: A number of years ago, I planted a red horse chestnut (*Aesculus* x *carnea* Briotii) at the church where my father gardens. Well, no matter what I did, that tree just refused to grow. It increased in height barely 4 inches a year and wouldn't bloom. Finally, last spring I was fed up and laid down the law—if the tree didn't do better, it would soon find itself mulching the perennials. Perhaps my threat did the trick; but the truth is, the tree probably broke through the hardpan of clay it had been growing atop all these years. In any case, last summer it added over a foot of growth. This spring, it adorned itself with gorgeous red blossoms. Patience paid off. I'll find other mulch for the perennials.
Steve Bender

stroy the azaleas, ferns, and rhododendrons growing nearby. How close can these plantings be?
Nancy Ford
Abingdon, Virginia
This hot airflow can injure nearby plants if pointed right at them. However, most modern units direct hot air upward. To avoid damage from units that blow hot air sideways, keep plants at least 10 feet away.

Japanese maple seeds: My Japanese maple produced a lot of seeds this year. I would appreciate some information on how to plant and grow them. *Mrs. Warren Taylor*
Morehead City, North Carolina
Japanese maple isn't an easy tree to grow from seed. The trick seems to be to collect fresh seed (green or red) before it dries and turns brown. Place the seed in a zip-top plastic bag filled with moist potting soil. Seal the bag, and place it in your refrigerator for three to five months. At the end of this time, remove the seeds from the bag, and plant about ½ inch deep in a seed flat. Place the flat in a sunny, warm location, and keep the soil moist. Some seeds may germinate almost immediately, but others may take a while. In any case, the seedlings will likely be different in appearance than the parent tree, due to genetic variability.

Jonquils: I have lots of yellow jonquils planted under a red oak tree. They will not bloom. Is there anything I can do to make them bloom?
Mrs. B. E. Wilson
Prentiss, Mississippi
There are several possible reasons why jonquils fail to bloom. First, you may have planted small bulbs, which often take a few years to bloom. Second, you may not have planted them properly. They perform best when planted 5 to 6 inches deep and 3 to 4 inches apart in loose, well-drained soil. If you need to take up and replant your bulbs, do it this spring when the foliage tells you where the bulbs are. Third, your soil may lack sufficient nutrients. Try fertilizing them in spring and fall with Holland Bulb Booster (9-9-6) sprinkled over the top of the bulb bed at the rate of ½ pound per 100 square feet. Finally, don't cut the jonquil foliage until it begins to yellow.

Lilies: Three years ago, we planted lilies in our garden. This year, the blossoms were exceedingly beautiful.

Should we dig up, separate, and re-plant the lilies this fall? If not, when should this be done? *Dallas Tandy Rogers, Arkansas*
Your question calls up the old adage: "If it ain't broke, don't fix it." If, years from now, your lilies become crowded and bloom less heavily than before, you may want to divide and move them. Let the foliage die down naturally in late summer; then dig up, divide, and replant in September or October. Space the bulbs about a foot apart, and plant at least 8 inches deep into rich, loose, well-drained soil.

Nandina: I'm considering planting nandina in my garden. Could you advise me what kinds of birds, if any, are attracted to its red berries?
Floyd Beach Powhatan, Virginia
Nandina makes an excellent winter food source for birds because it holds its berries all the way to spring. Here in Birmingham, we've noticed the berries attract mockingbirds, cardinals, sparrows, catbirds, and juncos. These birds should visit nandina in your area, too.

Naturalizing: Our area is called the Sandhills and features white, sandy soil and abundant longleaf pines. Most "lawns" here consist of massed shrubs and ground covered with pine needles. We do not want to plant grass, but want more to look at besides pine needles. Any suggestions?
Anne W. Ganley Jackson Springs, North Carolina
We applaud your decision to save time and trouble by not growing a large lawn. In its place, maintain a natural area covered with pine straw. Kill unwanted weeds by spraying them with Roundup according to label directions. To add extra color beneath the pines, consider planting sweeps of shade-tolerant perennials and shrubs. Plants that come to mind include mondo grass (*Ophiopogon japonicus*), Southern shield fern (*Thelypteris kunthii*), marginal shield fern (*Dryopteris marginalis*), Christmas fern (*Polystichum acrostichoides*), hostas, Lenten rose (*Helleborus orientalis*), oakleaf hydrangea (*Hydrangea quercifolia*), bottlebrush buckeye (*Aesculus parviflora*), piedmont azalea (*Azalea canescens*), mountain laurel (*Kalmia latifolia*), nandina, and holly. Before planting, supplement the sandy soil with plenty of organic matter, such as sphagnum peat moss, compost, or leaf mold.

Even with the extra organic matter, the soil will need more frequent watering and fertilizing than clay or loamy soil would.

Nutgrass: Is there any way to rid my flowerbeds of nutgrass? I've tried digging up the nutlets, as well as poisoning the plants with nutgrass killer. Nothing has worked. *Jim Watson Natchitoches, Louisiana*
You probably don't want to hear this, but the best way to rid your flower-bed of nutgrass is to pull it by hand. Keep at it, pulling some nutgrass every day until its numbers gradually decrease. Also, mulch your bed with several inches of pine straw so that nutgrass seed doesn't have sunlight to germinate. If you have nutgrass in an adjacent lawn,

EDITORS' NOTEBOOK

One thing a gardener quickly learns is that few plants behave like they're supposed to. A good example is chrysanthemums. They're supposed to bloom in autumn, right? Then why do those in my garden also bloom in spring? The answer is that in years past, older types of mums initiated flowerbuds only as a response to autumn's shortening days. But many newer types respond to both day length and temperature. When daytime is less than 12 hours long and nighttime temperatures hover around 60 degrees, bingo—you get blooms. For most Southerners, this happens in both spring and fall. If your mums surprise you with flowers this spring, don't panic. Enjoy the blossoms; then cut the plants back when they finish flowering. They'll bloom again this fall. *Steve Bender*

be sure to mow regularly to keep seedheads from forming.

Peach Trees: This spring, I discovered sap "bleeding" from the trunk of my peach tree. What can I do to stop this?
Raquel T. de Guzman Cushing, Oklahoma
Sap oozing from the trunk of a peach tree is often a sign of peach tree borers. Holes in the trunk filled with sawdust are another sign. To control borers, scrape away any mulch or soil that's up against the trunk. Then spray the trunk and around the base of the tree with methoxychlor or Dursban. Make three applications at two-week intervals, beginning in June. Be sure to follow label directions carefully.

Pear trees: We have three pear trees that are about 4 years old. One had about eight pears this year, but the others have never borne fruit. What do you suggest? *Bob Folsom Beaumont, Texas*
First, you may have planted "standard trees," which take longer to start bearing than semidwarf and dwarf trees. Second, most pear trees need a suitable pollinating selection to produce fruit. Your trees may not be compatible. Finally, you may not be growing the best selections for your area. Ask your county agricultural Extension agent for recommendations.

Peonies: My peonies were a disappointment this spring. The flowers weren't full—almost all the blooms had single petals. Also, there were no red blooms and very few whites. Is there any way to control the color and shape of the flowers? *Rick Kelley Fairfax, Virginia*
Usually, when people have trouble with peonies, it's due to plants set too deeply, fungus, or unseasonable or extreme weather (too warm, too cold, too wet, too dry). The single-flowered, early-blooming types perform better in the South. Perhaps this explains why some of your plants bloomed and why others didn't. Unfortunately, there is nothing you can do to change a peony flower's shape or its color, as both are determined genetically.

Peonies: I transplanted some very old peonies this spring. They all came up, but grew only about 10 inches tall, then withered and died. What went wrong? *Sherri Reid Piedmont, South Carolina*

Old, established peonies are very difficult to transplant successfully. Our guess is that your plants died from transplanting shock. The best time to transplant peonies is in fall, when the plants are dormant. But even carefully moving peonies in fall can set them back. That's why it's best to plant them where they can remain undisturbed.

Perennial problem: My perennials grow very tall before blooming. Then when they're in full bloom, they fall down and lie on the ground. What can I do to strengthen the plants?

Ruby Lutes
Easton, Maryland

It sounds like you're growing sun-loving plants in shade. The plants stretch toward the sun and fall over. There are several remedies you can try. First, move your plants to a sunnier spot. If this isn't possible, consider replacing them with perennials that enjoy light shade, such as astilbe, Japanese anemone, columbine, hosta, bleeding-heart, and black-eyed Susans. A third option is to use grow-through plant supports. Each support consists of a metal grid atop legs. Place the support over a perennial in spring; the plant grows through the grid and is held upright.

Photinia: Leaf blight has attacked our hedgerow of red tips that gave us privacy from the street. I've decided to pull them out. Can you suggest an alternative shrub that will grow 10 to 12 feet high?

M. Yost
Albemarle, North Carolina

Because Fraser photinia (*Photinia* x *fraseri*) is probably the South's most overused plant, the leaf blight may have been a blessing in disguise. Good replacements include wax myrtle (*Myrica cerifera*), Burford holly (*Ilex cornuta* Burfordii), or Foster holly (*I.* x *attenuata* Fosterii). All three plants are evergreen, fast growing, and care free. They will make a good, dense screen of the size you want.

Planting trees: Here in Montgomery County, Maryland, we have red clay. It doesn't drain well, especially in the heat of summer when the sun bakes it nearly as hard as rock. After watching my trees and shrubs die for no apparent reason, I concluded that lack of drainage was the problem. My solution was to plant new plants nearly on top of the ground with the bottom of the root ball only 2 to 4 inches below ground level. Next, I surrounded the root ball

with landscaping timbers and mounded good soil inside them. Then I covered over each mound with 3 to 5 inches of mulch. So far, my solution seems to be working. Any comments?

Bruce M. Leet
North Potomac, Maryland

Your method for planting trees and shrubs in what amounts to raised beds seems a logical solution to the problem you have with heavy, clay soil. However, because the plants are growing in a restricted soil mass essentially on top of the ground, they'll have shallow root systems. Therefore, they'll be more suscepti-

EDITORS' NOTEBOOK

It happens every fall. A panicked homeowner in a tizzy about his "dying" pine trees begs for the secret to save them. When I ask for the symptoms, the answer is "brown needles, dropping everywhere." Examine the branches closely, I say. If the newest growth—the needles growing on the tips of the branches—is turning brown, you have a real problem. Any number of things could be killing your trees. More likely, however, you'll discover it's the older, inner needles that are dying and dropping. No problem—this is perfectly natural. Pines may be evergreens, but individual needles don't last forever. Depending on the species, they live for two to three years before dropping. The heaviest drop occurs in autumn, but old needles shower down in every season. So if your tree looks like the one pictured above, relax.

Steve Bender

ble to drought, making careful watering essential for success.

Plants for solarium: Can you suggest plants with showy, blue flowers I could grow in a solarium that is attached to my living room?

Florence Wagner
Gainesville, Florida

You have many from which to choose. They include princess flower (*Tibouchina urvilleana*), cape plumbago (*Plumbago auriculata*), common ginger (*Zingiber officinale*), cape primrose (*Streptocarpus hybridus*), blue passionflower (*Passiflora caerulea*), and French hydrangea (*Hydrangea macrophylla*).

Plugging lawns: Can you advise me on how to plant Zoysia plugs into an existing lawn?

T. J. Keegan
Bradenton, Florida

If you're plugging Zoysia into a different kind of grass, first kill the existing grass by spraying it with Roundup according to label directions. However, if you're thickening up a Zoysia lawn, just set plugs into it. In either case, use a plugging tool, (available at most garden centers that sell grass plugs) spacing the plugs 1 foot apart in a checkerboard pattern across the lawn. Water the plugs thoroughly every rainless day for the first 3 weeks. Fertilize them with slow-release lawn food this spring and again in June. The plugs should fill in completely in 2 or 3 years.

Privacy screen: I'd like to plant an evergreen privacy screen along highway frontage. Can you suggest plants for my area that grow fast and require little maintenance?

Stella Smith
Johnson City, Texas

Needleleaf evergreens to try include Hetz Chinese juniper (*Juniperus chinensis* Hetzii), Afghan pine (*Pinus eldarica*), and Leyland cypress (*Cupressocyparis leylandii*). If you prefer broadleaf evergreens, consider thorny elaeagnus (*Elaeagnus pungens*), Burford holly (*Ilex cornuta* Burfordii), yaupon (*Ilex vomitoria*), wax myrtle (*Myrica cerifera*), firethorn (*Pyracantha* sp.), and Southern cherry laurel (*Prunus caroliniana*).

Spanish moss: Our magnolia tree is becoming a host for Spanish moss. We're afraid that it will eventually kill the tree. How do we get rid of the moss?

Norman F. Diment
Bradenton, Florida

One of the signature plants of the Deep South, Spanish moss is usually benign and quite ornamental. However, it occasionally grows so thickly that it weakens the tree. By far the best way to remove Spanish moss is to hire a tree service to do the job. Consider asking a local arborist to inspect your tree and judge whether removing the moss is warranted. Of course, removal won't stop it from gradually returning.

Sweet peas: Several years ago, I obtained a start of sweet peas. The blooms were very pretty, but had no fragrance. Why is there no fragrance?
Mrs. W. A. Latham
Jasper, Texas
Despite their name, not all sweet peas (*Lathyrus odoratus*) carry a sweet scent. Some selections, bred for large flowers or particular flower colors, have little or no scent. The only way to guarantee a truly sweet sweet pea is to plant a named selection, such as Maggie May, Leamington, and Royal Wedding, which has been chosen for its fragrance. Another possibility is that you may have a hardier, everlasting pea (*L. grandiflorus*). Everlasting pea varies in fragrance too. A good mail-order source for sweet and everlasting peas is Thompson & Morgan, P.O. Box 1308, Jackson, New Jersey 08527.

Sweet shrub: Four years ago, I bought a sweet shrub from a respectable nursery. It seems to be thriving, but it doesn't bloom. Did I buy a lemon?
Carol Cocke
Florence, Alabama
It's hard to say. Most sweet shrubs (*Calycanthus floridus*) sold by nurseries are grown from seed. Seedlings vary quite a bit in their characteristics, including blooming. Genetics may mean yours will bloom at an older age. If so, there is nothing you can do to change this. Another possibility, however, is that you're pruning your shrub in either summer or fall. This removes the flowerbuds for next year. The best time to prune sweet shrub is in late spring. May would be a good time in your area.

Tomatoes: What causes tomatoes to have hard, white spots on the fruit?
Lance Arnold
Nashville, Tennessee
This problem, called blotchiness, has several possible causes. They include fruit ripening when night temperatures fall below 60 degrees, compact-ed and poorly drained soil, and too little potassium in the soil. If the selection you're currently growing is so badly affected that you're throwing away tomatoes, try growing a different selection next year.

Tung-oil tree: While traveling in Charleston, South Carolina, this spring, we saw a tree with huge leaves and white flowers. We were told it was a tung-oil tree. Can you tell us a little bit more?
Shirley Parker
Aiken, South Carolina
A small, deciduous tree that grows 15 to 25 feet high, tung-oil tree (*Aleurites*

EDITORS' NOTEBOOK

No tree, in my estimation, surpasses the sugar maple for autumn show. But this mighty tree doesn't thrive in the hotter and/or drier parts of the South. Fortunately, three similar species (some say subspecies) make excellent substitutes. Two Southeastern natives, chalk maple (*Acer leucoderme*) and Southern sugar or Florida maple (*Acer floridanum*), fill the autumn woods with brilliant orange and yellow leaves. Though similar, these two can be distinguished through close observation. Chalk maple typically grows multi-trunked, 20 to 30 feet tall, and its leaves are velvety green beneath. Southern sugar maple grows 40 to 50 feet tall, most often with a single trunk. The undersides of its leaves are whitish green and fuzzless. Bigtooth maple (*A. grandidentatum*) is a good choice for the Southwest. Tolerant of drought and rocky, alkaline soil, it grows 50 feet tall and turns radiant red in fall. For mail-order sources, send a self-addressed, stamped, business-size envelope to Maple Editor, *Southern Living*, P.O. Box 830119, Birmingham, Alabama 35283.
Steve Bender

Fordii) gets its name from the large amounts of oil contained in its nutlike fruit. During World War II, the fine-grade oil was used to lubricate airplane engines. Today it's still used in paints and varnishes. Tung-oil tree grows fast, tolerates poor soil, and has few insect pests. It's winter hardy in the Coastal and Tropical South, as well as the milder parts of the Lower South. Clusters of showy white blossoms with orange markings appear in spring. The large green leaves turn orange and red in fall. In the right spot, tung-oil tree makes an interesting addition to the home garden.

Turnip Greens: Every year my turnip greens develop small, brownish spots that quickly cover the whole leaf. What causes this and how can it be controlled?
Mrs. Thomas Spencer
Talladega, Alabama
It appears your turnip greens are infested with leaf spot. To control it, pull off and discard any spotted leaves. Then spray your plants with maneb, zineb, or wettable sulfur every 7 to 10 days until the problem ceases. Be sure to carefully follow label directions, and wash the greens thoroughly before eating them. Water only in early morning, so that the foliage dries completely before nighttime. To keep leaf spot from returning, pull up and discard all turnips at the end of the harvest this fall. Next spring, plant the greens in a different section of the garden.

Winter care for azaleas and rhododendrons: Last spring I was given two Satsuki azaleas and two yellow hybrid rhododendrons. What sort of protection will they need to survive winter here in the mountains?
John L. Waldroop
Tuckasegee, North Carolina
The methods for protecting azaleas and rhododendrons in the mountains aren't much different than those for milder climates. First, shield the shrubs from winter sun and wind to prevent their foliage from drying. You can do this by planting them in shade or by erecting burlap windbreaks. Second, water the plants thoroughly this month before the ground freezes. After it freezes, mulch around each plant with 3 inches of shredded bark or pine straw. Finally, brush off snow from brittle rhododendrons to prevent broken branches. But leave the snow on Satsuki azaleas; it provides insulation.

Index

A

Acorns 200
African violets 200
Ajuga 89
Amaryllis *(Hippeastrum)* 185
    fertilizing 50
Ambersweet orange 160
Annuals 36, 50, 85, 100, 101, 118, 148, 178
    cool-season 178
    fertilizing 100
Ant control, tip 119
Antique Rose Emporium 77
Antique roses 77
Aphids 84
April notes 65
Ashes
    barbecue 200
    fireplace 190
Asparagus 178
August notes 135
Autumn Joy sedum *(Sedum* x *spectabile* Autumn Joy) 88
Azaleas 64, 100, 200, 205
    pruning 84, 135

B

Backyard design 73
Bagworms 148
Bath's pink *(Dianthus)* 72
Bedding plants 64, 84
Beets, tip 65
Benjamin fig *(Ficus benjamina)* 184
Bermuda grass 200
Bird feeders 36, 160
Bird-of-Paradise *(Strelitzia reginae)* 184
Blackberries 84
Blue star *(Amsonia tabernaemon tana)* 55
Books, gardening 50
Borers 84
Boston fern *(Nephrolepsis)* 184
Briarwood 128
Bromeliads 24, 184
Bulbs 118, 134, 172, 178, 185, 202
    daffodils 38, 100, 201

C

Caladiums 64, 160, 178
Callaway Gardens 142
Camellia scale 160
Cannas 118
Caterpillars 201
Chemical storage 190
Chinch bugs 100
Chinese chestnut 200
Chinese evergreen *(Aglaonema sp.)* 184
Chives 36
Christmas trees 24, 190, 196
Chrysanthemums 84, 155, 203
Citrus 36, 148, 178

ambersweet orange 160
Clematis 84
Cleome 160
Cold frames 190
Compost bins, tip 149
Composting 36, 148, 179, 190, 200
Confederate rose *(Hibiscus mutabilis)* 201
Concrete 43
Container plants 84, 134
    tip 191
Cornelian cherry *(C. mas)* 180
Corn plant *(Dracaena)* 184
Courtyards 124
Cover crops 24
Crepe myrtle *(Lagerstroemia indica)* 164
Crocus 173
Crosby Arboretum 126
Crown-of-thorns *(Euphorbia milii)* 201
Cut stone 43

D

Daffodils 38, 100, 201
Daylilies 134
December notes 191
Design 10, 13, 14, 16, 17, 18, 19, 44, 70, 73, 94, 107, 110, 124, 134, 140, 152, 153, 154
Dogwoods
    flowering *(Cornus florida)* 164
    planting 64, 201
Drainage 41, 140
Driveway 20, 154
Drying flowers 148

E

Eggplant 84
English ivy *(Hedera helix)* 184
Entry design 14, 17, 18, 70, 141
Espaliers 134
Evergreens 190
Exposed aggregate 43

F

Fairy ring 201
Fall color 162, 178
February notes 37
Fences 141
Ferns 190
Fertilizing 36, 100
Fire blight 190
Flagstones 43
Floral arrangements 32, 74, 134, 144, 148
Flower gardening 52, 166
Flowering plants 120
    source list 122
Flowers
    blue 204
    cool colors 118
    cutting 74, 134
    fertilizing 134
    planting 74, 85, 110, 160
Foliage combinations 198

Forced blooms 36
Foxgloves *(Digitalis purpurea)* 166
Front yard design 10, 13, 19, 152
Fruit 134, 203
    planting 178
    watering 100

G

Galax *(Galax urceolata)* 201
Gardener's apron, tip 101
Gardenias 118
Garden journal 24
Garlic 148
Gazebo 156
Gerberas 202
Gifts 190
Ginkgo *(Ginkgo biloba)* 164
Gladiolus 84
Gloxinia *(Sinningia speciosa)* 31
Goldsturm coneflower *(Rudbeckia fulgida Goldsturm)* 87
Grape hyacinth 175
Grapes 30
Grass
    in a basket 69
Greens 178, 205
Ground covers 89, 202

H

Harlequin glorybower *(Clerodendrum trichotomum)* 108
Heat pump 202
Heliconias 24
Herbs 24, 50, 84, 134, 148, 160
Hibiscus 178
Hickory *(Carya* sp.) 165
Houseplants 24, 32, 46, 160, 182, 185, 200
    insects 36
Hydrangeas
    pruning 100

I

Impatiens 202
Insecticidal soap 64
Interlocking pavers 43
Iris 118
    bearded iris 66

J

January notes 25
Japanese maple *(A. palmatum)* 165, 202
Jonquils 202
July notes 119
June notes 101

K

Kale 178
Kids, gardening for 45

L

Ladew Topiary Gardens 90
Lady palm *(Rhapis)* 184
Lawns 148
    Bermuda grass 200

centipede 118
chinch bugs 100
edging 24, 84
fairy ring 201
fertilizing 84
mowing 64, 118, 178, 179
naturalizing 203
plugging 204
shade-tolerant 50
tips 12
Leaf drop 64
Leu Gardens 199
Lilies 36, 91, 202
daylilies 134
Lima beans, tip 135
Loquats 190
Lubber grasshoppers 64

M
Magnolia trees 29
Mail-order plants 36
Mangoes 85
Mangroves 85
Maple trees 205
March notes 51
Marigolds 155
May notes 85
Mexican bean beetle 100
Mildew 85
Mold 119
Morning glories, tip 85
Mosquitoes 64
Mount Cuba Center 130
Mulch 85, 118, 161, 179

N
Nandina 203
Narcissus 174
Nasturtiums 36
Native plants 126
Naturalizing 203
November notes 179
Nutgrass 203

O
October notes 161
Onions, wild 51
Orchids, tip 25
Ornaments 197
painting 60

P
Palms 24, 85, 100
Pansies 160
Parking 21
Peach trees 203
Pears 118, 203
Pea gravel 43
Peas 50
Peppers 119
Peonies 179, 203
Perennials 86, 100, 148, 204
dividing 65, 149
fertilizing 36, 100
Periwinkle *(Vinca minor)* 200
Persimmon 100

Photinia *(Photinia* x *fraseri)* 204
Pine straw 161
Pine trees 204
Plant labels 65
Playground design 107
Poinsettias 36, 191
Poppies 186
Pools 123
Potpourri 25
Privacy screen 204
Privet 179
Pruning 28, 37, 135
Pumpkins 170
Pyracanthas 160

Q
Queen Anne's lace 115

R
Red horse chestnut *(Aesculus* x *carnea* Briotii) 202
Rhododendrons 205
Rose campion 100
Roses 25, 50, 65, 77, 101
disease-resistant 139
gall disease 119
pruning 37
tip 161

S
Salad vegetables 179
Salvias 150
Schefflera 184
Screening plants 26
Seedling trays, tip 37
Seeds 135
September notes 149
Shrubs 26
antique 56
fertilizing 36, 85
forcing blooms 36
mulching 101
planting 24
pruning 50, 135
red berries 192
transplanting 15, 25, 190
winter-blooming 25
Sidewalks 42
Slugs 119
Smoky Mountain Field School 75
Snowflake 174
Soil test 179
Solar greenhouses, tip 51
Sourwood *(Oxydendrum arboreum)* 165
Southern shield fern *(Thelypteris kunthii)* 86
Spicebush *(Lindera benzoin)* 171
Spanish bluebell 175
Spanish moss 161, 204
Stamped concrete 43
Starfish plant *(Stapelia* sp.) 200
Strawberries 149
Structures 105, 194
Succulents 184
Suckers 85

Sugar maple *(Acer saccharum)* 165, 205
Sunflowers 101
Sweet peas *(Lathyrus odoratus)* 205
Sweet shrub *(Calycanthus floridus)* 205
Sweet William *(Dianthus barbatus)* 166
Swiss chard 135

T
Tiles 43
Tilling 119
Tomato cages, tip 179
Tomatoes 205
in winter 102, 161
Sweet 100 cherry 50
Topiaries 168
Transplants 135
Trees 29, 93, 162, 202, 205
Chinese chestnut 200
Christmas 24
peach 203
pear 203
pine 204
planting 24, 25, 190, 204
pruning 28
transplanting 15, 190
wind endurance 85
Tropical plants 101
Tung-oil tree *(Aleurites Fordii)* 205
Turnip greens 205
Twig girdlers 50

V
Valentine basket 37
Vegetables 52, 191
harvesting 100
Mexican bean beetle 100
planting 37, 85, 119, 134, 135, 149, 160, 161, 178, 179
Verbena 119
Victory Garden 142

W
Water features 167
Watering 25, 119, 135, 191
fruit 100
Water plants 136
source list 138
Weeds 92, 101
White-flowering plants 90
Winter jasmine *(Jasminum nudiflorum)* 180
Wintersweet *(Chimonanthus praecox)* 180
Witchhazel, hybrid *(Hamamelis* x *intermedia)* 180

Y
Yarrow *(Achillea Millefolium)* 106
Yellow jackets 135
Yellow shrimp plant *(Pachystachys lutea)* 109